PORTO
GATEWAY TO THE WORLD

PORTO
GATEWAY TO THE WORLD

NEILL LOCHERY

BLOOMSBURY CARAVEL
LONDON · OXFORD · NEW YORK · NEW DELHI · SYDNEY

Produced for The Fladgate Partnership by Bloomsbury Publishing Plc

BLOOMSBURY CARAVEL
Bloomsbury Publishing Plc
50 Bedford Square, London, WC1B 3DP, UK

BLOOMSBURY, BLOOMSBURY CARAVEL and the Diana logo are trademarks
of Bloomsbury Publishing Plc

First published in Great Britain 2020

A catalogue record for this book is available from the British Library

Library of Congress Cataloguing-in-Publication data has been applied for

ISBN: 978-1-4482-1792-2

2 4 6 8 10 9 7 5 3 1

Typeset in Baskerville MT Std by Deanta Global Publishing Services, Chennai, India
Printed and bound in Great Britain by CPI Group (UK) Ltd, Croydon CR0 4YY

MIX
Paper from
responsible sources
FSC® C020471

To find out more about our authors and books visit www.bloomsbury.com
and sign up for our newsletters

For Emma, Benjamin and Hélèna

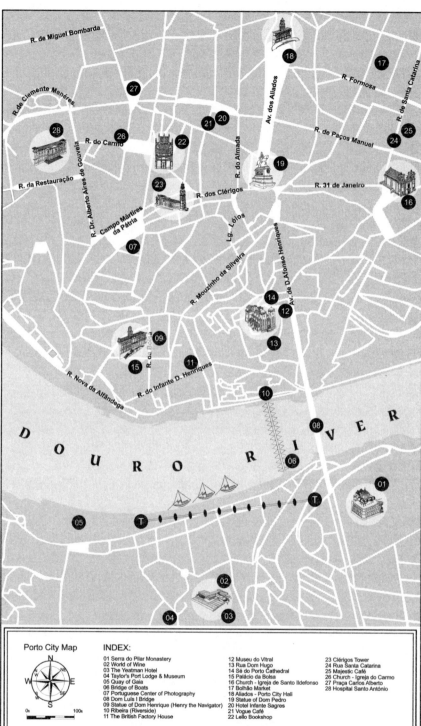

R. de Miguel Bombarda

R. de Clemente Menéres

R. da Restauração

R. do Carmo

R. Dr. Alberto Aires de Gouvela

Campo Mártires da Pátria

R. dos Clérigos

Lg. Lóios

R. Mouzinho da Silveira

R. Nova da Alfândega

R. do Infante D. Henrique

Av. dos Aliados

R. do Almada

Av. de D. Afonso Henriques

R. Formosa

R. de Santa Catarina

R. de Paços Manuel

R. 31 de Janeiro

D O U R O   R I V E R

Porto City Map

0ᴍ   100ᴍ

INDEX:

01 Serra do Pilar Monastery
02 World of Wine
03 The Yeatman Hotel
04 Taylor's Port Lodge & Museum
05 Quay of Gaia
06 Bridge of Boats
07 Portuguese Center of Photography
08 Dom Luís I Bridge
09 Statue of Dom Henrique (Henry the Navigator)
10 Ribeira (Riverside)
11 The British Factory House

12 Museu do Vitral
13 Rua Dom Hugo
14 Sé do Porto Cathedral
15 Palácio da Bolsa
16 Church - Igreja de Santo Ildefonso
17 Bolhão Market
18 Aliados - Porto City Hall
19 Statue of Dom Pedro
20 Hotel Infante Sagres
21 Vogue Café
22 Lello Bookshop

23 Clérigos Tower
24 Rua Santa Catarina
25 Majestic Café
26 Church - Igreja do Carmo
27 Praça Carlos Alberto
28 Hospital Santo António

Contents

Note from the Author

The story of the history of Porto is a rich tapestry of events and characters, which is best told by taking the reader on a grand tour around the important locations in the city where the action took place. In writing the book, I have grouped together key passages of time into specific places in order to provide a healthy flow to the narrative. Several strategically important points in Porto were obviously central to more than one conflict or series of events, so wherever possible I have highlighted these linkages.

This book can be read by visitors, and by those people who would simply like to know more about this beautiful city's long and distinguished history. It is written using both documentary and secondary sources, from a wide range of archives and existing accounts, with the aim of being of interest to all readers, including those who already know Porto and the region. Readers who have not previously come across the city, I very much hope will be intrigued and surprised by how central Porto has been in setting the political and economic development of the wider country and its efforts to establish the first truly global empire.

It is important to remember that the development of Porto did not happen in isolation. With this in mind, I have contextualised the history within the relevant international developments and trends of the era. Three foreign countries stand out most on this point: Spain, France and England (Britain). The reader I hope will find the attempts of each of these countries to exert influence and control over the city as interesting as I have done. Arguably, the most important of these foreign powers has been Britain, whose impact can still be seen with the Port wine industry that dominates the south bank of the River Douro.

Finally, with the development of better transport infrastructure, I have outlined some other key places of historical importance in the central and northern area of Portugal that can now be reached relatively easily from Porto. Learning a little about the rich historical heritage of the three cities of Braga, Guimarães and Coimbra adds much to the knowledge of the Porto region and the wider history of Portugal.

Introduction

I fell in love with Porto and I love it still.

I was enchanted by *fado*, the melancholy folk music that reflects the Portuguese themselves, who in my experience had a quietness and gentleness unique among Latin peoples I'd encountered so far. The city's spectacular bridges, its vertiginous riverbanks, steep with ancient buildings, the old port houses, the wide squares: I was entranced by them all.[1]

JK Rowling

PORTO HAS BEEN A refuge and a home for a number of foreigners, including the writer JK Rowling, throughout its long and proud history. Some outsiders, however, were more welcome in the city and the surrounding region than others. Invading armies have long identified the area as being rich in natural resources and, due to its geographic location, strategically important. As a result the city has been invaded, looted and, on occasion, had large parts of it burned to the ground. The city of Porto has always been more than simply an area located at the end of the River Douro and at the edge of the Atlantic Ocean. Its ancient name of *Portucale* (Portus Cale) forms the origin of the name of the state of Portugal, and today Porto is recognised the world over by its long and historic association with the Port wine trade. The city has enjoyed strong trading, political and cultural links with the outside world from its origins right up to the modern era. Important visitors to the city have paid tribute to its many attributes that link its past to the present day and the future.

You are the centre of a highly prosperous and industrious region that has contributed vastly to the growth of the country. But you also retain the character and beauty of your past, a past enriched by Portugal's exploring and seafaring traditions. Porto thus gives us a window on Portugal's international future as well as a window on Portugal's international past. And, of course, the wine that is produced here has, in turn, produced some of the best after-dinner conversations in the world; for centuries, it has facilitated the exchange of ideas between great minds, and has probably assisted in solving a few of the world's problems.[2]

'Porto: Gateway to the World' proclaimed Kofi Annan, Secretary-General of the United Nations, as he raised his glass at the end of his toast to the city during his visit to Porto on 7 August 1998.[3] His words illustrated a deep understanding of Porto's history and its relationship to Portugal, the Iberian peninsula, Europe and the wider world. The Secretary-General was not alone in highlighting the successes of the city throughout the ages. Countless foreign dignitaries who have visited the city have made similar remarks.

Another famous political leader who came to the city was equally enthusiastic about its significance. Speaking during her official visit to Porto in 1984, Margaret Thatcher talked of the important historical relationship between the city and Great Britain. Addressing businessmen in the *Palácio da Bolsa* in central Porto, she told the audience:

Yours is a beautiful and remarkable city—and its association with Britain is deep-rooted and famous... Oporto has played a vital part in the remarkable history of friendship between Britain and Portugal. It was not far from here in the municipality of Guimarães that the first Anglo/Portuguese treaty on trade was signed in 1372. It was from Oporto that the Fourteenth Century galleons set forth bearing their cargo of dried fruits, salt, honey and wax. It is largely from your region that our main imports

2

today of cork, pulp, textiles, come. Your justly famous wine has spread out of London's clubs, on to the supermarket shelves and into more and more British living rooms.[4]

The Iron Lady's personal relationship with Portugal ran deep. She had spent her honeymoon in the country during the 1950s and was a strong supporter of Portuguese democracy. As prime minister, she had been instrumental in lobbying for Portugal to be allowed to join the European Economic Community. Indeed, without Thatcher's support it is doubtful whether Portugal would have been able to become part of what British officials termed 'the rich club of Europe' until much later. Portugal eventually joined on 1 January 1986 and has been a keen participant in the European club ever since. The results of its relationship with what is now known as the European Union can be seen across the city of Porto and its strong trading relationship with European countries.

More recently, the 44th President of the United States, Barack Obama, talked about the beauty and importance of Porto when he spoke at 'The Climate Change Leadership Porto Summit' on 6 July 2018. Obama described climate change as the greatest threat to future generations stating that it should be addressed collectively.[5] The event was followed a year later with a three-day conference entitled 'Climate Change Leadership Solutions for the Wine Industry Conference' at which the keynote speaker was the former Vice-President of the United States, Al Gore.

The two conferences reflected Porto's position as a leading host city to major international gatherings ranging from business to high-tech meetings, and from cultural exhibits to sporting events. The collective result of this new-found status has been to further entrench the links between the city and the outside world and bring new investment and opportunity. Porto, as a result, has been transformed into a genuinely international city and sits proudly at the table as an elite location of Europe. What Kofi Annan saw at the end of the twentieth century in Porto has been confirmed and multiplied during the first decades of the twenty-first century.

Across Porto and in the surrounding areas there are a wealth of landmarks that illustrate the importance of Porto to the development of Portugal, and especially its historical relationship with the outside world. This book takes the reader across the city and the region, telling the most important tales of the events, people, and wars that helped shape its long and distinguished history. Many of the landmarks mentioned in the book are marked on the map to aid those wishing to explore the key parts of the city and the region.

The most appropriate starting point for the visitor to Porto is one of the vantage points from World of Wine (WoW) located on the south bank of the River Douro. Standing here, the visitor is treated to a panoramic view of Porto from the riverside up to the city centre. The colourful houses of the Ribeira stand out, framing the upper heights of the city with its more austere granite buildings. Porto is a city of bridges, and much of the city's long history is linked to attempts to cross the River Douro. Today the river is easier to cross than in olden times due to the advent of additional bridges and ferry services that shuttle people from Porto to Gaia and vice versa.

From the viewing points of WoW, buildings that represent the three pillars of the Porto region throughout the ages can be seen across the river: administrative (Câmara Municipal do Porto), judicial (the court house and prison, today the Centro Português de Fotografia) and religious (Sé do Porto, known in English as Porto Cathedral). The latter is all the more important given the pre-eminent role of the Catholic church throughout the history of the city.

The visitor can also witness the last twists and turns of the majestic River Douro as it winds its way between the two administrative districts of one great city: Porto and Vila Nova de Gaia, which occupy its north and south banks before it spills out in dramatic fashion into the Atlantic Ocean. Best viewed either early in the morning or prior to sunset, the visitor can see how the river has been central to the development of the Porto region. In truth, the Douro is a river no longer: the construction of a series of large

4

dams upriver means that it no longer flows freely from its origins in Spain.

The city of Porto that rises up from the banks of the river is very distinct from Lisbon, Portugal's capital. Indeed, the two cities could not be more physically different: Lisbon appears more Mediterranean, and Porto more European. The granite buildings that define much of the city's architecture are in sharp contrast to the pastel-coloured plastered buildings that dominate much of the Lisbon skyline. Much of Lisbon's city centre was destroyed by an earthquake in 1755 and rebuilt under the leadership of Sebastião José de Carvalho e Melo (Marquês de Pombal). The centre of Porto, while subjected to the horrors of bombardment during international conflicts and a civil war, has remained much less physically changed in recent centuries. While downtown Lisbon was laid out in a neat grid-like form by the Marquês de Pombal, Porto city centre is much less regimented offering the visitor a very different experience to that of Lisbon.

There is a natural rivalry between the two cities which runs throughout the history of Portugal. Lisbon has been known as the seat of government for centuries, while Porto has been home to much of Portugal's successful industry and commerce. While Lisbon governs the country, Porto makes money, and there is a different mindset between inhabitants of the two major cities of Portugal. In recent years, the competitiveness has been most visible on the football field as Benfica and Sporting, the two leading clubs of Lisbon, contest with FC Porto to win the Portuguese league and cups. The recent exploits of Porto's football team make it most probably the second most internationally recognised brand of the city after Port wine.

Portugal's two major cities do share one thing in common: both are extremely hilly. In Porto, as in Lisbon, the visitor needs to be prepared for steep climbs and rapid descents, towards and away from the river. Some of the most interesting aspects of the city require a willingness to go off the beaten track. The climbs, however, are worth the effort. A large number of key viewing areas provide excellent balconies to see the splendour of the city.

Throughout history important foreigners, such as the Duke of Wellington during the Peninsular War, have stood on the same high ground surveying the city in order to make strategic decisions on how best to proceed. As many people have recounted over the ages, it is worth remembering that Porto is best viewed from a vantage point in Vila Nova de Gaia and vice versa. Today the viewing points provide ample opportunity for Instagram moments and Porto is fast achieving the status of one of the most photogenic cities in Europe.

Geography has been central to the history of Porto and its relationship with the world. The city is located on the very western edge of Europe where the land ends and the ocean starts. The Atlantic coastline of Portugal runs from the Minho in the north to the Algarve in the south. Through the ages, the majority of the inhabitants of Portugal have lived along or near the coastline. This is because the Atlantic Ocean has been historically the single most important feature in Portugal's creation, development, battles for independence, and ability to survive independent of Spain. Hemmed in by the mountain ranges that dominate large parts of the border areas with Spain, Portugal has looked to the sea as a means for securing trade, expansion and power.

It is important to remember that Portugal is located on the Iberian Peninsula, on which Spain occupies approximately 80% of the land area. As writers are keen to point out, 'Portugal looks towards the ocean and has turned its back on Spain'.[6] After rejecting integration with Spain, Portugal has had to look outside of the Peninsula.[7] With poor overland connections to the rest of Europe, and rivers that were not navigable, the ocean has proven to be an attractive and lucrative alternative for Portuguese traders.

Over recent centuries, Porto has played an important role in the exporting and importing of goods, with the city developing a reputation as the major centre for trade in the country. There has been a strong and prolonged international dimension with regard to the British-dominated Port wine trade. As we will see, the city of Porto and the Douro region remain full of references to the wine trade and the colourful individuals who built up the trade and who thrived in the city. Though by no means the only export from the city, Porto will always be linked to Port wine.

Relations between the wealthy British traders in the city and the inhabitants of Porto have generally been of a friendly nature. The British community linked to the Port wine trade has existed as an almost unique colony: a small enclave set amongst the wider country. Much of the development and redevelopment of Vila Nova de Gaia is being undertaken by old Port family-run businesses, such as Taylor's. At key moments, however, there have been tensions between the British community and the local Portuguese. Reasons for these sporadic quarrels range from a sense of envy from the latter towards the former, to more specific economic issues.

The ocean and the river have not been the only factors that explain the development of Porto. The climate, characterised by plentiful rain and relatively mild summers, has made the lands in the Porto area more attractive to farm than in the south of Portugal (and in the interior) where summer temperatures can often reach forty degrees Celsius. In ancient times this made it easier for families to live off smaller plots of land. The presence of metals was also an important feature in the region's development. From the beginning of time the area has been rich in metals found in the soils. Ores, most notably wolfram (tungsten) and gold, have been of such great importance that foreign powers have at times considered invading Portugal in order to secure control over them.

Rich in minerals, with access to the ocean and with a major river running through it, the Porto region has been throughout time an attractive place to live. Who came, and for what reasons, who stayed and who left? Which foreign armies invaded, and for what reasons? How did the politics of the city become intertwined with the developments outside of Portugal? These questions are central to understanding the history of Porto and its relationship with the outside world. In helping to answer them it is best to take the visitor through the streets of Porto and let the city reveal its stories and hidden secrets.

PART ONE

DAY ONE – MORNING

1

Arrival

Our history teaches us that the periods of greatness of Portugal are those in which the country is open to the world and that the periods of decay, and even the loss of independence, coincide with periods of isolation that are always an attitude of provincialism and insufficiency.[1]

Francisco Sá Carneiro

TODAY, THE EASIEST WAY for the visitor to arrive in the city is by air via the Francisco Sá Carneiro Airport, located eleven kilometres northwest of the city centre. In its current form, it is a multi-award-winning airport with a sleek modern spacious terminal, which was inaugurated on 15 October 2005 after a five-year construction period. In recent years, the facility has increased the annual passenger capacity of Porto Airport to over six million. Architecturally it is best known for its use of natural light to provide calm arrivals and departures areas for visitors to Porto. The local population has become very proud of their airport, which has helped transform access to the region, and encouraged it to develop its potential as a resort for tourists from all over the world.

For those visitors who arrive from the south the final twenty minutes of the flight should (cloud cover permitting) offer spectacular views of the Douro and of the monuments, buildings, and bridges of the city of Porto as the plane flies over before banking to the right to head towards the runway. When arriving from the north the town of Vila do Conde, one of the oldest settlements in northern Portugal, is visible as it struts out from the coastline to the Atlantic Ocean. On a clear day, just prior to landing, it is possible to see several of the historic buildings including the Santa Clara Convent.

Porto Airport first opened, without much fanfare, on 3 December 1945. Its primary role was to connect Porto with Lisbon, and for some time the only scheduled flight into and out of the airport was from the capital city. Indeed, it did not handle its first international flight until nearly eleven years later in 1956. Porto Airport was originally named Aeroporto de Pedras Rubras (Reddish Stones) after the area in which it is located. In 1990 it was renamed in honour of the Porto-born Francisco de Sá Carneiro, the former prime minister of Portugal who died in a plane crash, soon after taking off from Lisbon Airport on a flight to Porto on 4 December 1980. At the time of his death Sá Carneiro was the first centre-right prime minister since the Portuguese Revolution of 25 April 1974 had ended the authoritarian rule, known as the *Estado Novo*, which had run the country since 1933. Prior to Sá Carneiro, the centre-left had dominated Portuguese politics in the democratic era.

The cause of the plane crash has been the subject of much debate and speculation in Portugal. Over the years, different theories have been put forward as to why the light aircraft came down. It has been suggested that there was evidence of a bomb being placed on board the aircraft or other forms of sabotage. Many Portuguese remain convinced that Sá Carneiro was assassinated and various conspiracy theories have been put forward as to the motive. These include the possibility that the prime minister was not the intended victim. One theory suggests that the Defence Minister, Adelino Amaro da Costa, who was also travelling on the aircraft was the target. The minister was thought to be about to expose a political scandal related to the period of instability that had followed the Revolution.

Sá Carneiro was a young, charismatic, modern leader who connected with large parts of the population, and his death robbed Portugal of one of its most capable and promising post-Revolution leaders. To some extent, the unexplained nature of his death invites some comparison with the assassination of United States President

John F. Kennedy, and the resulting decades of investigations and speculation about potential motives. To the visitor, it might appear a little strange or macabre, to name an airport after a person that died in a plane crash, but Sá Carneiro remains one of Porto's favourite sons and the city wanted his name honoured.

The expansion of the airport in recent years has helped open the city up to visitors from near and far. As the visitor walks through the arrivals hall, they will pass passengers from all over Europe, North America, Africa, Asia, the Middle East and South America. Porto has become a truly international destination for tourism and business. The national airline, TAP, runs an hourly air bridge between Sá Carneiro Airport and Humberto Delgado Airport in Lisbon, which has created further connections out of Porto to cities across the globe.

In the spirit of naming airports after famous sons, Lisbon chose a man who, despite being born in the interior of the country, came to be linked to the city of Lisbon and specifically the opposition to the authoritarian *Estado Novo*. Humberto Delgado was murdered by an agent of the Portuguese secret police in Spain on 13 February 1965. His death remains one of the most controversial events of the *Estado Novo* era in Portugal.

The democratic leaders of Lisbon chose to honour him by renaming Lisbon airport after him on the 50th anniversary of his murder. However, Delgado also had links to the city of Porto – particularly during his attempt to win the Presidency of Portugal in 1958. When he visited the city during the campaign, there was a massive turnout in Porto of nearly 200,000 locals in support of him. The General eventually lost the election, which was widely perceived to have been rigged in favour of the candidate who was loyal to the *Estado Novo*. Pictures of Delgado being greeted by the people in Porto (still wearing his military uniform and trademark hat despite leaving the Air Force some years before) were largely censored by the government in Lisbon.

There remains an additional link between Humberto Delgado and Porto. In 1945, Delgado was the first passenger to arrive at the newly opened Pedras Rubras Airport on board a flight from Lisbon.

At the time, Delgado held the position of Director do Secretariado da Aeronáutica Civil and was still very much a part of the *Estado Novo* regime. Later, when he broke ranks and called for the sacking of the authoritarian leader, António de Oliveira Salazar, Delgado became a figurehead for the opposition to the regime.

The journey from Francisco Sá Carneiro Airport into the centre of the city is unspectacular and unmemorable as the visitor quickly passes through a hinterland defined by industry, car sales stands, and the largest shopping centre in the area. Thankfully the trip is brief and soon the high-rise buildings of the outer city centre make way for the more pleasing and colourful *praças* (squares), churches, shops, and homes of the inner circle of the city. Here almost every road and avenue contains a wealth of tales from the past that tell the story of the city from its origins until the present day. Unlike many larger cities, much of the story of the Porto region is contained in this small area that clings to the two banks of the River Douro, rising up steep hills on both sides of the river that create several pleasing viewing points.

Prior to the advent of the international airport, Porto and its region were most easily accessed from the sea, or by road. Arrival into the city from the ocean, however, was not straightforward. The strong currents that swirl around the area where the river meets the ocean at the affluent coastal town of Foz made navigation into Porto hazardous, even for the most skilled of sailors. Many trade ships, as a result, were lost in the final approaches into the city, their cargos washed up on the sandy beaches and coves that run north all the way from Foz to the Spanish border and beyond. Whilst no arrival from the Atlantic Ocean was easy, pilots were on hand to help the captains dock their boats. English writer William Kingston, whose father worked in the Port wine trade observed:

> The shades of night had just closed over the world (as the poets sing) when we arrived off the mouth of the Douro. The darkness mattered little as the night was beautiful, the sea calm, and Nossa Senhora da Luz (Our Lady of the Night), shone benignly forth to welcome our approach and guide our course. This lighthouse

stands on a hill about quarter of a mile from the mouth of the Douro, on the north side, and just outside the town of St João da Foz. The paddles were stopped, and a gun was fired to call the attention of a pilot, whose boat is always kept in readiness to land the mailbags and passengers.[2]

An additional problem for ships' captains in previous centuries was the lack of alternative ports to Porto. If access to the port proved too treacherous then ships faced a long diversion, either south to Lisbon, or more likely, north to Viana do Castelo. This re-routing would add days, or weeks, to the arrival of goods into the Porto region. The construction of a new deep-water port to the north of the city became a priority during the twentieth century as the size of ships increased, making access into Porto by way of the River Douro even more difficult to navigate.

For the sailors and passengers in the past, once safely out of the ocean, the view of the city soon came into focus as they made their way cautiously thorough the twists and turns of the river as it started to narrow. William Kingston described the view upon arrival from his steamer, which came as far as Foz:

> In daylight, from the decks of the steamer the city of Oporto can be clearly discerned, standing about three miles from the shore; the most conspicuous objects being the Torre dos Clerigos, a high conical arabesquely ornamental tower, the church of Nossa Senhora da Lapa, which shews a dazzling white front. The city appears as if standing on the summit of high cliffs, on each side of the gap in the land through which the river flows.[3]

For those aboard the ships this was the first sight of land for weeks, or even months. As the ships docked, they were greeted by a hive of activity. A small army of officials, traders, and labourers to remove the cargo and load the next would spring into action. How strange this must have seemed for the people on board after the calm and quiet of the voyage, to be so dramatically replaced by the sounds of the city. The ocean air was rapidly replaced by the rich smell of fish and Port wine.

The approach to Porto by road was no less hazardous or dramatic until funds from the European Union helped construct a network of motorways from the border with Spain into the Porto region. The highways, with their impressive series of long viaducts which slice through the mountain ranges, opened up large parts of the region to overland trade with Europe. Today the visitor can reach Porto relatively quickly, in a matter of only a few hours from the Spanish border along these well-maintained roads. For the visitor who chooses to drive, the views reflect the changing climate and geography between Spain and Portugal. This tells us much about the differences between the two countries and helps, in part, explain the historical reasons for the conflict between the two nations.

The dry and arid wide-open areas of the western Spain are soon replaced by more green and fertile lands as the visitor enters Portugal. The contrast could not be starker. Portugal, although a small country of only ten million inhabitants, has lands in the mountains and along its 561-kilometre Atlantic Ocean coastline which are able to support farming and this, in the past, gave it a greater potential for self-sufficiency in food production.[4] The Porto region is very much two distinct lands, as is much of the rest of Portugal. The heavily populated area near the Atlantic coast and the more under-populated interior areas.

Indeed, the visitor will be struck by how unevenly the ten million population is distributed throughout the country. The urban areas of Porto and Lisbon account for over one-third of the total population. The density of the population has placed strains on the Porto region all though the ages. Much of the reason for this distortion was that the pace of industrialisation in Portugal outstripped the development of the agricultural sector.[5] Indeed, the former had a negative effect on the latter with the population shift from the countryside to the city. The division of the agricultural sector in the north of Portugal has been different to that in the centre and parts of the south of the country. While Porto and the north has been characterised by small or medium sized estates, in the Alentejo region to the east and south of Lisbon the size of the farms has been significantly larger.

Despite the lands being fertile and the climate more hospitable than across the eastern border in Spain, there has been a historical pattern of emigration from Porto and the surrounding countryside. In the middle of the last century there was a substantial increase in the numbers who left. Political and economic reasons were the main cause of this exodus. Some left to get better paid jobs in northern European countries, where the salaries would often be more than double than that of Portugal.

Others fled, fearing political persecution from Salazar's secret police, and many simply got out before they were conscripted into the army and sent to fight in one of Portugal's colonial wars. While some of the emigrants were city dwellers, a large number came from villages away from the major population centres. Such was the extent of the exodus that some villages became deserted – abandoned like little ghost towns. Several other villages were left with ageing populations with the younger generations all leaving and not returning until retirement. An additional factor was the remoteness of many of the villages from Porto in the era before the highways dramatically reduced journey times.

One of the great joys for the visitor who chooses to drive towards the Porto region along the A4 are the spectacular views it offers, in places, of the Douro valley countryside. The opening of a new tunnel – known in Portuguese as the *Túnel do Marão* – has transformed the accessibility of parts of the Alto-Douro to the city of Porto. The tunnel measures over five and a half kilometres and cuts the driving time as well as the stress of travelling on the old road, which clung to the side of the mountains that the new tunnel slices through. The Alto-Douro is now accessible for day trippers from Porto who are able to arrive there from the city in just over one and a half hours.

Once remote towns, such as Pinhão, that have grown up along the banks of the River Douro and that have been central to the Port wine trade are today playing host to an increasing number of tourists arriving by road. One of the best viewing points in the town is from the garden of The Vintage House Hotel. Here the visitor can see for themselves the vineyards and the terracing that are cut precisely into the side of the steep hills that rise from the riverbank into the clouds. In early mornings, when the mist hangs over the mountains, it is not possible to see their peaks. Lower down, the lines of vines appear to go on forever. The view of the river reveals how much change has taken place in the area in recent decades. The construction of the dams has tamed a once fearsome current and it now looks like a calm lake, which is what it has now become.

Sitting in the garden of The Vintage House Hotel, it is possible to imagine how different Pinhão used to be. The sounds of the boats being loaded with the pipes of Port wine to sail down the river to the warehouses at Vila Nova de Gaia and from there to the great cities of the world. With the freshness of the air, it is easier to detect the slightly sweet smell of the Port mixed with the odour of the oak barrels. Today, the town remains important to the Port wine trade and is one of the gateways to the more remote parts of the Alto-Douro where the finest Ports are still produced. It also remains one of the most popular destinations for cruise ships, which make their way up the River Douro from Porto on tours that can take the visitor all the way to the ancient university city of Salamanca across the border in Spain.

On this occasion, if the visitor is keen to arrive in Porto, it is more than possible to leave a tour of the one of the most breathtakingly beautiful parts of Europe until the end of the trip to the region. Instead, take the motorway which heads towards the city. It passes along the outskirts of another picturesque town, Amarante, which the British and French fought for control over during the Peninsular War. There it is possible to see the River Tâmega, an impressive tributary of the River Douro. The origins of the town go as far back as those of Porto and its strategic location has made it important to foreign armies wishing to gain access to Porto.

In 1955 the French photographer Henri Cartier-Bresson published two photographs taken in Amarante in his book on post-World War II Europe, *The Europeans*. One depicted a scene in a forest on the outskirts of the town. The other became an iconic photograph of the town, taken from the riverbank with two women folding up the washing that had been left to dry. Bresson's book was largely about the state of the post-war continent where many people still lived in ruins and had little to eat. In some ways, the book reflected a search for a common European identity in order to avoid another war. In retrospect, the choice of Amarante to form part of his Portugal section in the book was highly appropriate given the town's history of conflict.[6]

After Amarante disappears in the rear-view mirror, there is not much for the visitor to see as the motorway winds its way down towards the coast and to its eventual destination, Porto.

Nondescript dormitory towns appear and just as quickly disappear again. Small industries have grown up in some of the towns, such as furniture manufacturing, and more recently service industries have started moving out from the city to cheaper offices. Closer to Porto, new cities have developed, such as Maia, near to the airport and linked to Porto by a Metro line. These places are full of grey, concrete, soulless estates; lacking in history, but offering larger living spaces with cheaper house prices and rents to those of Porto. They are best passed by the visitor who may well feel, at this stage, a mixture of weariness from the drive and expectant excitement at the prospect of arriving at the final destination. Before then, the motorway joins the same intersections as those visitors who have travelled by air. The journey through the hinterlands of Porto, as a result, is a very similar one to those who arrived in the city from Francisco Sá Carneiro Airport.

2

Origins

Here, unlike the rest of continental Europe where they could roam at will over vast areas, these wandering tribes found themselves hemmed into a cul-de-sac bound by the sea. Those communities that had already settled had to put up with unwelcome new arrivals and coexist with them in what was a comparatively limited space.[1]

José Hermano Saraiva

I T IS NOT UNUSUAL for river mist to hang over the city of Porto, covering it in a blanket of damp grey cloud long into the mid-morning. This can occur during any of the four seasons, but is most likely during the spring and autumn months. The mist adds to the feeling of mystique, as the sun tries to get up enough strength to burn it off, heralding a deep blue midday sky. For those visitors who are able to arrive at the riverfront early in the morning it is worth crossing the river, either by the ferry service, located near the Dom Luís Bridge, or by using the narrow walkway on the lower tier of the bridge itself. The ferry service saves the visitor much valuable time and offers an opportunity to view the double-decked metal bridge mid-river from below its lower tier. The bridge, however, is not the first objective of the morning.

After crossing the river to the Gaia side, the visitor should start to walk towards the ocean along the dedicated walkway. Hug the riverbank past where the Port wine houses end and the sparse, often semi-derelict buildings start to dominate the south bank of the River Douro. Just prior to where the river widens, on the site of a new hotel project, lies the origins of the Porto region. Excavation works have a habit of revealing hidden histories, and here recent new finds help chronicle the origins of the city of Porto and the nation that came to be known as Portugal.

Evidence of the early settlers is still being uncovered, as archaeological digs being undertaken prior to major construction projects in Vila Nova de Gaia reveal interesting and potentially new details about their lifestyles. As the earth is gently excavated, each layer produces evidence that suggests the importance of the area. The site can be seen from the walkway on the Gaia side of the river. Sheltered by the slight bend in the River Douro from the chilling winds of the Atlantic Ocean, there is evidence of the existence of early settlement.

Visitors to the Portugal Region Across the Ages experience (PRATA) at WoW are able to see colourful visualisations of the lifestyles of these early settlers. The exhibit highlights the development of these settlers and the probable first permanent trading post by the Phoenicians. It then illustrates the fortified settlements of the Iron Age: the lifestyle and trade, moving onto the Celtiberians, the Gallaeci and Lusitanians. Finally, it focuses on the Barbarian Invasions, highlighting the differences between the various groups of warriors. Although much of the information about the early period of settlement still remains incomplete or is disputed between historians, there is a consensus on the importance of the ocean and the presence of a wealth of mineral resources.

During the Bronze Age the Porto region was sought out for its mineral resources, and basic trading links were established with the outside world. New immigrants came hoping to exploit these resources and the arrival of each new group helped introduce new developments and skillsets. For example, the Celts, who arrived on the Peninsula in around 1000 BC, were said to be skilled metalworkers. The key to understanding the early development of the area is how the outsiders interacted with existing groups within the context of conquest, wars and invasions.

Today the visitor can stand next to the recently excavated site on the banks of the River Douro and imagine the reasons that the location was chosen by the various groups of early settlers: shelter, fertile land, and access to the river and the ocean. A careful look upriver provides the visitor with a detailed panoramic view of its twists and turns and the reasons for the development of larger communities along both its banks. From early origins to the present day Porto has been a trading area. Starting with the exploitation of its natural resources in ancient times to the export of Port wine over the last 350 years, the area has interconnected with the outside world in order to survive, to develop, and to prosper. Over time the products have changed, but the formula has remained the same.

Standing on a quiet part of the bank of the River Douro, it is possible to sense that the area does not only mark the end of the Peninsula, but also that of continental Europe. Today it is thankfully a peaceful setting. One in which the visitor can pause to think about the themes of its past. In doing so, it is worth remembering the following points that connect its ancient past to its more recent history.

The story of the Porto region through the ages is a tale of conquests, loss, and reconquests, of development and near collapse, of invasion and resistence, and of civil war and strife. It is also a part of the story of Portugal, Iberia, and Britain, along with the rest of mainland Europe, Africa, Brazil, and the other Portuguese colonies that formed part of its global empire during the golden era. Put simply, the city has attracted the attention, sometimes undesired, of foreign powers even before the nation of Portugal was founded.

A brief summary of the groups that invaded the western edge of the Peninsula in the centuries prior to the creation of Portugal is required to help understand the development of the land, the creation of key trading towns, and the military battles that took place. In the first instance, it is important to understand why each of the foreign armies invaded the lands that today comprise Portugal. A recurring theme is that of economic motives, as the foreigners understood the quality of the farming lands and the presence of different metals, many of which were easy to mine and available in large amounts. Moreover, how did these foreigners instil their cultures and customs into local populations, changing society and power structures in the process? The creation of new trade routes, especially during the era of Roman domination, also led to new industries being started.

The reaction of the local population to the invaders needs to be given consideration. The ability to continue armed resistance, as well as its consequences for the population, merits investigation. In the main, much of the armed resistance that took place was of limited success with, arguably, the exception of key moments during the direct rule from Rome. What is clear is that the foreigners thought the lands to be highly exploitable for their own benefits and they looked to extract as much as possible from them.

The geographic divisions of the lands were largely established during these centuries: the south, the centre, and the north were all distinct from one another and offered different resources. An additional division was soon established between lands close to the Atlantic coastline (including those that today form Porto) and the interior. The climate along the Atlantic coast was damper, while temperatures in the interior reached over forty degrees Celsius in the summer months.

All the invading armies brought positive, and well as negative, development to the area. Often, however, the newly arriving army would destroy all that had gone before them. This was usually a mixture of direct intention or was simply caused by houses, villages, and even towns being badly damaged, or completely destroyed during the fighting. Despite this wanton destruction we can still see and find influences of the invaders in the Porto region.

On this score, the greatest legacy was the development of infrastructure that encouraged communication and ended isolation. For the Romans this was all about roads, roads, and roads. From south to north and west to east they constructed a road system that served the lands and the local population for centuries. The Romans, however, were not given a warm reception by large parts of the local population when they marched into the Peninsula. As a result it took them an extremely long time to defeat the locals and develop their plans to exploit the lands for their own uses.

The Romans first invaded eastern Iberia in 218 BC in order to prevent their enemies, the Carthaginians, of important resources: men, horses, and mineral wealth. In other words, for economic reasons. In around 202 BC they invaded and conquered south-western Iberia and from there started to move northwards. The further north they went the greater the resistance the Roman army faced from independent Celts, who the Romans called Lusitanians. Events turned even nastier after the Romans implemented plans to trick the Lusitanians into signing a peace treaty with the incentive of promising them access to better lands.[2] After gathering a large number of the Lusitanians in one place the Romans massacred them, killing thousands. Those lucky enough to escape death were taken prisoner and subsequently sold into slavery.

Despite this apparent mortal blow, the remaining Lusitanians continued to resist Roman rule. A new leader, a shepherd called Viriathus, assumed command and enjoyed a great deal of success against the Roman armies by employing hit-and-run tactics as well as mounting larger scale ambushes against them. The success was not to last. The Lusitanians fell for the same Roman trick of offering friendship to end the conflict. An unsuspecting Viriathus was killed while he slept in his bed, by assassins who had been employed by the Romans.

Following the death of Viriathus, the Romans once again murdered thousands of Lusitanians and sent the survivors into slavery. The name of Viriathus, however, lives on in Portuguese culture, immortalised by Luís de Camões, one of Portugal's greatest poets, in his most well-known work, *Os Lusíadas*. Even after the death of Viriathus, resistance continued from the Lusitanians from their mountain hideaway. Eventually the Romans were able to pacify the population, ending local opposition in 19 BC and bringing to a conclusion the Lusitanian wars.

As part of an effort to control the local tribes, and to enforce greater central administration in the area the Romans constructed a network of roads that connected areas that had previously been isolated. In terms of the development of new settlements, the building of the south-north route was the most important. This encouraged better communication along the Atlantic coastal areas and encouraged new settlements.[3]

Other Roman projects included the establishment of new towns, the location of which were largely based on economic criteria. The Romans introduced, or encouraged, a wide range of economic activities in Lusitania. Among the most important were agriculture, fishing (and the preserving of fish), raising cattle, metal working, and the mining of the rich resources. In terms of exports to Italy, wheat, olive oil, and wine, all from the Alentejo, were among the most sought-after goods.[4] The Romans also developed quarries to help supply the materials for buildings, paving stones, and for inscriptions. Marble was also in plentiful supply in the centre and north and was mined by the Romans. In open-cast mines, gold and lead were extracted in the north, and copper and iron in the south.[5]

The Roman general, Decimus Junius Brutus Callaicus, who conquered the region, founded the Roman city of Portus Cale in around 136 BC. The town continued to attract the attention of foreign invaders after the Romans were defeated. Two more groups sought control over the lands in the Peninsula. The result of the second was a near total depopulation of the area that is now the city of Porto.

The first group of barbarians invaded the Peninsula in 409 AD after defeating the, by then limited, Roman resistance. Unlike the Romans, their contribution to the development of the western part of the Peninsula, and specifically Portus Cale, was limited. During the invasion, towns that had been built by the Romans were abandoned; many were never reoccupied and left to decay.[6] A period of uncertainty followed during which there was a counter invasion, organised by the Roman Emperors. New political and social systems emerged with the warrior class at the apex of the pyramid of power. A king was drawn from the warrior class, and the clergy did very well for themselves – often living in large palaces they were influential in policymaking. The Jewish minority controlled large parts of the trading economy. Disliked by the other parts of the elite, they were rich but often persecuted. The lands were farmed by a large peasant class and under this group was a slave class, many of whom were forced to serve in the army. Disaster struck in the year 700 due to two factors: crop failure and disease. This coincided with the attempts of Arab and Berber pirates raiding the southern Peninsula from the Mediterranean. This was the precursor to another full invasion of the Peninsula, this time from the south and brought another wave of immigration into the area.

The initial Moor (Arab) invasion took place in 711 when they crossed the western Mediterranean at one of its narrowest points. In the north of Portugal, what is today the Minho, the control of the Moors lasted only for a very limited time. However, in the Alentejo, and the Algarve, it continued for around five centuries.[7] The cultural and religious impact on the north, as a result, was much less than in the southern areas. Initially, relations between the different religious groups were peaceful. Muslims, Jews, and Christians were essentially segregated from each other, living next to one another with their own places of worship (mosque, synagogue, or church).[8] People were not categorised by the language they spoke or by their race, but simply by religion. Those who elected to continue to follow their own religion were able to do after the payment of a tax.

As a result, the impact of the Arab culture and language on those who lived in areas fully under the control of the Moors varied. Some inhabitants continued as if little had been changed by the invasion. Continuing to speak their own language and maintain their way of life they went about their business as essentially a community within a community. Other groups of Christians, who maintained their religious identity, assimilated into Arab culture in a much deeper and more profound manner. Many adopted the language of their conquerors and after things turned nasty with the era of the Reconquest this group became known as *mozarab* (Arabised). Those Christians that went even further and converted to Islam were termed as *muwallad* or *muladi*.[9]

Economic changes and developments under the Moors were arguably not as profound as during the period of Roman rule. There was a shift towards smaller agricultural holdings, in contrast to Roman times when the sectors producing wine and grain had been scaled up to create large holdings. The Moors introduced the use of water to help power mills and better methods of irrigation in orchards. The latter produced a big saving, cutting down the need to use manual labour in the process. Other advances came in the form of mapmaking and shipbuilding as well as in science and technology.[10] Education was embraced and encouraged with the aim of developing a greater understanding of the world. In the north, the near ever-present military conflict, comprising of raids, retaliation, and counter-attacks did not create the necessary conditions for economic advancement.

There is much debate among historians about what came to be known as the 'Reconquest'. What is clear was that it represented one of the last pieces of the jigsaw in the creation of Portugal. The term 'Reconquest' is employed as a label to describe the long process of the re-establishment of Christianity in the Peninsula. The Reconquest did not fully end until 1492, with the capture of Granada in the south of the Peninsula by the Catholic kings. Its starting point is a little more contentious, and seemingly far less dramatic. Most historians point to the Battle of Covadonga in 718 as the start of the Reconquest. However, the Portuguese historian, José Hermano Saraiva, thought this starting point was a little overdramatic. He describes the allegedly legendary battle as 'little more, in fact, than the successful ambush by guerrillas of a small band of Moors sent out to smoke them out of their Asturian fastness.'[11]

Generally speaking, the Reconquest did not really get underway until the middle of the eighth century, starting more as a rebellion with the catalyst being the arrival of waves of noblemen and soldiers migrating into the area.[12] Much of the era of the Reconquest was bloody, violent, and, in the north, involved high levels of population displacement and the destruction of well-established towns. Initially, the rebels in the north made massive territorial gains, and soon occupied all of Galicia. The Moors, however, were far from finished and struck back with devastating military campaigns in 764, 791, 794 and 840.[13]

The result was the near-total destruction of Galicia. For over a century its lands resembled a battlefield or dangerous 'do not enter' borderlands. The area contained badly burnt-out towns that were mostly deserted. The population had largely survived by fleeing the towns and moving into the forests and other safer parts of the countryside in the area to the south of Galicia – in the lands between the River Douro and the River Minho (today between Porto and Portugal's northern border with Spain). Repopulation of the abandoned areas did not start until the middle of the ninth century.

Two towns became extremely important: Chaves, in the north, and in the south, Portus Cale (Porto). Both became administrative centres as the Christians expanded their control over territories in the north. In 868 the old Roman fort of Cale was finally permanently secured by the Christians. It had changed hands several times during the era of the Moorish occupation. The area extended in the north to the River Lima, in the east to Beira Alta, and in the south to the River Douro.[14] Once again, their military successes proved short-lived and the Moors launched new raids bringing back destruction and disorganisation. This time, it took the Christians the best part of three-quarters of a century to reclaim the ground they lost.[15]

The geographic, social, and religious significance of Portus Cale continued throughout the pre-state period of the nation, and it was to play an important role in the creation of Portugal, which derived its name from the city. The Moors were not to be the last foreign army to invade the Peninsula, and to conquer the city of Porto, ransacking it and terrifying its inhabitants.

In order to recount these tragic events, the visitor needs to move on, and leave one of the finest views of the city at river level. The silence of the location is only broken by the occasional passing car, and by the distant noise of conversations from afar on the river boats that carry excited tourists up and down the river. Looking directly upriver, the boats looked like a carefully arranged flotilla as they sail in almost perfect unison before making the sharp bend past the last bridge to head back towards the city. The calmness of the leisurely cruise is only broken by happy shouts coming from children enjoying a day out. How very different it is from the bloody history that dominated the early history of the city, and which returned with vengeance.

3

French Invasion

Next morning, which was to prove a day of blood and sorrow, broke with a lovely blue sky: the earth had been refreshed by the rain and the defenders' appearance had also benefitted thereby; the orgies of a night were to be succeeded by a frightful reckoning. From their tents, the Portuguese soldiery heard the sound of drums and the shrill note of the bugles. Looking over the ramparts they saw the glitter of thousands of bayonets. The attack was about to commence in earnest.[1]

Charles Sellers

AN IMPORTANT REMINDER OF arguably Porto's darkest hours can be found by the visitor retracing their steps along the walkway on the Vila Nova de Gaia bank of the river. Very quickly the calm and quiet of the archaeological dig is replaced by the bustle and noise of the Quay, with tourists heading off to WoW and the Port Houses pausing to take pictures of the colourful houses in Porto's Ribeira district set against a splendidly deep blue sky. Take the Cable Car from the quayside, which offers stunning views of Porto and Gaia. The trip is 600 metres long and brief at approximately 5 minutes. Dismounting from the car you are some 63 metres above street level in Gaia. Ignore the temptation to immediately head to the top tier of the Dom Luís I Bridge, instead pass through the Jardim do Morro and cross the Avenida da República. From there head to one of the vantage points located next to the bridge that offer views over the river and into the Ribeira district of the waterfront.

Looking to the left and to the right, notice a number of bridges that cross the River Douro and link Gaia with Porto. Road, metro, motorway, foot, and rail bridges are all options for crossing the river with ease. Imagine, however, a time when these metal and concrete structures did not exist. Instead, during the era of the Peninsular War, there were only two ways of making the crossing from Gaia to Porto: by boat and across a single pontoon-bridge. The latter was over 200 metres long and was comprised of twenty boats anchored in the river with a timber-framed walkaway built across the top of them. Constructed in 1806, it was the first semi-permanent crossing point between Porto and Gaia. The bridge was cleverly designed and built in a way that allowed it to move up or down with the tides, and to move upstream or downstream with the current. Importantly, it was possible to remove some of the boats from the bridge to allow ships to pass and sail up or down the river. It was also possible to dismantle the entire bridge when flooding or other adverse weather was forecast. Designed by the architect Carlos Amarante, it was based on a similar type bridge that had been constructed in Rouen, France. Locally, it was known simply as 'The Bridge of Boats'. During the French attack on Porto, it came to play a central role in the tragedies of that fateful day.

The complex causes, and the military campaigns of the Peninsular War, go beyond the remit of this book. In summary, the war was a reflection of political changes in Europe, especially in France, and was a conflict between the leading European powers of the era: Great Britain and France. Both Spain and Portugal had hoped to sit out any conflict between the two powers, but, largely as a result of French manoeuvrings, they were drawn into the fighting. For Portugal, there was the additional complication of an ancient alliance with Britain and the closeness of its trading ties with London. For its part, Britain exploited Portugal's Atlantic-facing ports and waters to try to essentially impose an economic blockade on France by denying it access to the Mediterranean.

As the crisis between the two European superpowers deepened, France bullied Portugal to try to weaken Britain, and London made it clear that it regarded Portugal as essentially a protectorate and that they would continue to exploit its geographic importance and economic trade.

From the perspective of Portugal, the Peninsular War involved a number of invasions (three in total), but for Porto it was the French invasion and occupation of the city that became the most traumatic. For the visitor with a strong interest in the war there remains a huge volume of work on it, written by British, French, Portuguese, and Spanish scholars. There is also a healthy supply of eyewitness accounts of the fighting, including the campaigns that took place in Portugal, and specifically Porto. All of the above illustrate the continued importance of the war: the military strategy, the divisions it caused in Portugal, the consequences for the Portuguese royal family, and the impact on Brazilian independence. For although it was a European war, its effects reached well beyond the shores of the continent. In this respect, it was one of the first truly global conflicts.

In Porto, the Bishop who ruled over the city, the British Port wine traders, the Portuguese armed forces, and the inhabitants of the city all understood that the French were on their way. As in past conflicts, Porto knew that it was a prime target for an invading army into the Peninsula. The river, access to the ocean, a successful working port, and the British Port wine trade were all attractive to the French invasion force. By following the route of the French garrison and its battles along the way, the Bishop concluded that the city had three weeks to prepare its defences in order to prevent the French from entering the city. The decision to fortify the city indicated that two strategic decisions had already been taken. First, and most important, was that Porto would fight. It would not lie down and try to appease the French by coming to a formal agreement or memorandum of understanding with them. Second, and most problematic, it indicated that the Bishop and his military commanders believed that they had a chance of defeating the mighty French army led by Marshal General Jean-de-Dieu Soult.

This self-confidence proved to be very misplaced when the reality of the city's precarious position became clearer.

There was another aspect to this programme of fortifying the defences of the city, one which is often overlooked; namely it was a unifying factor for the heavily divided population of Porto. Putting the people to work appeared a good plan. There had been rioting in the streets as news reached Porto that Braga had fallen to the French.[2] In the three-week period prior to the arrival of the French on the outskirts of the city, much work had been undertaken and completed. Under the Bishop of Porto's leadership, guns had been placed in the west of the city on fortified buildings, such as at the old fort in Foz known locally as the *Castelo do Queijo* (Cheese Castle). Artillery was placed in lines next to houses on the outskirts of the town and also on the commanding monastery over the river in Gaia, which overlooked the quays in Porto. In total there were approximately 200 artillery pieces in place to repel any French attack. In the city, there were secondary lines of defence. These were of a more primitive nature: barricades and cut down trees lay across the main arteries of the city.[3] The numbers of men in the city ready to face the French was not fully clear. There were approximately 9,000 armed inhabitants of the city and more or less 5,000 regular troops (although many of these were highly inexperienced, and for a large number this was to be their first and last experience of combat).[4] In addition, there were thousands of Portuguese from outside the city who had taken refuge as other cities and towns in the north of Portugal fell to the French[5].

Prior to the arrival of the French on the outskirts of the city, the Bishop of Porto crossed the river and moved to the relative safety of a retreat on the hilltop in Gaia overlooking the city. Before doing so, he handed over control of the defence of Porto to his generals.[6] The imminent arrival of the French had led to increased tension and fighting amongst the inhabitants of Porto. Anybody accused of passively or actively supporting the French was killed. Those in prison for similar crimes were taken out and killed, their bodies dragged around the city as a punishment and a warning to others. Underneath all the noise of the songs and the banging of drums, a deep sense of anxiety and forboding prevailed among even the most hardened of the regular fighters. The military strategists among the fighters understood that they were backed up against the river. There was no exit route, except for the Bridge of Boats across the river to Gaia. It was widely presumed, correctly, that the French would very quickly control all other exits from the city by land.

Marshal Soult did not have much of a track record of entering into negotiations with the Portuguese in order to avoid a battle, with its resulting human casualties and damage to the city. As the French forces massed and readied themselves to attack Porto, it was difficult to see any other outcome other than a French victory, despite the local efforts to build up the defences in and around the city. On this occasion, however, the marshal decided it was worth making an effort to come to an arrangement with the Bishop of Porto. If he really thought that there was any chance of success, then he was to be disappointed. More likely, the French commander wanted to at least make the offer safe in the knowledge that it would more likely than not be rejected by the Bishop, whose rhetoric indicated that he and the rest of the city were up for the fight. Easy to say for the Bishop when holed up in a monastery in Gaia out of harm's way for at least any initial assault on Porto. Soult was very direct in warning the Bishop to avoid the 'horrors of a sack' of the city.[7] He went on to make the case that France came not as an enemy of Portugal, but rather as a liberator to free them from England and its controlling hand.

The messenger sent to the Bishop by Marshal Soult was carefully chosen. A Portuguese major who had been captured during a previous battle for Braga. As the major reached the first line of the defences for the city, he staked his claim to be allowed to enter. Mob rule characterised the mood of many of the outposts which were run by irregulars and locals. The life of the quick-thinking messenger was only spared when he informed those manning the barricade that he had come to offer the surrender of the French army to the Bishop as Marshal Soult was appalled by the strength of the defences around the city. That such a story was believable to people reflects the sense of unreality and collective macho bravado that was present among the irregulars. The answer from the Bishop of Porto and his generals did not take long. Just as Soult expected, it was defiant and challenging. In retrospect, a terrible mistake. It was quickly transmitted to the French commander who prepared his forces for the assault on Porto, which he decreed would start early the next morning.

Soult decided against ordering a replay of the frontal attack that he had employed so successfully in the taking of Braga. Instead, with 16,000 men available he opted to attack on each of the Portuguese flanks, concentrating on the west where he believed the defences to be at their weakest. His hope was that the Portuguese would have to reinforce this by moving men and artillery away from the north of the city; the central zone. By holding back his men from attacking here, Soult believed that the Portuguese would weaken their centre. At this moment the division he had hidden would attack and cut the Portuguese line in two and this would allow French troops to rapidly reach and take the city centre and move down to the riverfront. In terms of military strategy, it was not a complicated plan, but Soult felt that it would help render much of the heavily defended areas to the north of the city much easier to take, helping to reduce French casualties and ensuring a quick victory.

In the early hours of the morning of 29 March 1809, all appeared quiet. The French garrison was resting, preparing for the assault on the city due to commence at dawn. Inside the city, there was persistent movement as Portuguese regular and irregular soldiers continued with last-minute additions to their defences. Much of this activity was cosmetic, but it provided a welcome distraction from thinking about what lay ahead. The city contained a strange mixture of veteran locals and outsiders drawn from all parts of northern Portugal. There was a deep sense of nervousness about what was going to happen. The outsiders brought with them tales (some true, but many exaggerated) about the behaviour of the victorious French army in Braga and throughout the north of Portugal. The intention of the storytellers was to help fuel anti-French sentiment among the inhabitants of Porto. Instead, it created anxiety, and a sense that if the city was overrun that the local population would not be spared by an allegedly ill-disciplined and tired French army. Among the women of the city, the tales of rapes and mass killings in northern Portugal caused alarm. As Porto prepared for battle it did so with a strange mixture of defiance, bravado, and trepidation. Few showed the latter feeling, internalising it, and the songs that people sung highlighted the former two emotions.

Tensions were heightened by the constant ringing of church bells across the city. Orders were issued that the bells should be rung all night. They were meant to reassure and remind the inhabitants of the city that God was on their side and that they would prevail. They sounded more like the music for the damned, the impending doom, and the sounds of death and destruction. As darkness fell the skies were clear, promising a clear bright morning for the battle the next day. Then, as so often happens in Porto with its proximity to the Atlantic Ocean, a new weather front rolled in without any warning. The bright stars that lit up the city soon disappeared as a cloak of darkness hung over the city, making navigation around the narrow high-walled streets of the centre all the more difficult. The wind that had hitherto been absent started to gather pace, whipping up mini dust-storms around the barricades. Preparing for the next morning's battle, the majority of the French troops slept through the change in the weather. The defenders of the city remained too absorbed in their own thoughts to pay it much attention.

At 3.00 am, torrential rain started to fall, followed soon after by a thunderstorm and a hurricane that crossed the city from a north-westerly direction. In all the ensuing confusion – the flashes of sheet lightening, the roar of thunder – some Portuguese thought that the French attack had started. Quickly manning their positions, they started firing their heavy guns, which added to the commotion. Soon small arms fire was heard across the city. As Charles Sellers wrote:

Suddenly there was a vivid flash of lightening accompanied by a terrific squall which, whistling among the tents, made the Portuguese imagine that the French were on them. Running to their guns, fuse in hand, a terrific cannonade commenced from the 200 guns while the infantry discharged their pieces, and what with Heaven's artillery and the reply of the 50 guns from the Serra the terror-stricken inhabitants of Oporto rushed wildly about the streets not knowing where to go for safety.[8]

Lying down in the open, the French forces were drenched by the thunderstorm. Soult decided to postpone the attack for an hour to give the French soldiers time to dry off, eat breakfast, and for the condition of the wet and muddy ground to improve. The respite for the tired and weary Portuguese defenders, who had been awake most of the night, was short-lived. At precisely 7.00 am the French launched their attack on the Portuguese flanks. As Soult had expected, his men made rapid progress on the western flank, forcing the Portuguese to reinforce, while the French then intensified their efforts on the eastern flank. During this time, Soult refrained from attacking the central lines. The plan worked, as the Portuguese were forced to reinforce the east flanks with troops from the centre, thus weakening this crucial area. When the attack on the centre came it was swift, massive, and decisive. The French soon broke though the defences and took two forts. Two French battalions moved to attack the left flank of the Portuguese from the rear, to prevent any chance of them re-entering the city. Soult's plan to split the flanks and drive through the middle was tactically complete.

What followed could politely be called mopping up operations, or more accurately a free-for-all. As French forces burst through the centre, killing all who stood in their way regardless of whether they were combatants or women and children, they created an intentional wave of panic among the largely leaderless local inhabitants. The local Portuguese commander in charge of the central zone, General Parreiras, left the battlefield soon after the French central thrust. He fled over the Bridge of Boats with the apparent purpose of reaching the Bishop of Porto in Gaia to warn him that his army had been routed by the French and that Porto was on fire (in case the Bishop could not see this for himself from his hilltop vantage point over the city). Much of the rest of

Porto followed close on the heels of the general. A few inhabitants bravely continued to man the barricades, although the battle was lost, and paid with their lives as the French battalions ruthlessly, without mercy, stormed though the city towards the riverbank.

As news spread of the impending defeat, the pressure on the quays area of the city intensified as people tried to escape to the apparent safety of Gaia across the river. Almost instantly, the bravado and self-confidence of the previous days and weeks had been obliterated by the swift French advance. Resilience quickly turned to panic as the terrible reality of defeat dawned on Porto. French soldiers entered the narrow cobblestoned streets that make their way down to the quays. Using their bayonets they cut down anything, and everybody, that they came across during these hours of madness. As rumours spread of massacres carried out by the French forces on the outskirts of the city and the defeat of two flanks of the Portuguese defences, the only thing left to do for the inhabitants of the city was to save their own souls. In the centre, the French raced down to the quays in the hope of cutting off any retreating Portuguese cavalry and artillery. Their orders were to make the victory as total as possible and to prevent any reforming of Portuguese lines across the river in Gaia, especially on top of the Serra.

The flow of traffic across the Bridge of Boats was enormous. Women, children, irregular and regular soldiers all trying to reach what they envisaged to be safety in Gaia. Then disaster struck. An unknown Portuguese officer, operating without orders from higher authority, ordered the drawbridge on the central pontoons of the bridge to be raised to prevent the French from following the fleeing Portuguese across the river into Gaia. The drawbridge had originally been installed to allow shipping to sail upriver, something of a game changer for its era. Different reasons were offered for this act of madness. It was said that the order was given by the fleeing commander of the garrison in Porto to prevent his capture by the bridge. Others surmise that the drawbridge was raised to protect Gaia and the Bishop of Porto without any understanding of the enormous volume of people who would try to escape using the Bridge of Boats.[9] Some second-hand eyewitness accounts speculated that the cause of the disaster was simply that the middle of the bridge could not take the excessive weight of the people and that the boats simply sank, creating the sizeable gap in the middle.[10] Most first-hand accounts, however, report seeing the drawbridge raised.

Whatever the reasons for this incomprehensible decision, the consequences were devastating. The first group of people reached the gap in the bridge and ground to a swift halt. The pressure of the traffic still entering the bridge was too much. In all the confusion it was impossible for those people at the edge of the river to see that the drawbridge had been raised, so they kept coming. Scared, believing that their lives were in danger, they started to push. The congestion and the pushing got worse.[11] The noise was truly terrifying. Shrieks, screaming, and shouting of the most terrible words. Those unlucky enough to be nearest to the raised drawbridge could feel the air being squeezed out of their lungs, suffocating and searching for air they turned around and tried to move back towards the riverbank. This created a sandwich with those pushing to get to Gaia and those pushing back to Porto. Still more people tried to get onto the bridge. The French were getting ever nearer. Those people still on the quays could hear the sounds of boots and the shouts in a foreign language. The screams of people being butchered by the lead soldiers reached the riverbank, echoing through the built-up streets like a bugle, warning of impending doom.

Suddenly out of the shaded streets the first French soldiers appeared in the bright sunlight of the quays. With muskets already loaded they immediately opened fire on both the quays and the bridge. Their aim was indiscriminate. The screams of those trying to escape from the bridge were drowned out by the noise of the guns. Fire; reload, and fire, the routine took only a short time to repeat. Watching the horrors from the safety of the Serra do Pilar monastery in Gaia, the Portuguese commanders gave the order for the twenty guns that were perched on its high hill to open fire on the French. The noise of the artillery being fired in unison must have been deafening. This made it impossible for those trapped on the bridge to communicate with those still trying to push their way onto it. The artillery fire directed from Gaia was not wholly accurate with several shells landing short. Caught between French muskets and Portuguese shells, people saw gaining access onto the bridge as the only hope of survival.

In the middle of the bridge people were being pushed by the mass of bodies into the river. The volume of people pushing the centre was greater than those trying to get back to the riverbank. Soon the forty-foot gap in the middle of the bride was filed with drowning and dead people. The pressure on the bridge increased even more with the arrival of the remnants of a group of Portuguese cavalry, trying to escape to Gaia after their exit to the east of the city was blocked by the French. Galloping into the crowd, trampling everybody in their way at the bridgehead they continued to try to drive forward until the sheer numbers of people meant that they could proceed no further. The actions of the cavalry pushed more people onto the bridge from the riverbank, and more poor souls into the river in the gap by the raised drawbridge. After nearly thirty minutes, the number of people falling into the gap reduced, but the weight and pushing on the bridge led to some of the wooden guardrails breaking, throwing additional people into the water. It was a terrible scene with people disappearing under water, reappearing, and then disappearing again, dragged under. A few people made it across the river to Gaia. The majority did not.

The French soon realised that those fleeing onto the bridge were not returning their fire. Noticing that the people were mainly women, children, and non-combatants, they ceased their deadly firing. Instead, soldiers started to rescue people caught in the river, helping them back onto the shore. Turning their muskets round, French soldiers used the butts of their weapons for crowd control purposes. They moved the vast crowds at the riverbank away from the bridge, sending them up very same streets that the French had charged down. This reduced the pressure on the bridge, allowing a more orderly evacuation of those on it back towards the city. Later that afternoon, French engineers fixed the bridge and, under fire from Portuguese forces from across the river, proceeded to cross into Gaia. Soon after they were able to pacify the Portuguese force and stormed up to the Serra, seizing the artillery guns that had fired upon them earlier in the day.[12]

In Porto, French forces spent the remainder of the day brutally mopping up pockets of Portuguese resistance. The costliest for the Portuguese was at the Bishop's Palace in the south of the city where hundreds of irregulars had been holed up. After breaking down the large gates to the palace, French soldiers bayonetted all they found after entering the building. While the soldiers who had to deal with the disaster at the Bridge of Boats acted in a disciplined and honourable manner, much of the rest of Porto was subjected to the 'sack' that General Soult had tried to avoid. Rape, looting, and arson attacks were widespread, carried out by French forces drunk on their victory. Civilians were often killed for no reason other than being in the wrong place at the wrong time. Soult went out of his way to stop the crime spree, ordering his officers to rein in their men.

The people of Porto, so confident of resisting the mighty mechanised French army only twenty-four hours earlier, were downcast and angry at the failure of the military leadership. All military defeats are terrible for the losers, but the unexpected swiftness of the French overrunning of the city and the consequences of the occupation were hard to comprehend. Local inhabitants were also guilty of atrocities in the heat of battle:

> Every street and house now rung with the noise of the combatants and the shrieks of distress; for the French soldiers, exasperated by long hardships, and prone like all soldiers to ferocity and violence during an assault, became frantic with fury, when, in one of the principal squares, they found several of their comrades who had been made prisoners, fastened upright, and living, but with their eyes bursted, their tongues torn out, and their other members mutilated and gashed. Those that beheld the sight spared none who fell in their way.[13]

For Marshal Soult, the overall military operation had vindicated his strategy of pushing on one flank at a time to divert enemy troops away from the heavily guarded centre ground, before a mass push through the midpoint when the two flanks were cut off and weakened. French casualty figures were remarkably low for taking such a heavily defended city as Porto. Total French losses were put at under eighty dead and 350 wounded. Estimates on the number of Portuguese who died in the attack range from 4,000 to 20,000. Most historians lean towards the lower figure.[14] A number of the defeated Portuguese returned to fight in later battles of the Peninsular War. An unknown number of people drowned in the Bridge of Boats tragedy; most estimates are in the region of thousands, rather than hundreds. The damage to the economy included the confiscation of agricultural lands near the city, animals, and foodstuff, as well as the general climate of political uncertainty.[15] The French took over what they could: the finest buildings for their officers and the garrison was well supplied by produce from the Porto region.

For Marshal Soult, the victory in Porto provided him with a key central operational base that allowed the French forces to conduct an orchestrated campaign of warfare in Portugal. The fruits of his victory included gunpowder and 197 pieces of seized working artillery. An additional bonus was the capture of the thirty English ships, which had been wind-stuck in the river, unable to get out to sea. The ships were carrying wine and food for their voyage.[16] Following the sacking of the city, Soult adopted a conciliatory tone and tried to repair relations with the city's population. He ordered the return of some of the plunder that the French had seized, called for the inhabitants of the city to be treated fairly, and for those who had left the city to return. He promised to stop any additional violence from his men directed against the city. Opportunities were offered to key local traders and noblemen to collaborate with the occupying power: an offer several locals took up.

For the visitor to fully comprehend the magnitude of the events of 29 March 1809, it would be misleading to simply call them a French sacking of the city. The attack on Porto represented an important point in the implementation of Napoleon's aim of invading Portugal, southern Spain, and the Levant that would bring this phase of the war to an end in France's favour. He outlined his plans to his generals at the start of the year and believed that the war could be over by the summer. Napoleon believed the political situation in Portugal and Spain made them ripe for a swift takeover. Despite notable successes, such as Porto, progress was not as rapid as Napoleon had hoped and there were an increasing number of setbacks to match the successes of Marshal Soult. The capture of Porto was important for the French, but circumstances were changing and the retention of control over the city proved to be more challenging than its capture.[17] France's position in northern Portugal weakened during the later spring and early summer as Britain, with the important help of Portuguese troops, mounted a fightback.

4

Liberation Day

Our gaining possession of Oporto was a scene the most animating and impressive I shall most probably witness. Where we crossed the river a large white flag with a black cross was hoisted, fragments of the bridge, and those burning, were floating on the water, reports of cannon and musketry were heard in every direction, and the waving of handkerchiefs by the nuns through the grating of their convent accompanied by loud acclamations of 'Deliverers' from every window increased the natural eagerness of our soldiers to meet the French.[1]

John Aitchison

AFTER LEAVING AVENIDA DA República, and its viewing area over the city, the visitor should walk back towards Gaia for a hundred metres and then up a rather steep, inclined road to Mosteiro da Serra do Pilar (Serra do Pilar monastery). The monastery proudly stands overlooking the Dom Luís I Bridge and the entrance to central Porto, like a sentry watching over its guard. Today, it provides the visitor with a panoramic view over the city and the river to the west. For those who enter its gardens it is also possible to view the river to the east of Porto as it snakes and starts to head towards the interior of the country. In 1996, the monastery was designated a UNESCO World Heritage Site, making it one of several sites in the Porto region to be recognised by the United Nations.

There are few areas of the city that are not visible from this elevated location. Naturally, in times of war and invasion, the location became strategically important to foreign armies that were either defending, or invading, the city. In the past, tall trees obscured the view to the city, and more importantly made it difficult for armies based in Porto to be able to see the manoeuvrings that were taking place on its forecourt or in its garden. Most famously, the British commander, Sir Arthur Wellesley (awarded the title of the Duke of Wellington in 1814) exploited the strategically important position of the monastery to launch a surprise attack against the French garrison that were occupying Porto during the Peninsular War. The operation became one of the most famous of Wellesley's career and led to the rapid withdrawal of the French forces from the city. It also proved to be the nail in the coffin of the French presence in the north of Portugal. It was not, however, a totally successful action against the French forces. Controversy remains as to how, and why, the British were unable to rout the rapidly retreating French army, and instead allowed the vast majority of Soult's forces to escape through northern Portugal back into Spain.

Despite the eventual British victory, the war resulted in changes in Anglo-Portuguese relations, not all of them positive. In a letter to the British from an (anonymous) seemingly influential Portuguese person who wished to highlight the perils of close relations for the Portuguese with Britain wrote on the Peninsular War:

> After the French invasions, the Portuguese soldier could well ask himself what benefit he had obtained by vanquishing Napoleon's general's, when Wellington's general's took their place, or whether they were merely substituting one tyranny for another... The two nations were bound by a political alliance, but there was neither friendship, nor sympathy between the two people.[2]

The comments, while not totally representative of Portuguese opinion, revealed the long-lasting deep sense of frustration at the injustice suffered by Portugal at the hands of Britain during, and after, the Peninsular War. Here it is important to remember two salient facts: a large number of Portuguese irregular soldiers had served with the British during the war, and many were killed or wounded during the fighting. Much of the Portuguese landscape was a battleground between the British and French armies and was either partially or totally destroyed in the fighting, resulting in major food shortages. It was not only the land that fell victim to the war; the Portuguese population was subjected to brutal treatment by the invading French army. Local uprisings were put down by brute force and intimidation of the civilian population was widespread as the occupiers tried to cement their control over the country. The British commander Arthur Wellesley commented on this ill-treatment by the French in his dispatches from the Peninsula, as he chased the French out of northern Portugal:

> Their soldiers have plundered and murdered the peasantry at their pleasure; and I have seen many persons hanging in the trees by the sides of roads, executed for no reason that I could learn, excepting that they have not been friendly to the French invasion and usurpation of the government of their country, and the route of their column on their retreat could be traced by the smoke of the villages to which they set fire.[3]

The Portuguese population was not slow to take their revenge, often killing French prisoners in the most brutal manner. A British soldier involved in the retaking of Porto by British forces wrote home 'the inhabitants of Porto were most severely punished for their insubordination and want of animosity, but they provoked the cruelties that were practiced by the French'.[4] In Porto, Arthur Wellesley was concerned enough by the reaction of local population to the retreating French that the British posted a warning sign that read:

Inhabitants of Porto!

The French troops have been expelled from this town by the superior gallantry and discipline of the army under my command,

I call upon the inhabitants of Porto to be merciful to the wounded and prisoners... they are entitled to my protection... these unfortunate persons... can only be considered as instruments in the hands of the more powerful who are still in arms against us.[5]

All the retribution that was the result of the invasion and the occupation should not obscure the brilliance and simplicity of the British victory over the French at Porto. The attack helped confirm Wellesley's reputation as a first-rate, fast-thinking, strategically flexible commander. Standing on the terrace of the Serra do Pilar monastery, hopefully on a day when there is a deep blue sky and good visibility across the city (just as the British forces enjoyed) it is easy to visualise the challenges that Wellesley faced on that bright morning on 12 May 1809 as his forces gathered on the south bank of the River Douro in Gaia. The visitor needs to imagine the river with no bridges. The French army had blown up the Bridge of Boats. To make matters worse for the British, the French had taken all the boats from the south bank over to the city of Porto on the north bank. Boats used to transport Port wine, small fishing boats and those used to ferry people over the river were either destroyed or taken to the north bank.

For their part the French commander, Marshal Soult, believed the city to be secure in French hands with the deep wide river between his French forces and the British on the other riverbank. His only concern was a potential British attempt to use boats that had been used to land additional troops at Ovar, a small coastal town to the south of Porto. Marshal Soult believed that the most likely course of action for Wellesley would be to use the boats to ferry his men to a point in the estuary to the west of the city, near the small resort town of Foz where the river depth was at its lowest point. As a result he gave the order for the French to carefully patrol the whole riverbank between the city and Foz.[6] The vast majority of French forces were therefore stationed either in the centre of Porto or to the west of the city. This proved to be a fatal mistake. At the time, the French commander believed that his forces would be able to repel any river landing by the British by rapidly introducing reinforcements from the city centre into any battle taking place to the west of Porto.

The French were already planning an orderly retreat from Porto. Marshal Soult was intent on remaining in the city for just as long it took another part of his force to secure the route out to the east of the city through the town of Amarante, onto Vila Real and from there over the border to Spain. Soult wanted to keep his army intact and its heavy weapons for use in future battles with the British forces. The potential exit from Porto was proving to be more difficult however, as British forces had been dispatched to the east of Porto to cross the river upstream and try to block the expected escape route for the French. Both Soult and Wellesley understood that a French retreat in a northerly direction from Porto towards north-western Spain would prove to be much more hazardous. The mountain terrain and narrow, winding, poorly marked tracks, did not lend itself well to a retreating army accompanied by its big guns. Soult concluded it was worth remaining in Porto for a while longer to hold out for the easterly route, with little danger of the British being able to launch a major offensive across the river without the necessary boats. He presumed that it would take Wellesley days, perhaps even weeks, to head east towards the Douro where his forces would be able to cross the river.

Standing on the balcony of the large luxurious villa where he had based himself since his arrival in Porto, Soult could survey all the river valley from the west of the city right out to Foz and the start of the Atlantic Ocean. His views to the eastern part of the city were for the first part excellent, but the hill on the top of which sat the Serra do Pilar monastery blocked his view any further. At that point the river bends, taking a small turn to navigate its way around the steep heights of the land on the southern bank making the river invisible from the north bank of the city centre. Soult did not think this area worthy of stationing a battalion along the riverbank or in the buildings that overlooked that part of the river. Had either he, or one his commanders, paid greater attention to the area they would have noticed that the riverbank on the Porto side of the Douro offered good protection for a river crossing. Olive groves and high-walled gardens with pathways wound towards the river. The riverbank itself was covered with thick weeds that grew to over a metre high. Everything rested on boats. Along the riverbank were a couple of ferries that had been brought to the northern bank of the river, but they had not been scuttled. The French had not even posted guards to watch over them. Perhaps the area was simply out of sight and out of mind for Soult who wanted the vast majority of his forces to concentrate on the centre and western approaches.

The morning of 12 May 1809 was hot. Not quite the heat of summer, but the sun was already strong enough to break up any mist that hung over the river between the two armies. British and French soldiers were taking a rest after days of battling to the south of the city. There was little expectation of action on this day as it was clear to all that the British had to cross the River Douro from the south bank and all the boats had been destroyed or were moored on the north bank. French officers believed it highly improbable that Wellesley would mount a direct attack across the river in broad daylight on his first day in Gaia. There were early morning rumours that the British might march up the river, as Marshal Soult thought they would, and cross over further inland. The French garrison was busy patrolling the areas to the west of the city looking for any boats trying to enter the river from the Atlantic Ocean at Foz. Soldiers based in the city centre when not on patrol looked for shaded cover from the sun in the narrow cobblestoned streets. Soult had gone to bed believing his plan for an orderly retreat to the east was going well.

Wellesley had moved his troops up into Gaia with his leading forces located on top of the hill next to the Serra do Pilar monastery. The position of the troops and heavy guns was shielded from the French by large trees, orchards, and vineyards. Other parts of the force were hidden by the natural incline of the hill which made it impossible to detect them from Porto. Wellesley spoke with several Portuguese nobles, many of whom had come across the river the previous day and who were well acquainted with French troop positions on the Porto side of the river. Wellesley had arrived with no real plans as to how to remove the French from the city.[7] Standing in the small, but beautifully maintained, garden of the monastery, he surveyed the scene in Porto through his glasses. He saw a hive of French activity by the north-eastern gate to the city where large columns of infantry were gathering. In mid-morning, the soldiers headed off along with a number of wagons. This was the start of the French evacuation of 'sick and reserve artillery' going in the direction of Amarante.[8] In the centre, he saw the narrow streets opening onto the riverfront where there were several boats. French forces, he noted, appeared to be heavily concentrated in this area.

It was when he turned his glasses to the right from the monastery's garden that Wellesley sensed the possibility of an opportunity. Looking upstream he noticed that things appeared much quieter. The riverbank was quite rocky with good cover and the few isolated buildings looked to be deserted. Initially, Wellesley was a little suspicious of the seeming calm of the scene. He feared that French troops might be hiding in the buildings. His mood improved when his intelligence officers, who had earlier been dispatched upriver, returned with an important piece of information. A ferry boat moored four miles upriver at Barco d'Avintas, which the French had damaged, had been quickly (and quietly) repaired by the local villagers.

Better still came the news that Colonel Waters, one of Wellesley's best scouts, had come across a local barber who had crossed the river in a small boat, which he had hidden in the reeds on the bank. The barber confirmed that the opposite bank had been left unguarded by the French and that there were four wine barges moored there with no signs of damage to any of them. There was one large isolated building, which was soon identified as the Bishop's Seminary, and this was surrounded at the back by a garden with a high wall and an overgrown pathway down to the riverbank. The building was isolated with the ground around it fairly open. This made it easier to use artillery fire from the monastery on the south bank to protect a British landing. Wellesley sent his men back down to the riverbank to scout the location and to double-check for any French movements. There he was assured that if the British could get enough men across before being detected by the French they would be able to reach the old the Bishop's Seminary building. It was risky, but the British commander had to weigh up other factors as well.

Wellesley was keen to move quickly to take Porto and then give help to British forces operating to the west under Marshal Beresford. His decision to attack was made easier by what he viewed as the French lack of alertness. As the sun burnt down, the French appeared to be napping. He gave the order to go immediately:

> It was important with a view to the operations of Marshal Beresford that I should cross the Douro immediately, and I had sent Major General Murray in the morning with a battalion of the King's German Legion, a squadron of cavalry, and two 6 pounders, to endeavour to collect boats, and if possible, to cross the river at Avintes, about four miles above Porto; and I had as many boats as could be collected brought to the ferry, immediately above the towns of Porto and Gaia.[9]

After persuading a slightly reluctant barber to ferry a small team of British officers to the north bank, they headed off and soon returned with the Port wine boats. The crossing had been uneventful, confirming that the area was free of French forces. As the first wave of around twenty-five troops loaded into the leading boat, Wellesley went down to the riverbank to bid them farewell. Fifteen minutes later the first British troops landed and ran up into seminary closing its big iron gate. The other boats soon landed on the northern bank of the river and the troops secured the outer walls of the seminary. Wellesley watched the whole operation through his glasses. For over an hour, he feared that if their presence on the northern bank was detected the operation could have failed. A second and then a third crossing of the boats was made, still without any shots being fired by the French.

When the first French shots rang out, breaking the peaceful calm of a sweaty spring morning, a full hour had passed since the first wave of British boats had set out to cross the river. The French commanders had been caught off guard, just as Wellesley hoped. Marshal Soult was still sleeping, and a number of his senior officers were taking their morning coffee in the city. Upon hearing the news that 'the English had got into the town' a furious Soult gave the order to move a large amount of his men and heavy guns to the east of the city to drive the English back into the river.[10] The crossing had first been discovered by the French at around 10.30 am, but it took another hour before they were able to launch a sustained attack on the seminary building.

Watching from the gardens of the hilltop monastery on the south side of the river, Wellesley gave the order for the impressive range of British guns to open fire on the French assault on the seminary on the northern bank. Time and again the French were driven back by fire from inside the seminary, and from a near-constant wave of artillery shells fired from the monastery. In a last gamble, Soult brought in the French division that had been guarding the quays in the centre of Porto. He wanted to have one last go at removing the British, and if that failed, to start a withdrawal in the direction of Amarante.[11] It was a mistake of gigantic proportions. As soon as the soldiers moved, and the quays were no longer adequately guarded, the local population came out of their houses, made their way swiftly down the narrow streets to the riverbank and launched all the boats that the French had moved to the northern bank on the previous evening. Very soon the boats were picking up British troops and heading back to Porto. The swarms of British soldiers arriving at the quays in Porto charged up the hills, meeting only token resistance from French stragglers.

The British soldiers then headed towards the seminary to help relieve the soldiers under fire from the ongoing French attack. Within thirty minutes, the soldiers reached and engaged the flank of the French force that was firing on the seminary. A brief battle continued before Marshal Soult understood that the situation was hopeless and ordered the French to pull out of the city. It was a sorry sight, a full-scale retreat at speed with a startling lack of organisation. News soon spread through the city, and the local population came out to celebrate and to seek revenge on the unfortunate French prisoners and wounded that were left behind. Additional fighting continued in the Douro region, as the British missed a golden opportunity there to inflict a decisive defeat on Soult. The French did suffer. Cut off from their planned route of retreat they were harassed as they made their way through some of the most challenging terrain in Portugal as they headed north for Galicia. The weather did not help; it rained incessantly during the retreat. French forces eventually reached the Spanish border on 18 May, but only after almost being trapped by the British. The cost to Marshal Soult was enormous: 4,000 dead, his big guns lost, and the remainder of his fighting force was out of action until the end of the summer.[12] British losses during the Porto campaign and the resulting chase were minimal when compared to the French numbers.

The taking of Porto from the French presented Wellesley with a much-needed victory, and an unexpectedly rapid one. His frustration at not being able to finish off Soult shone through in his letters back to England. He wrote to the Duke of Richmond from Porto on 22 May 1809:

> I have just returned from the most active and severe service. I have been on the pursuit, or rather chase of Soult out of Portugal. We should have taken him if Silveira had been one or two hours earlier at the bridge of Melgaço, or if the captain of the militia of the province had allowed the peasants, as they wished, to destroy it. We should have taken his rear-guard on the 16th, if we had a quarter of an hour's more daylight, but in the dark our light infantry pursued by the road to Rivaes instead of by that of Melgaço. But as it is, the chase is out of Portugal is a pendant for the retreat from Coruña. It answers completely in weather: it has rained torrents since the 12th.[13]

For the inhabitants of Porto, the ending of the French occupation brought to a dramatic conclusion a difficult chapter in the city's history. The feeling that the country was not yet free from the horrors of the Peninsular War proved to be well-founded. An interesting counter-narrative history to Wellesley's decision to seize the moment on the first morning was that the rains that arrived and washed out much of the rest of May would have made any crossing of the River Douro all the more difficult. Fortune favoured the brave.

PART TWO

Day One – Afternoon

5

Absolutism versus Liberalism

Iberian civil wars follow, in recent centuries, a pattern. It
is a war between constitutionalism and absolutism, liberty
and tyranny, liberalism (often with a little Freemasonry
thrown in) and clericalism; in brief between Left and Right.
Carlist wars, Miguelist wars, legitimist wars, uncles against
nieces, dictators against republicans: whatever form they
assume, their basis is the same. The same too is the cleavage
of opinion about them abroad: liberals support one side,
conservatives the other.[1]

Rose Macaulay

THE EXPULSION OF THE French from Porto did not mark
the end of the Peninsular War. Many major battles followed,
along with another French invasion of parts of Portugal,
culminating with the famous British and Portuguese defensive lines
at Torres Vedras, some 200 kilometres south of Porto. When the war
eventually ended with France's defeat in 1814, Portugal entered a
new period of crisis and instability leading to civil war and the Siege
of Porto, bringing much hardship to the inhabitants of the city. The
catalyst for the crisis was the leadership vacuum in Portugal caused
by the Peninsular War. The ingredients included royalty, nobility,
freemasonry, and the British, all vying to control the heart and soul
of the political direction of the country. Once again, Porto found
itself centre stage, in the thick of the debate, its lands fought over
by rival factions trying to secure hegemony for their vision of a
political system over that of their bitter rivals. In the end, the choice

came down to a war between two brothers from the royal family who became figureheads of the dispute between absolutism and liberalism. Before recounting the story of royal versus royal and the resulting civil war, the visitor should first make their entry into the city of Porto from Gaia.

As the visitor makes their way down from the monastery and heads towards the Dom Luís I Bridge to cross into Porto, there are fine examples of a more 'positive' French influence over the city. Walking over the top tier of the often incorrectly labelled 'Eiffel Bridge' into Porto, upriver, the old single-track metal railway bridge (which Eiffel did contribute to), has now been replaced. The previously mentioned Bridge of Boats was dismantled in 1842, replaced by a suspension bridge built by the French engineer, Stanislas Bigot. The bridge was single-tiered, running from the riverbank in Porto straight across to the opposite side. It represented a massive improvement over the Bridge of Boats, but its single deck was not adequate to carry the increasing amount of traffic crossing the river.[2]

Before any final decision was taken to construct a new road crossing, the city opted to build a railway bridge to bring the Lisbon to Porto railway service across the River Douro and into the city. Gustave Eiffel's proposal won the competition to build the bridge; his company's proposal was said to be considerably cheaper than the rival bids. The bridge made of wrought iron, eventually opened to much fanfare on 4 November 1877. Said to be one of the longest iron arch bridges at the time of its construction, running to 353 metres, at its highest point it was sixty metres above the river level. Its supporting arch was no less spectacular: at 160 metres, it was the largest in the world. Various names were put forward for the bridge, before settling on Maria Pia Bridge, after the queen consort of the serving monarch, King Luis I. Its design attracted rave reviews at its opening, but there were persistent questions about its structural integrity. At the start of the twentieth century, the single track, six-metre-wide bridge had a speed limit of 10 km/h imposed on the trains chugging over the top of it. On windy days, the sway of the bridge was noticeable, unnerving, and, at times, downright scary for passengers. As well as serving the Porto to Lisbon line, a number of regional services used it, connecting Porto with Gaia, and the hinterland towns and villages along the Atlantic coast.

For much of the twentieth century concerted efforts were made by Portuguese and international engineers to try to reinforce the platform and the support structure of the bridge. It was a race against time as train travel was becoming more sophisticated and the weight of locomotives and carriages grew heavier, putting additional strain on the bridge. Cement was pumped into the foundations to reinforce creeping joints. The electrification of the Lisbon to Porto line imposed additional challenges for engineers. The bridge was eventually closed to rail traffic in 1991, replaced by a new dedicated rail bridge linking Gaia to Porto; the Ponte de São João. At the time of its closure, trains operated only on a single line with a maximum speed of 20 km/h. Local gossip claimed that every time a train went over the bridge a bolt fell out of it into the river below. Since its closure, a number of proposals have been submitted to find a use for it, including turning it into a cycle bridge, illuminating it at night as a tourist attraction, or using it as a tourist train linking the centre of Porto with the Port wine companies in Gaia. Despite its lack of use, it remains a beautiful reminder of an era when wrought-iron bridges were considered to be futuristic in design and train travel slightly exotic and exciting. It must have been quite a sight to watch a steam locomotive making its way over the bridge, white smoke bellowing out its chimney, set against the backdrop of the shiny metal of the bridge and a deep blue summer sky. And for all its structural failings it completed the link between Portugal's first and second cities. No mean achievement.

As the visitor walks across the Dom Luís I Bridge, there is much to admire about the bridge prior to the arrival into the city of Porto. The linkage of Gustave Eiffel to the bridge is threefold, beginning with his presentation in 1879 of a detailed project to construct a single-tier bridge across the River Douro. The plan was rejected, not being considered radical enough to meet the increased growth in road traffic between Porto and Gaia. The preference was for a two-tier bridge, along the lines of the finished bridge seen today. The thinking behind this was to use both tiers for traffic with the top tier giving quick access into the centre of Porto, especially Avenida dos Aliados, an area undergoing a lot of development at the time. The lower deck was to link the two riverbanks, essentially replacing the original road suspension bridge. It was an ambitious project, reflecting the positive spirit of the era to construct infrastructure that would allow the area to develop and continue its trade links with the outside world into the twentieth century.

In 1880 the formal competition to construct the bridge was announced. Eiffel's company entered the competition, but it did not win. Disappointing for the Frenchman but not a disaster; his company went on to secure many other contracts, particularly related to railway infrastructure. The competition for the bridge was won by the Brussels-based company, Société de Willebroek, whose bid was considered to have represented the best value. The work for design and the construction of the bridge was given to the German-born Théophile Seyrig, who, when working for Eiffel's company, had designed the Maria Pia Bridge. Work began in 1881 and was not finished until 1886. The finished bridge resembled the wrought-iron railway bridge, but with the addition of a lower deck. In order to help pay for the cost of the construction of the bridge a toll was levied on those using it until 1944. Upon its completion, it dominated the river valley, sending a strong signal to the rest of Portugal, and the world, that the elegant industrial city of Porto was open for business. Locals wryly noted that Porto had constructed a modern bridge to link it with areas to the south of the city, while Lisbon had no similar bridge crossing the River Tagus to its southern satellite towns. Nor would it until the Salazar Bridge (renamed 25th April Bridge following the 1974 revolution) was inaugurated in 1966, eighty years after the Dom Luís I Bridge first opened. *Lisboetas* would probably point out that its bridge was 2,278 metres long, compared to the 395.25 metre length of the bridge in Porto (at its longest point), owing to the greater width of the River Tagus over the River Douro.

Nonetheless, as the visitor leaves the upper deck of the bridge, heading up a slight hill before descending into the city centre of Porto, the symbolism of having such a bridge was important to the local inhabitants. As the visitor walks past the imposing Sé do Porto (Porto Cathedral) on the left, to which they will return later, the most important building on the right is the magnificent São Bento railway station. Here, it is worth taking a moment to enter the building, the construction of which was another piece in Porto's jigsaw of creating a city fit to meet the challenges of early part of the twentieth century. The station building was a significant addition to the city centre, when it was officially inaugurated in 1916, but it was the tunnel, linking the city centre to the existing Campanhã station, located on the eastern outskirts of Porto, which was the greater engineering feat. Work on the tunnel had begun much earlier, in 1890, taking several years to construct.

The station building was designed by José Marques da Silva. Today, trains depart from it to head in a mainly northerly direction, linking Porto with Braga and Guimarães in the north, and Aveiro to the south. The most enjoyable train route however remains the line out to the Douro which provides views of the magnificent scenery of the Douro Valley as the trains run alongside the river. The train is often best combined with a boat trip to make for an enjoyable day out of the city. Boat up the river and train back, or vice-versa, offers the opportunity to observe the UNESCO area from different perspectives and to return to the city in a single day.

A big attraction of São Bento railway station is the *azulejos* (tiles) painted by the artist Jorge Colaço (1868-1942). There are approximately 20,000 *azulejos* created between, approximately, 1905 and 1916. The tiles depict a range of narratives: the history of transport in Portugal, landscapes, and a selection of Portugal's defining historic moments, including key battles. Colaço was one of the leading tile-painting artists of his generation and another example of his work can be found at Igreja de Santo Ildefonso in Porto. The *azulejos* in the station building tell us much about Portuguese history and culture, the battles to secure independence of the nation from foreign armies, and the importance of the warrior royal. Naturally, there is a great deal of focus on those that were fought against Spain.

On the north wall we find the key figures: Egas Moniz, a Portuguese nobleman, and Alfonso VII of León, a king of Galicia and Castile. On the south wall, there is a painting of the entrance to Porto of King João I and D. Filipa de Lencastre on horseback, as they celebrate their wedding in 1387. The visitor can learn much about the importance of symbolism in Portugal by studying the tiles and reflecting upon their meaning. Portugal has faced a historic quest to gain and retain its independence from foreign control. For large parts of its history it was not successful in achieving this aim, and the importance of royalty, inter-marriage, and court intrigue has been a central feature of the history of the nation. The final destination of this short walk from Gaia to the centre of Porto will reveal one such example of the type of destructive forces that can be unleashed by deep-rooted divisions within the royal court.

From the railway station, a gentle walk down the hill towards the Praça da Liberdade and, once in this central area, head for the large statue that dominates it. There, sitting on top of his horse, is Dom Pedro IV. The bronze statue, erected on its ten-metre high column, dominates the area and is a reminder of the role he played in securing the eventual victory of the liberals in the city after a siege had brought the inhabitants of Porto to their knees. Dom Pedro IV did not fit the mould of most royal heroes. Indeed, it would be difficult to think of a less likely hero than this man whose personality and early leadership traits did not single him out to be such an influential part of Portuguese, and Porto, history.

In order to recount the story, we need to return to trace the origins of liberalism (constitutionalism) in Portugal. Liberalism was first introduced to Portugal by the American and French revolutions, but it was not until after the end of the Peninsular

War that it grew in strength and challenged the hegemony of the monarchy.[3] A crucial starting point was the introduction of freemasonry by foreign merchants operating in Portugal, and especially in the Porto region.[4] In 1818 a group of freemason intellectuals from Porto set up a covert underground group known as the *Sinédrio* (from a Greek word meaning assembly).[5] Their aim was to spread liberal ideas and to win support from the military for their ideas. The French invasions helped disseminate liberal ideas among the Portuguese middle classes who, although small in number (around 200,000 out of a population of three million), sought greater social and economic advancement. New radical ways forward for the nation were also discussed by influential Portuguese exiles living in London and Paris, who had observed the development of political systems in these countries. The exiles were politically active, holding meetings, disseminating their ideas into Portugal by way of smuggled newspapers, and leaflets. These radicals sought to rebuild Portugal along the lines of France by creating a constitutional monarchy to replace the existing absolutist monarchy.

Calls for political change were also sparked by necessity. Much of the country had been destroyed by the Peninsular War, the north of the country suffering especially badly. Damage to buildings, looting of valuable assets, and unfavourable trading terms all contributed to a difficult state of affairs. Many Portuguese felt that their British allies were most to blame for the problems. London was dominating the lucrative trade market with Brazil, to the direct detriment of Portugal, at the same time as the nation's expenditures were increasing, with around seventy-five per cent devoted to its armed forces.[6] British control over the country during this time was strict, self-serving in its national interest, and detrimental to the development of Portuguese freedoms in both politics and trade.

From 1808 until 1821, Portugal was officially a British protectorate with Marshal William Carr Beresford, a British officer, in charge of Portuguese forces and serving as a viceroy-type figure to the country.[7] Beresford did not restrict his remit to only military affairs; he sought influence in political life in Portugal as well, and his interventions and tactics were not welcomed by all. Portugal during this period was not only under British influence. The Portuguese royal family, along with much of the country's elite, had left Lisbon and gone into exile in Brazil as the French forces entered the capital during the Peninsular War. The court in exile had a profound impact on relations between Portugal and Brazil, and the problems deepened when the royal family refused to return to Portugal at the conclusion of the Peninsular War. The politics of the Rio de Janeiro-based Royal Court of the time centred on intra-family disputes over the thrones of Portugal and Brazil, succession struggles, and disputes over whether the court should return to Lisbon. In the meantime, Marshal Beresford's influence grew, as did local resentment of his power and authority.

Much of the ill-feeling towards Beresford arose from a series of events in May 1817 when he had been made aware of an alleged conspiracy among Portuguese army officers. As head of armed forces, Beresford felt he had little choice but to inform the government of the potentially treasonous plot. The plot was crushed with a brutal show of force by the British, keen to make an example of those involved to act as a deterrent to any future would-be plotters. All of those officers involved in the plot were subjected to swift justice and were hanged. Among them was General Gomes Freire Andrade, the grandmaster of the Portuguese Masons and the leader of the liberal movement in the country.[8] Beresford was blamed by the Portuguese for the executions which were greeted with widespread revulsion and dismay in the country. The death of the general and his alleged fellow plotters did not end the march of the liberal cause in the country; instead it helped energise those calling for profound change to the political system.

The situation was complicated by developments in the Portuguese royal court. After nearly a quarter of a century of suffering from insanity, Queen Maria I died and the prince regent was proclaimed João VI. The new king had developed strong connections in Brazil, and having created a court and a government, pronounced that he did not wish to immediately return to the motherland.

Naturally, this reluctance helped stoke the fires of the liberals in Portugal who became ever more critical of the monarchy. In March 1820, the increasingly unpopular Beresford travelled to Brazil in order to try to persuade the reluctant king to return and to raise funds in order to help pay the army. Beresford's absence from Portugal encouraged the liberal influence within the army to increase. This was most noticeable in the Porto region. It would prove to be only a matter of time before the liberal supporters in the military struck.

On 24 August 1820, the army in Porto revolted, creating a provisional junta which seized control of the government of Portugal until a formal constitution could be framed. The leaders of the revolt argued that the monarchy had been bypassed because it had been unable to successfully resolve Portugal's lengthy financial crisis.[9] Upon his return from Brazil, Beresford was barred from re-entering Portugal and returned to England. At this stage the liberals appeared to be in control, pushing home their advantage by holding indirect elections for a constitutional *Cortes* in December 1820, which was first convened the following month in January 1821. Needless to say, the majority of people elected to the *Cortes* were mainly supporters of constitutional monarchism and wanted to reduce the king's role with parliament doing the governing. The king would have power to delay legislation, but not to block it indefinitely. They argued for a greater range of civil liberties to be introduced and that although Catholicism would be the religion of the state other religions, including Judaism, would be allowed to exist alongside the official religion. The latter proved too much to take for several leading members of the Catholic Church, including the cardinal-patriarch whose vociferous protests about the proposed constitution led to him being forced into exile.[10] Later the same year, on 23 September, the constitution was finally approved.

At approximately the same time, King João VI decided that the time was right for his rather tardy return to Portugal. In truth he had little choice. The *Cortes* in Lisbon demanded his presence, or he would risk losing the Portuguese crown. Upon his arrival in

Lisbon on 4 June 1821 he agreed to uphold the forthcoming new Portuguese constitution. Queen Carlota-Joaquina, however, refused to swear the oath to the constitution and moved to the palace in Queluz, near Lisbon. The queen was the sister of the Spanish king, Ferdinand VII, and a die-hard absolutist. Despite continued efforts to get her to change her mind she steadfastly refused, and eventually punished by losing her citizenship and exiled. Before the punishment could be enforced, however, ten doctors declared her unfit to travel overseas so she was merely confined in a convent near Sintra.[11] The royal couple were not particularly normal partners. The queen was pushy, highly ambitious, and ruthless by nature. She had once come close to having her husband committed for insanity.[12] A British soldier serving in Portugal wrote an apt description of her:

> She was a woman of very violent spirit, entering into party politics with an ambitious view of seizing the reins of government. To gain her ends she fearlessly hazarded her own life and those of her adherents; but she calculated the king's weak character. When in Rio de Janeiro she showed her daring and violent spirit by firing a pistol at Lobato, the Viscount of Villa Nova, the king's favourite, as he came out of his master's room. She was an accomplished mother; her conversation was full of wit and spirit; she was a good mother, if to offer rigid precept with bad example be the duty of a good mother.[13]

The royal couple had two sons: Pedro and Miguel. Both children were more Brazilian than Portuguese. They had sailed out of Lisbon with their parents when the French invaded the city. Pedro was nine and Miguel five as their ship sailed down the River Tagus and headed into the Atlantic Ocean. Miguel returned to Portugal with his parents and, like his extremely conservative mother, refused to swear an oath to the constitution. Instead, he was to plot with his mother against the liberals and his own father.

The king's eldest son, Pedro, remained in Brazil despite similar demands that he return. Brazil was itself undergoing profound political changes that would impact upon Portugal. The Brazilian liberal movement grew, drawing inspiration from the independence of the United States and the efforts of Brazil's neighbours to gain freedom from Spain, calling for the independence of Brazil. On 7 September 1822 Pedro stood up and made his famous remarks 'Independence or Death!'. The former was eventually declared on 12 October 1822, and Pedro was proclaimed as the constitutional emperor of the newly created state. The implications for Portugal of the loss of Brazil were mostly in the arena of trade. Portugal had just lost its historically most lucrative colony at a time when its own finances were in a mess.

By local standards, the new constitution in Portugal was nothing short of radical. It created a constitutional monarchy with sovereignty based on the will of the nation. In essence, following the traditional liberal model, it created three branches of government: legislative, executive, and judicial. The legislative power was an elected chamber of deputies, executive power rested with the king, and judicial power was placed in the hands of the court. Crucially, the king and his secretaries of state were given no representation in the chamber of deputies and had no executive powers to dissolve parliament at any point.[14] The establishment of a constitution is a dramatic, potentially dangerous, moment in the history of all countries. It was in Portugal and, given the small size of the middle class who supported it, all the more hazardous. Opposition to the constitution was widespread, and it was not long until the absolutists made their move. The major cleavage in Portuguese society as a result became between the liberals (or constitutionalists) who defended the constitution, and the royalists (or absolutists) who opposed it, favouring absolutism, where the monarchy remained the supreme authority and was not restricted by any written rules.

On a chilly winter's day in February 1823, in Trás-os-Montes (north-east of Porto), the first insurrection against the constitution took place, led by the Count of Amarante, a strong absolutist. The count subsequently led an even more serious rebellion at Vila Franca de Xira, to the north of Lisbon, on 27 May 1823.

The armed forces that rose up against the constitution there were joined by forces from Lisbon and, intriguingly, by Miguel, the second son of João VI and his mother's favourite. The king used the uprising as an excuse to suspend the constitution of 1822. It was a highly risky, but cleverly calculated move, with little opposition forthcoming to his decision. The liberals simply did not have enough support in the country to implement their radical ideas. The Catholic Church and the large land-owning nobility remained the strongest groups in Portuguese society and their preference was to maintain a status quo of absolutism, which best protected their interests.[15] Portugal, as a result, was governed by 'moderate absolutism'.[16]

The empowered, petulant son Miguel was not satisfied, and wished to challenge his father's authority, with the help of his scheming mother. Following the *Vilafrancada*, as the uprising is known, Miguel was awarded the title of *generalissimo*.[17] Efforts were made to limit his powers, but he intended to use them for his own purposes. In April 1824, he made his bid for power to replace his father. The absolutists made their move and part of the Lisbon garrison came out into the main square, Rossio. Miguel was quick to take control of the revolt and was hailed as king by the plotters. He issued a proclamation that made allegations of a plot to murder the royal family, using this as a pretext to arrest the chief of police and other opponents. He then appointed key supporters in their places.[18] The queen could barely contain her joy as she arrived back in the capital. Her happiness was to be short-lived. An isolated and shaken João VI initially signed a decree on 3 May agreeing to his son's demands, but changed his mind a few day later. Central to the king's decision-making process was the arrival back in Portugal of Marshal Beresford. The British officer was horrified by the plot and got to work rallying the diplomatic corps to help save João VI. The king sought sanctuary on a British ship, *HMS Windsor*. Once safely on board the king sent for his upstart of a son, informing him at the same time that he had been relieved of his rank. When Miguel arrived, his father further informed him that he was being sent into exile in Paris. His mother was removed from the palace in Ajuda and sent to be locked up in a dungeon in Sintra. João VI continued to rule Portugal until his death on 26 March 1826. His son, Miguel, proceeded to irritate the elite society of Paris, before moving on to Vienna with his bad manners, self-importance, and inappropriate attitude towards women. João VI was widely seen as a moderately successful king who disliked violence and wished for his subjects to be happy.[19]

6

War of the Brothers

Dom Miguel was educated, if education it could be called, as a Portuguese prince; ignorant of everything he did not choose to learn; therefore it may well be supposed, that he was more apt at athletic exercises than in his literary studies. His governor, during his youth, had been the Count of Rio Mayor, but he had little power over the prince; and it is much to be doubted whether the king himself was very anxious on the subject of the education of his sons: perhaps he might have had a jealous feeling of their knowing more than himself.[1]

Anonymous

THE DEATH OF JOÃO VI created a number of problems that led to the war between his two sons, the resulting Siege of Porto, and a prolonged period of political instability across Portugal and Brazil. Like most civil wars, the fighting was bloody, bitter, and often pitted neighbour against neighbour, colleague against colleague. The royals were not the only divided family over the issue of absolutism versus liberalism. While the 'War of the Brothers', as it is known, was an essentially ideological war about the political direction of the nation, the dispute over power should not be ignored – Miguel was certainly in part guided by this motivation. The outcome of the war did not resolve the political crisis in Portugal, rather it helped provoke another period of instability that, for a time, threatened to lead to an additional civil war in the country. Such a war was prevented only by the intervention of the outside powers, bringing together the parties under the flag of gunship diplomacy. While the capital city of Lisbon was established as the seat of government, much of the political intrigue, calls for reforms, and fighting took place in the city of Porto and its surrounding areas. The city's role as the home of liberalism was fully established during this difficult era in Portugal with several notable liberal leaders, thinkers, and artists coming from the city.

Following the death of the king, the first problem needing resolution was the tricky question of succession. With both his sons overseas (Pedro in Brazil and Miguel in exile in Vienna), the king had chosen his second daughter, Maria-Isabel, to lead the Council of Regency to resolve the succession issue. A delegation travelled to Brazil to offer allegiance to Pedro. The council seemingly ignored the hazy issue of whether Pedro was still a Portuguese national now he had become head of an independent Brazil. If he was not, he would not be eligible to inherit the crown of Portugal. This argument was later highlighted by the absolutists as a reason not to accept Pedro's inheritance of the crown. Pedro jumped at the chance of becoming king of Portugal, announcing that he would instil the country with a constitutional charter similar to that of Brazil and France. The charter was to prove the catalyst for the civil war, but despite the fighting over its contents, it continued to form the basis of a political system, with some cosmetic changes, until the end of the monarchy in Portugal.[2] The charter was signed on 29 April 1826 and, as planned, Pedro announced that he was to abdicate in favour of his daughter, Maria da Glória. At the time she was only seven years old, and Pedro set the condition that when she became of age she would marry his brother, Miguel. His younger brother indicated his support for Pedro at the time of the announcement, but this did not last long.

The constitutional charter left behind by Pedro represented something of a fudge in trying to find a way to unite the liberal and absolutist camps in the country. To do this Pedro attempted to make significant changes from the 1822 constitution which had led to the revolts by absolutist supporters. The 1826 constitutional charter created four branches of government with the legislature being divided into two houses. The upper house resembled the British House of Lords and was known as the Chamber of Peers. It comprised of peers (life and hereditary) and clergy all appointed by the king. The second chamber came to be known as the Chamber of Deputies and had 111 deputies who were elected to a four-year term. Its members were elected by an indirect vote of local assemblies. These assemblies were themselves elected (or selected) by people of social and economic rank such as landowners. As in the previous constitution, the power of the judiciary remained in the hands of the courts. The provision for executive power was much changed in the new constitution. In essence, it rested with the ministers, mixed with some powers for the king who also held a veto over all legislation passed by the legislature.[3]

The constitution was flawed to its core and reflected the personality traits of Pedro, that included his deep sense of paternalism, which he had inherited from his father.[4] Pedro's character was a strange mixture of the romantic liberal with a deeply held belief that this was the best way forward, mixed with more autocratic traits that reflected his position and upbringing. It must have been difficult to shed the influence of his strongly absolutist mother. His impulsiveness was another trait that did not bode well for the future. He was said to have dashed off the constitution in a great hurry, reflecting his passionate engagement with framing it. He was not a man for detail but rather a headline, or soundbite, king before the phrase was even invented. To make matters worse the Portuguese people that the constitution was being dashed off to govern were like aliens to Pedro. He had left Portugal as a child and had no idea of the wishes, hopes, and aspirations of his new subjects. Moreover, he did not understand the composition and hierarchy of Portuguese society and the cleavage between rural and urban Portugal (generally defined as the cities of Porto and Lisbon).

Arguably his greatest shortcoming was a near-total blindness to the international dimension of the implementation of the constitution. In this respect there was a Spanish and a wider

European dimension to Pedro's efforts. Once again, his mother and the absolutist groups were all laying traps and preparing rebellions. Deep in his heart, Pedro, as a liberal, believed that the objections of the absolutists could be overcome. An early warning of the difficulty in achieving this came when absolutists mounted a rebellion before heading over the border to Spain where they were protected by the Spanish government who refused to disarm them. Amidst fears of a possible Spanish invasion of Portugal, the British sent a small force to Lisbon, which did the trick in the short run as the absolutist forces that had re-entered Portugal returned to Spain and, on this occasion, were disarmed by the Spanish authorities. In short, given the continued importance of Portugal to the European powers, developments in the country were watched with some concern.[5]

Divisions arose in London over whether to support the efforts of Pedro to reform Portugal. Among those who did offer support there were disputes over how involved Britain should allow itself to become. Politically, the general rule was that the Tories supported the absolutists and the Whigs favoured the liberals. On a personal level, there was not much love for either Pedro or Miguel. The Duke of Wellington (formerly Arthur Wellesley) was said to have thought Pedro to be a 'ruffian', and the constitution he introduced awful. Before Miguel returned to Portugal from his exile to swear an oath of allegiance to Pedro's constitution, he visited London. The impression he left with his hosts was not favourable, despite the general ideological sympathy many had with the cause of the absolutists.

...They had not taken to the young fellow (Miguel)... He had disgusted everyone in Paris by his boorish manners; he came to England to be instructed in his behaviour as a Regent, pledged to observe the constitution that Britain was pledged to support. Wellington found him unbusinesslike, he had to stay at Strathfieldsaye, together with the Marquis [Duke] of Palmela, while Wellington and Palmela discussed the form of the oath he was to take, the backward young man (who no doubt had no intention of taking or even keeping an oath at all) paid no attention, but sat flirting with Princess Thérèse Esterhazy. 'This will never do', said the Duke to Palmela. 'If he is so careless in an affair of such moment, he will never do his duty'. To which Palmela had answered, 'Oh, leave him to us, we will manage him'.[6]

As it transpired, the concerns of the Duke of Wellington turned out to be very well-founded. On 22 February 1828, following his stint enraging London society (just as he had done in Paris and Vienna), Miguel landed in Portugal to take the oath of allegiance to the constitution and to take the regency. Taking the oath of loyalty to his brother and the constitution on 26 February, Miguel was installed in the position of Lieutenant-General. His supporters, however, had other ideas and plans were soon afoot to start a process that would lead to his challenging the legitimacy of Pedro and the constitution. Initially, Miguel was said to have favoured accepting the constitution, but was soon convinced otherwise. The hidden hand of power was once more exercised by Pedro and Miguel's mother, Carlota-Joaquina who returned to Lisbon in order to influence events in favour of the absolutists. The queen mother was keen to settle scores and had produced lists of friends and enemies. From the outset, she encouraged Miguel to appoint ministers who were absolutists. As a result, there were major protests in key liberal areas. In a sweeping purge of liberals, the queen mother encouraged the sacking of local governors and military commanders who were not absolutists. The month after his return, Miguel moved against the legislature, dissolving the Chamber of Deputies and the Chamber of Peers. The absolutists were seizing power, and the pace of their attempts gathered speed.

The liberals tried to resist. On 18 May 1828, the armed forces in Porto declared their loyalty to Pedro, his daughter Maria da Glória, and the constitution. The uprisings soon spread to other urban areas, the traditional strongholds of the liberals.[7] The response of Miguel and his absolutist supporters was swift, brutal, and provocative. *Cortes* were dissolved and a ban introduced on pro-Pedro demonstrations.

Thousands of liberals were arrested and thrown in jail without due process. As the situation on the ground worsened, both radical and moderate liberals started to flee the country with many taking refuge on British ships anchored in Porto and Lisbon. Those seeking sanctuary in London included the Duke of Palmela who, when he had met Miguel in England prior to his return to Portugal, felt that he had undergone change and would uphold the constitution.[8] Local officials were told to send petitions calling for Miguel to be pronounced king.

The *Cortes*, purged of any liberal opponents, met in June and decreed that Miguel was the rightful heir to his father and therefore the constitutional charter produced by Pedro was null and void. On 11 July 1828 Miguel was crowned, much to the delight of his mother and the absolutists. As a sign of the lack of international support for his coronation, only representatives from the United States and Mexico attended the lavish ceremony. The absolutists were not unduly worried by the no-show by the international community. They correctly calculated that there was little appetite for international intervention to support the liberal cause in Portugal. Even in Britain, the favoured destination of many of the liberal refugees, there was not a great deal of sympathy for the predicament of Pedro and the liberals.

With Miguel sitting on the throne, there followed a five-year period of repression and purges. Before her death on 7 January 1830, the queen mother remained at the centre of much of this activity, freely expressing her extremist views and turning her attention to individuals who she viewed as being soft, or more moderate, absolutists.[9] The result was that the extremists were able to eclipse the moderates, who were driven from positions of influence. With the hardliners in charge, the pace and intensity of the repression increased. There followed a steady stream of executions of liberals, waves of arrests, and deportations followed as Miguel tightened his grip on power. There was a policy of zero tolerance for liberal opposition. As they attempted to regroup outside of Portugal, the liberals plotted and strategised how best to challenge Miguel. Central to this was Pedro.

The liberals waited anxiously for the response of Pedro to the events in Portugal. His grip on power back in Brazil was coming under greater scrutiny and threat. In 1831 he chose to abdicate, leaving his son Pedro II to take the throne. Pedro then sailed to England from where he arranged a military expedition to the Azores Islands, in the middle of the Atlantic Ocean. During his stay in London, he arranged what amounted to a very large loan in the name of his daughter and recruited a number of British soldiers to form the backbone of his army.[10] When Pedro arrived in the Azores, the islands were already in the hands of the liberals and later, on 3 March 1832, the ex-emperor, now preferring to be known simply as the Duke of Braganza, announced himself regent and the protector of his daughter.[11] Put simply, he declared a government in exile. Pedro spent his time on the beautiful islands planning his military and naval expedition to the Portuguese mainland. His strategy to occupy the city of Porto was to lead to the famous siege of the city by Miguel and his armed forces.

Miguel's naval forces imposed a blockade on the islands in the hope of preventing the liberals from sailing to mainland Portugal. The ships blockading the islands, however, were attacked by the French navy. The liberal army was able to sail to Portugal and chose to land in an area that had been abandoned by forces loyal to Miguel. The forty-seven vessels of Pedro's men arrived off the coast of Portugal on the evening of 7 July 1832[12]. The liberal army of over 7,000 men chose to land and disembark at Mindelo, to the north of Porto, on 8 July.[13] There they rapidly established a beachhead and prepared to march into Porto to seize control of the most important city in the north; the birthplace of liberalism in Portugal. Pedro's armed forces were relatively well-armed, but not well-prepared for battle or versed in the strategies of defensive and offensive warfare. At the time it was not certain what they would find in mainland Portugal, or the extent to which Miguel's forces would engage them in the Porto region. Among the force were two influential names associated with the siege of the city of Porto; Almeida Garrett, a popular writer and soon-to-be liberal politician, and Alexandre Herculano who was to become a famous historian and poet. There was also a contingent of a British international brigade to help prepare the defences of the city, most of whom were the soldiers that had been personally recruited by Pedro during his stay in London.

The next day the liberal army marched unopposed for the ten miles into Cedofeita, in the centre of Porto.[14] Large crowds greeted the army, many though merely attended out of curiosity to catch a glimpse of Pedro as he returned to mainland Portugal for the first time as an adult.

It was a triumphal march, a pageant such as the Portuguese delight in. The citizens of the loyal city received them with open arms, and his brother laid siege to the place.[15]

The outpouring of local support for Pedro was not forthcoming outside of the Porto region. In the countryside, the majority were for Miguel and the absolutists. Given the levels of repression exercised by the absolutists against liberal supporters in previous years, people might justifiably have been rather nervous about making public shows of support for Pedro and the cause. Almost immediately Pedro's 7,000 men were besieged by an army of 13,000 men loyal to Miguel. The siege of the city by Miguel's forces started one of the most bloody episodes in the history of the city. The War of the Brothers had well and truly commenced.

7

The Siege of Porto, 1832

In duration of time, in severity of suffering, and in the patient endurance with which those sufferings have been borne, the modern history of the world offers no parallel to the Siege of Oporto! And, withstanding the privations we all experience, and the personal dangers to which we are all exposed, still the most painful feelings which are connected with a residence in Oporto at the present moment arise from the melancholy scenes of want and private distress by which we are surrounded.[1]

Thomas Sorell, British Consul at Porto

A S THE VISITOR STANDS next to the statue of Dom Pedro in the centre of the city it is important to imagine what the Siege of Porto was like for its citizens trapped in the city and the liberal army charged with defending it. Shelling from the forces loyal to Miguel, much of it indiscriminate and designed to terrify the civilian population, was a constant source of fear. Miguel's troops hoped that the shelling would be sufficient to force the city into surrender. Local inhabitants came to recognise patterns to the attacks, shelling from specific batteries at certain times of the day. Whilst it never became routine, there was a gallows humour towards the risk to life and limb among the population. Food shortages were equally serious, as Miguel's forces hoped to starve the population into submission. Water was also in short supply with the resultant problems that this brought. Disease in Porto was rife. In parts of the city centre there appeared to be more rats than humans as they swarmed around the streets going through the uncollected piles of rubbish and human excrement. The smells were overpowering. On hot days, the city was unimaginably unpleasant. People complained of a feeling of permanent dizziness, caused in all probability by the pungent smells that emanated from the drains, clogged and overflowing with human and other waste. The river, the beautiful golden River Douro, no longer shone in the sun, instead resembling a watery wasteland of a city under siege. The city was a ghost town during the day with people afraid to roam freely for fear of copping one of Miguel's shells or bullets.

On 10 July, the first serious exchanges took place with shelling in Gaia and musket fire between the two forces.[2] People continued with their daily lives for as long as possible in the hope that the shelling and musket fire would take place in other parts of the city. Elizabeth Noble, a member of the English community in Gaia, wrote in her diary for 12 July, 'Walked out early to see Dom Pedro... and met many of the grandees.' Two days later, Elizabeth went to the resort of Foz, to the west of the city with a friend to spend a leisurely afternoon, and her next entry referred to the celebrations for her mother's birthday on 15 July.[3] These entries were among the last not to talk of shelling or rumours and news of the conduct of the war. Most entries from this point onwards refer to the endless cycles of shelling, gunfire, and the resulting fear, chaos, and confusion.

As the siege grew longer, the local population adopted a fatalistic and slightly macabre attitude. Baron Forrester was one of the most influential men in the Port wine trade, and arguably the most important Scotsman to live in Portugal. Forrester resided in Gaia on the south bank of the river, a stronghold of Miguel's forces, while his uncle James Forrester lived in Porto, where Pedro's army was trapped. Baron Forrester wrote movingly to his uncle:

> Those who have been made familiar with danger will confess that familiarity soon produces indifference to it. Soon after the entry of the Constitutionalists [liberals] into Oporto the city was besieged by the Royalists [absolutists] from the south side of the river. At first, the greatest alarm and anxiety prevailed amongst

the inhabitants, but as the shells were busting over their heads at almost every instant of the day and night, I may assert without the smallest exaggeration that many persons arrived at such a pitch of ability in calculating the curves each shell would take, that were enabled to decide with the greatest nicety where the destructive engine would fall...[4]

Forrester's comments on the almost routine nature of the shelling cannot hide the terror it spread among the population across the whole city. The artillery batteries of Miguel's forces were strategically placed to bring as much of the population as possible into range of its guns. They also acted as a jailer, blocking any exit point and turning the city into one giant prison. Now, nobody was safe from the shelling as they went about their daily business, no matter from which side in the war. Forrester himself was caught up in this one day:

...Six shells fell within a few yards of me, and before I could cross the square I was making every haste to a more sheltered spot, when whiz, whiz, whiz came a grenade close to me, but not so near to prevent my throwing myself flat on some bags of rice on the floor of a grocer's shop. The grenade afterwards immediately burst, and one of the pieces struck a poor girl who was seated on the counter spinning, she was struck on the calf of the leg and pinned thereby fast to her seat. The blood flowed plentifully and the first intimation I had of her misfortune and my own escape, was the blood trickling down from her wounded limb on my face, as I still remained in my horizontal position on the ground.[5]

During the initial stages of the siege there was a sense among the British soldiers fighting with the liberals that they had been lured into Porto by Miguel's armed forces (popularly referred to as the Miguelites) in order for them to have an excuse to destroy the city: the cradle of liberalism. The idea of a trap was compounded by the numbers of men and cavalry available to Miguel compared to his brother. From the outset, the armed forces of Pedro (known as Pedroites) made strategic mistakes that allowed the Miguelites to lay siege to the city. The major error was not to cross the River Douro into Gaia soon after their arrival to take advantage of the confusion and fear caused by their disembarkation and arrival in Porto.[6] A second mistake was not following up on their initial successes in battles with a greater deployment of troops when they did eventually cross.[7] The Pedroites held the strategically important monastery, with its ideal artillery placements, but the Miguelites continued to dominate much of the rest of the area on the south bank.

Arguably the biggest mistake for the Pedroites was the failure to make their first blows count in the war. As a British officer fighting with the Pedroites put it:

> The first blow of a campaign, if struck with dash and decision by small bodies of troops, is always fortunate. The enemy is caught unawares, idle and in stupor; not yet awake to busy strategy. A charlatan will win it with *eclât*; but he must be a soldier who tries the second; if the enemy is then alert, and the golden opportunity is lost. So it was with the Pedroites; for their first blow, although prettily done, was only half struck... They had nothing to lose, all to gain; yet when they tried their second, by moving to the north, the Miguelites had then been entered into fire, and they had become more confident in their cause; they had lost the fear of long beards, and the horror of fighting against royalty.[8]

The result of the initial military failings of the Pedroites in the Porto region caused panic among the population of the city who feared being overrun by the Miguelites. At this juncture, Pedro took the decision to abandon any offensive operations against the Miguelites, instead opting to fortify the city and wait to see what materialised.[9] The retreat into Porto by the Pedroites was a mistake and unnecessary: a strategic error of judgement that illustrated the shortcomings of the Pedroite officers. The Siege of Porto was inflicted upon the people of Porto by the mistakes of the Pedroites. As a result, the city paid an enormous price in destruction and human suffering. The siege could have, and should have, been avoided by more competent military leadership.

The withdrawal into the city could have proved even more of a disaster for the Pedroites on 25 July when an attempt to destroy their army by setting fire to the barracks almost proved successful. The soldiers were sleeping, exhausted by the battles of the previous days, when three priests allegedly set fire to the barracks in the Convent of St. Francis at 1.00 am. The soldiers escaped just in the nick of time as the fire swept through the building. There was speculation at the time, unproven, that the sub-plot to the fire was an attempt on the life of Pedro. It was thought that, as per usual, he would lead the efforts of his men – in this case to put out the fire. [10] Elizabeth Noble described the drama:

> I had not been in bed long before mama came to tell me that the bells were ringing in town and that a large fire had broken out in the Convent of St. Francis... The fire did not extend further than the convent. The fifth *Caçadores* [the elite light infantry troops of the Pedroites] and other troops about 500 had been quartered in the convent, and the friars set it on fire hoping they would all perish. Fortunately, they all escaped, but walked to the Vittoria in the evening when the fire was still burning. [11]

The fortification of the city by the Pedroites was a more successful military operation. Given the failings of their initial military adventures and the resulting fears in the city, there was unanimous support for the creation of lines of defence around Porto. The fortifications started at Quinta da China to the east of the city, reached down to the River Douro and to the lighthouse at Foz, to the west of the city along the Atlantic coastline. Fortifications were built on high grounds with a series of moderately deeply dug ditches connecting the forts. Soldiers were given instructions that under no circumstances were the Miguelites to be allowed to break through this defensive line. The major debate about the fortifications was whether to include Gaia. In the end, Pedro decided not to, and this was probably the correct decision. Instead, the Pedroites contented themselves with solely defending the monastery which they controlled on the south bank. They simply did not have the number of soldiers required to place a garrison on each bank of the river. Any attempt to protect a larger proportion of Gaia beyond the monastery would have resulted in a dangerous over-stretching of the lines of the Pedroites.

The biggest financial mistake the Pedroites made was not to move the stocks of Port wine out of the warehouses in Gaia. This came to cost them, and the British Port wine traders, later in the campaign. All wars take money to fight, and the Pedroites were running a little short of finance. In order to try to resolve the shortfall, the Duke of Palmela was dispatched to London to try to negotiate some credit to help finance the struggle. The only security that Palmela could offer to secure a loan was the enormous amount of Port wine stored in readiness for export in Gaia. Prior to Duke's departure, it was agreed that the wine should be removed with immediate effect in case it fell into the hands of the Miguelites. Given the long history of anti-British rhetoric from Miguel and his absolutist supporters there was a strong fear that his forces, if given the opportunity, might attack and destroy the British Port wine houses.

Due to its financial importance to the Pedroites, Palmela begged that the operation of moving the wine be made an absolute priority. Needless to say, it was not. Day after day, the removal operation was put off as the leadership of the Pedroites focussed on the fortifications on the north bank of the river, ignoring the financial importance of the wine. Soon it was too late; the wine fell into the hands of the Miguelites and its financial advantage was lost to Palmela as he frantically tried to raise funds in London. Despite calls for the resignations of some of the senior officers of the Pedroites for these failings, nobody was discharged, but there were reassignments and a general reorganisation of some of the senior staff. In truth, the quality of several of the senior officers was questionable.

For the foreign soldiers serving in the Pedroites, the retreat back into Porto provided them with an opportunity to get to know the city and to admire its beauty and cuisine. One British officer offered the following observations:

> The nights were beautiful and clear, when I often wondered up and down the hilly, ancient streets and *praças*, struck with the beauty and solidity of the churches and convents and mansions, all built of granite, upon hills of the same rock. The churches were visited by a few of the faithful, the convents deserted; and the houses of the Miguelite nobles, who were with 'their king,' were now turned into barracks and billets. In a backstreet, at a small eating-house, I found I could get a meal for seven *vintems*, consisting of salt fish or sardines, bread, potatoes, and a bottle of pure port, very new, thin, sour and highly coloured; but as for meat, there was none to be had.[12]

The motivation of these soldiers was generally strong; fighting for both ideological reasons and financial reward they did their best to ignore the increasing shortage of food and lack of complete payment of their wages. Among these soldiers there was a deep respect for Pedro, his cause, and several of his senior officers. One of the names mentioned in the most flattering terms was Coronel José Antonio da Silva Torres who was in charge of the defence of the Serra do Pilar monastery and who was 'one of the bravest and energic officers' among the Pedroites. 'To see him was to respect and like him'.[13] Torres needed to be good – the strategically important position of the monastery, overlooking the city of Porto, was much sought after by the Miguelites, especially as they tightened the siege.

To many Pedroites it remained a major mistake on the side of Miguelites that they had not fortified this position before the arrival of the Pedroites – they could have easily defended and held it against any attack. This oversight represented arguably the single biggest error of the Miguelites during the initial stages of the war. In other words, both sides made major strategic blunders at the start that came to damage the strength of their respective positions as the war progressed. From the outset, another problematic area was the management of the potential for desertions from one side to the other. This was of particular relevance to Miguel whose forces saw a number of its men desert at the very start of the war. This number soon dried up, in all probability due to the Miguelites imposing strict and brutal punishments on any deserters they caught. The fact that the Pedroites had performed so badly in the opening battles of the campaign probably also led to a reduction in confidence among potential side-swappers that they would prevail in the war.[14] There were also examples of soldiers crossing sides in the opposite direction, including two individuals from the English contingent who had originally been fighting for the Pedroites.

The lines of the conflict were quickly established and the shelling from the Miguelites into the city became a near-constant worry for the Pedroites. Over the summer months there were skirmishes as both sides concentrated on consolidating their positions in and around Porto. Occasionally, night attacks on specific strongholds held by the Pedroites were tried by the Miguelites, but with little success. The lack of military discipline, inexperience, and confusion contributed to the failure of these operations, most notably on the Serra do Pilar monastery on 8 and 9 August; typical attacks by the Miguelites were described by Elizabeth Noble in her diary:

> Attack on Porto. Began about 8.00 in the morning. The attack was chiefly directed against the Serra where the enemy was completely routed... Firing from artillery on both sides. One of the enemy's pieces soon disabled. Bridge taken away... Musketry all day... Two attacks on the Serra, both fail.[15]

The failures were not confined to the Miguelites; an offensive operation by the Pedroites to inflict damage on the forces besieging the city ended in failure with heavy casualties sustained, including a disproportionate number of officers.[16] The presence of heavy fog which hung over the city during many summer mornings was thought to favour the Miguelites who could use it as cover to mount a surprise attack. The Pedroites, as a result, were placed at action stations from 2.00 am each day until the fog lifted from the city.[17] However, the expected attack did not materialise. The Miguelites contented themselves with a series of operations to try to take the Serra do Pilar monastery but they were repelled on each occasion.[18]

As the siege continued, food became scarce with the population trapped in the city reaching the point of starvation. The Pedroites saw their rations reduced. 'We began to draw daily rations – 1lb beef, 1lb bread, half a pint of wine', wrote a serving officer whose daily allowance was greater than that of the general population.[19] As winter approached, food shortages in the besieged city worsened. It was primarily for this reason that the Pedroites attempted to break the siege:

> Oporto was not provisioned in any way for the support of its inhabitants and the army. The winter was approaching, and the bar at the mouth of the river was almost impassable by reason of the tempestuous weather. Under these circumstances Dom Pedro resolved upon a sortie on the north, to attack and destroy entrenchments and batteries in that direction, fire the enemy's camps, and in a measure open the way for the entry of food.[20]

The operation was a partial success with several positions belonging to the Miguelites destroyed, allowing food and provisions to enter the city for a few days afterwards. The Pedroites, however, paid a high price for the temporary relief with around 200 men killed and wounded, including seventeen officers. The Miguelites responded with furious shelling of the city in an attempt to force a surrender without having to launch an assault on it. The thick granite buildings of central Porto, which were often two or three feet thick, absorbed the pounding. Civilian casualties grew in rapid numbers. It was no longer safe to move around the city to collect food and provisions during the hours of daylight. The

One of Porto's most famous sons from the Age of Exploration, Infante Dom Henrique (Henry the Navigator).

A panoramic view of Porto from the River Douro in 1791.

Dom Pedro, the 1st Emperor of Brazil and King of Portugal.

Baron Forrester completed the first illustrative map
marking out the entire River Douro region.

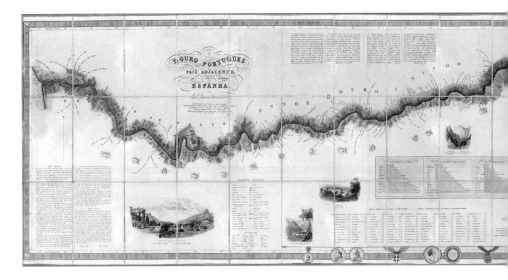

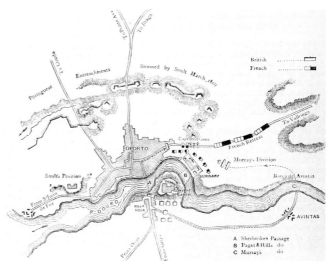

Map of the French positions
and entrenchments in Porto,
with British positions and plans
for crossing the Douro river.

Plan of The Passage of the Douro
made for the British Army under the
command of Sir Arthur Wellesley.

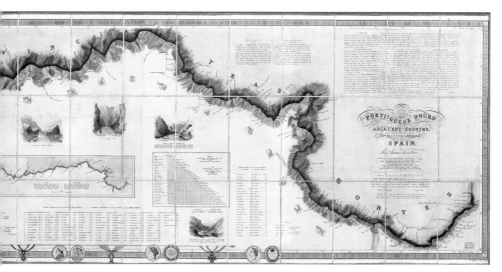

A cartoon illustration of Lord Beresford, commander of the army in Portugal (left) and Lord Wellington (right), in 1811.

The defensive lines of Porto during the Peninsular War.

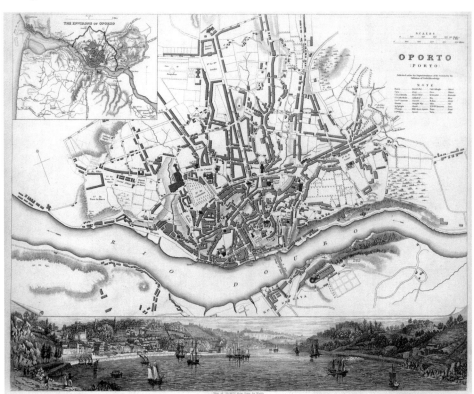

Dom Miguel, brother of Dom Pedro. The War of the Brothers culminated in the Siege of Porto.

Portrait of Sir Arthur Wellesley, the Duke of Wellington.

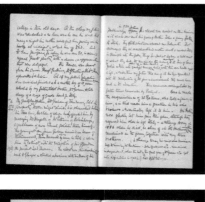

Diary of Elizabeth Noble; she recounted the drama of living through the Siege of Porto.

A map of the fortifications and entrenchments of the Porto Lines.

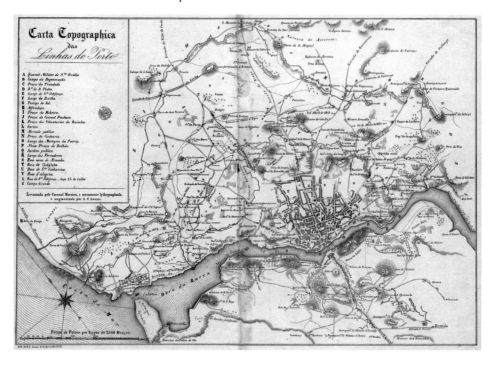

After the defeat of the Miguelites in Porto, Dom Pedro (centre) proclaims his eldest daughter (right) Queen Maria II of Portugal.

O Regenerador was the newspaper of the Porto based political party called The Regenerators.

The Municipal Guard take up cannon positions to prevent rebel Republican troops from advancing on City Hall during the Porto Revolt of 31 January 1891.

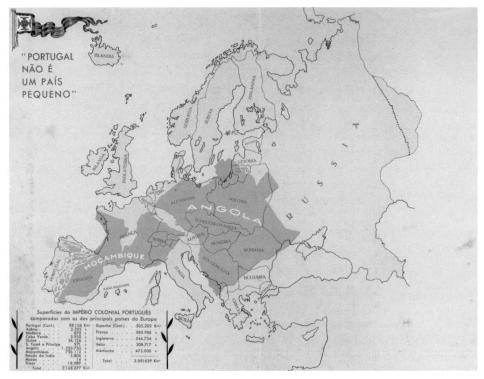

A propaganda poster from the Estado Novo to highlight
that 'Portugal is not a small country'.

Façade of the Palácio do Cristal and gardens in 1934, at
the time of the Portugal Colonial Exhibition.

The two riversides of Porto and Gaia, in 1948, with a view of the Douro river towards the Atlantic.

The city of Porto in late 1940s.

Clerigos Church with its tower rising above the Porto skyline, designed by Nicolau Nasoni.

One of the many attractive squares across Porto.

Dom Luis I Bridge: an icon of Porto.

Statue to commemorate the Peninsular War at Rotunda.

The city of Porto in 1948 reminiscent of the view from 1791 as well as present day Porto.

PORTO · PORTUGAL

A typical tourist postcard of Porto from the 1960s.

The first of a series of lighthouses located where the River Douro meets the Atlantic Ocean in Foz.

The town of Amarante was strategically important in the Peninsular War.

St James's Anglican Church of Porto and cemetery has served the British community for centuries.

British architectural influences of the 18th century can be seen across Porto, most notably in the Santo Antonio Hospital.

The University of Porto, from where many important local cultural and political figures graduated.

The view from Serra do Pilar monastery, from where
Wellington devised a military plan to cross the River Douro.

The edge of Europe, the lighthouse from the river estuary
at the Atlantic Ocean.

The statue to Dom Pedro.

Façade of the Infante Sagres Hotel, home to Vogue Café.

View of the extensive art deco gardens of the Serralves Museum of Contemporary Art.

Pedroites, as a result, launched a series of operations to try to push the Miguelites back to a more comfortable distance from the city.[21]

Additional operations were conducted for different aims, but for the soldiers the motives were no less important. On 17 December, an operation was launched by the Pedroites to cross the Douro from Porto into Gaia in order to obtain supplies of wine from the warehouses. Secrecy was not a strong suit of the Pedroites and, as usual, details of their intended operation reached the Miguelites. Around 2,000 men were ferried across the River Douro to capture wine belonging to the Oporto Wine Company, which was said have been sympathetic to the Miguelites.[22] They crossed the river as artillery fire was exchanged by both sides in a ferocious reminder of the deadly power of shells.

Disaster struck the operation. With all the boats loaded with wine and heading to the north bank of the river, the Pedroites were left stranded. Instead of taking up defensive positions to await the boats' return the soldiers advanced too far. They had been given orders to clear an area around the Convent of San Antonio, whose grounds and building had been used for attacks on the monastary still held by the Pedroites.[23] They soon came under sustained enemy fire. Their plight worsened when the boatmen refused to return with their boats after unloading the wine, and there were no soldiers around to force them to make another journey across the river.[24] The stranded men fled in any little boats they could find, with others swimming out to one of the British merchant ships anchored in the middle of the river. Several men were not so lucky. Their frozen bodies disappeared into the cold wintry currents of the river before being dragged under. Some of the dead were later washed up on the shore, but most were never recovered.[25]

The operation illustrated the often amateurish nature of some of the military operations conducted during the siege. A better way to have undertaken the exercise would have been to divide the boats into two divisions: one to transport the wine, and the other to stand by if needed to evacuate the soldiers. Given that the Pedroites understood that they were heavily outnumbered by Miguelites in the area this would have been a sensible precaution.[26] A large of amount of wine had been taken, but at a high price. As the soldiers drank well into the evening, they reflected on their casualty figures for the day's work: '...seventy-four, including five officers and a general, killed'.[27] The price of a bottle of wine had never been higher. Nearby, the Miguelites involved in the days fighting were being reviewed by their leader Dom Miguel, who congratulated them on their good work.[28]

8

Decisive Battle

Firing continued all the night and musketry all around
the lines. At daylight the attack was made… From the top
windows we could see the men advance. After several hours
fighting they were obliged to retreat with the loss of about
1500 and 100 on our side. The Scotch behaved very well.[1]

Elizabeth Noble

F OR THE FIRST FIVE months of 1833, the Siege of Porto
continued in much the same fashion as it had for the last
part of 1832: exchanges of artillery fire, attempts to place
guns in new positions, attacks, and counter attacks in order to repel
the Miguelites. The war was starting to enter its crucial phase with
each side probing the other looking for signs of weakness. The
soldiers on both sides were increasingly tired and also trying to
save energy for what they knew would be the bloody major battles
to come as the weather became more settled in late spring. On the
Pedroites side there was a sense that the Siege needed to be broken
at least before the end of the year. The people of Porto could not
be expected to hold out for another winter. The Miguelites were
considering one major concerted push to defeat key enemy positions
and to force their way into the city.

As the soldiers of both sides tired, carelessness became a greater
problem with terrible results for both the belligerents and the
civilian population. On 17 January 1833 a shell which was being
prepared at the Serra do Pilar monastery had exploded due to an

officer smoking his cigar too close to it. The explosion killed two officers and four men and wounded many more.[2] The intensity of the shelling however increased, and so did the civilian casualties. Other civilians, such as Baron Forrester, were much luckier. His house suffered a direct hit on 8 March, but he was unhurt. The following day, another British resident, Mr Simpson had 'two balls' land on his house.[3] Increasingly tired soldiers became less precise with their targeting.

A tragic example of shelling occurred around the same time in Gaia. A stray cannon ball hit the house that belonged to the manager of Croft Port. A letter recounted the story of a Mr Wright who was inside the house at the time:

> News from Porto to communicate and it is news that I have to inform you with a feeling of deepest distress of the very unfortunate disaster that has befallen your Mr Wright having been struck by a cannonball (a 24 pounder) whilst sitting in his house, which so dreadfully shattered his left arm as to render immediate amputation necessary…Frankly I know how acutely you will feel as we all must not only for him in his truly disaffected situation but also for his dear wife who appears deeply fond of him, and (no) doubtfully will be in an agony on receipt of this heart rendering intelligence (news)…[4]

The one factor that appeared to prevent the shelling was adverse weather: rain, river mist or fog, and heavy cloud silenced all the guns, but as soon as the weather broke there was a swift return to artillery and musket fire. 'Rain: tolerantly quiet' was a frequent insertion in Elizabeth Noble's diary.[5] Strategically little changed on the ground. Both sides continued to probe one another with limited success, leading to a status quo in terms of positions. The good news for the Pedroites was that their fortification of the city of Porto had withstood any concerted assaults from the Miguelites. Efforts to break the siege, however, had been less successful. The numerical advantage of the Miguelites made breaking out by land highly risky and prone to failure.

The month of June 1833 proved to be pivotal in the war. It was clear to the liberals that foreign intervention was required if they were to emerge victorious. The conflict had become a test of resources and military strength, rather than any reflection of the political support each side enjoyed in the country. Orders were issued to the commanders of the Pedroites to go on the offensive in order to strike a deadly blow against the Miguelites. The previous emphasis on defence was shed and plans laid for a series of offensive attacks:

> All of Porto were in lively expectation that some grand blow was to be attempted, though it was doubted whether it would be successfully struck. The army, however, became exceedingly elated at the prospect of shaking off their chains.[6]

A Royal Navy veteran, Captain Charles Napier was brought into serve as an admiral for the Pedroites, along with a group of sailors that he had personally chosen. Known amongst the Pedroites by the alias of 'Carlo Ponza' he was 'not to be trusted except in the hour of danger, and then performs prodigies far beyond all calculation.'[7] The arrival of Napier brought a new, more offensive and seaborne element to the liberal cause. Among the rank and file soldiers he was much liked:

> Admiral Napier's unassuming manners had already won hearts. He appeared in plain clothes, the simple country gentleman. His conversation betrayed nothing of that prompt and daring spirit he was known to have so often exhibited in the navy of England.[8]

Not everybody was happy with the appointment of the Scottish-born naval officer. Much of the High Command of the Pedroites felt that the campaign was going as well as could be expected, given their numerical disadvantage to the Miguelites. There was also a natural deep suspicion of foreigners and the motives they held for joining the campaign, plus the financial rewards being offered to them in contrast to those paid out to the Portuguese officers.

Suspicion is often a two-sided coin; Napier's initial impression of Pedro was not very flattering:

> I came next and was received at the door by the Emperor (Pedro), who stood with his hands behind him, looking very angry, and speaking as roughly as he looked. Not being accustomed to such company, I began to consider whether this was an uncivil or only an imperial manner of receiving a person who had come to render him a service. My mediations were soon disturbed by his majesty, in rather a brusque manner, asking if I wished an expedition immediately; to which I replied, I have come for that express purpose.[9]

It was not only Pedro's manners that worried Napier. In contrast to the senior Portuguese officers in the Pedroites, he felt that their campaign, until this moment, had proven to be something of a strategic failure. Much of these shortcomings could have been avoided with clear and more unified leadership among the ranks of the Pedroites.[10] Competition and internal power struggles were rife among the senior officers. Issues that had been simmering for months came to a head with disputes over how best to break out of Porto, end the siege, and move towards the eventual defeat of the Miguelites in the nation. One plan supported by key officers called for an attack on the Miguelite front lines in Porto. Another idea was to organise an expedition of 5,000 men which would sail from Porto and land along the coast of Lisbon in order to seize the capital city. The majority of senior commanders were against both proposals. They argued that any frontal assault would expose their men to being outnumbered and outgunned by the Miguelites. Nor were they keen to commit such a large force being deployed to Lisbon as it could threaten their present positions in Porto. In the end, the liberal leadership settled upon a different course of action. They proposed to send a smaller expedition force of between 2,500 to 3,000 men to the south of the country. Once there, they were to disembark at a convenient point along the Algarve coastline.[11]

On 21 June 1833, the liberal fleet sailed away, in full view of the inhabitants of Porto, the Pedroites, and many of the Miguelites. Napier recorded his exit from Porto:

> The steamers got away the day before, joined in the morning, and with a fine breeze we stood to the southward, our hearts leaping with joy at the brilliant prospect before us[12].

Amongst the population of the city there was a double feeling of anxiety; fear for their own increasingly perilous position as the defensive garrison was reduced by thousands of men and concern over the fate of the naval fleet which many incorrectly speculated was set to attack Lisbon. The force was commanded by the Duke of Terceira who had had his men embarking onto the ships quietly at night since 12 June.[13] The fleet's departure represented bold new thinking from a reshuffled leadership of the Pedroites. As shells rained in on Porto from the Miguelites, the Pedroites sensed an opportunity to push home an advantage; rumours continued to circulate in the city as to the whereabouts of the liberal fleet. On 23 June, reports circulated that it had landed in the small fishing village of Cascais, at the western end of the Lisbon coastline.[14] Other reports speculated that they had tried to land at Figueira da Foz, but had been repelled. It was not until 29 June that news arrived of the expedition force having disembarked in the Algarve.[15] Back in Porto, Elizabeth Noble celebrated news of the landing by taking an evening stroll. 'Beautiful nights', she wrote in celebratory mood in her diary.

More good news for the Pedroites was to follow. On 9 July, while Porto was marking the first anniversary of their entry into the city, came the news of the defeat and capture of the Miguelite fleet off the coast of Cape St. Vincent by Admiral Napier's boats.[16] For many inhabitants of the besieged city, the defeat marked the beginning of the end for the Miguelites. Few, however, could barely believe it:

> It was so unexpected, so improbable, under the consideration of their relative forces and weight of metal that it was scarcely

credited by the besieged until fully authenticated. Dom Pedro sent a flag of truce to the Miguelites, to communicate the intelligence and to offer an ample amnesty for the past, and proposals for entering into further arrangements, that the effusion of blood might be stopped. As was expected, the officer was not permitted to leave his letter.[17]

The messengers were 'allowed to enter the enemy's lines and were treated very civilly'.[18] The Pedroites who had remained to guard the city feared one last desperate effort to take the city by the Miguelites. On the night of the 9 and 10 July, the Porto skies were lit up by illuminations and rockets. Pedroites in the city were placed under arms from 2.00 am onwards in the expectation of a major assault. None materialised. The next day expectations of an attack were heightened, the Pedroites were still under arms, but the day passed with only a few shots exchanged at night-time.[19] The threat of an assault increased tensions in the city, especially among British residents. Elizabeth Noble complained that the preacher at church on Sunday gave 'a most stupid sermon, which we did not understand, and perhaps he did not understand himself'.[20] Even the usually unflappable British consul was showing signs of nervous strain:

> The British consul, Colonel Sorell, was nearly worn out by the continued anxious inquiries of timid newsmongers, and by the difficult task of maintaining a due equilibrium with Pedroites and Miguelites, English and Portuguese. He kindly offered his house to those of his countrymen who might wish for that asylum, and he stood ready for the approaching crisis, confident in the flag and painted arms of England. He had no other protection or defence; yet how weak must that barrier have been, had the town been taken by assault.[21]

News from the south of Portugal reaching Porto was reassuring. The Pedroites had faced only token opposition in the Algarve and were marching through the sun-drenched wide-open plains of the Alentejo towards Lisbon. Disease, and the heat of the Alentejo summer sun, became the major enemies of the Pedroites rather than the Miguelites. Support for Miguel remained strong in the countryside with only the major urban centres supportive of Pedro. Peasants continued to send food supplies and recruits to the Miguelites and helped sustain them. On 24 July, however, the Pedroites entered Lisbon.[22]

The evening of 24 July in Porto proved to be the quiet before the storm. In places, the lines were close enough for soldiers to be able to exchange verbal insults. 'We're going to eat you up tomorrow' cried the Miguelites. 'We're too tough to digest' replied the Pedroites. The summer heat had arrived bringing balmy nights and hot days. One soldier noted:

> The weather was now very fine, the fields were covered with bright grass, the vines were in full leaf, shading many a jaded sentinel from the hot sun's rays; and the patches of Indian corn with its beautiful foliage waved gracefully in the breeze. The months of shelling and pounding with shot had opened the walls of many a garden and orange grove… The flowers had run wild, grass and weeds were growing on the paths… In many instances the doors had long been wrenched off their hinges and used as firewood.[23]

The expected grand attack of the Miguelites came at 6.00 am on 25 July 1833. It opened with a barrage of artillery fire, some originating from new positions, preceding a series of full-frontal attacks, with the Miguelites advancing in large columns, and directed from several points across the city. The aim was clear: to overrun the positions of the depleted forces of the Pedroites and storm the city. The main part of the battle lasted until 4.00 pm. Advances of the Miguelites were swiftly driven back by dogged resistance from Pedroites. The forces of the Miguelites were well organised, their aims achievable, but while the Pedroites were heavily outnumbered theirs was the strongest motivation. Women and children played an important role for the Pedroites 'biting off the ends of cartridges and keeping them supplied with water'.[24] At 4.00 pm the fighting stopped; an eerie silence replaced the sounds of artillery and musket fire. The lines of the Pedroites had held. Just. 'I think the Miguelites never fought so well as they did this day, and it was just touch and go that they didn't get the better of us', admitted a British soldier in the Pedroites.[25]

The casualty figures were high; on the side of the Pedroites the losses were 322 men, including thirty-nine officers.[26] Losses for the Miguelites were estimated at around 5,000.[27] The failure of the hugely numerically superior Miguelites to take the city on this fateful day has been the source of much debate among military historians. Arguably the most salient explanation came from Charles Napier:

> The failure of this attack must be attributed to the great dislike of the Miguelite troops had to attack entrenchments. The heads of the columns, instead of keeping firm and filling up the spaces, became vacant by the killed and wounded, and, marching boldly up, invariably broke into skirmishing parties, securing themselves as well as the nature of the ground would allow, thereby exposing to a desultory fire, probably from its duration more destructive than the bolder and more decided attack of the bayonets would have entailed upon them.[28]

The battle of 25 July proved to be the decisive defence of the city. It would only prove a matter of time before the Siege of Porto would be lifted.

Later the same evening, church bells started ringing out in Porto and in Foz. News had reached the city of the Pedroites' takeover of Lisbon and that Dona Maria II, daughter of Pedro, had been proclaimed queen the previous day.

It was a rare double good news day for the Pedroites.[29] With the failure of the efforts of Miguel to storm Porto safely defeated,

Pedro decided to go to Lisbon. During the afternoon of 26 July, he toured his troops to thank them for their efforts before dining at his headquarters. Under the cover of darkness, he headed for Foz, where he, his ministers, and staff boarded a ship and headed to the capital. He left the Duke of Saldanha in command of his forces in the city.[30] He arrived in Lisbon two days later to try to develop liberal control over the nation.

9

The Wine is on Fire

Still in the most awful state of suspense as to what may
be the fate of Villa Nova, if but one tithe of the apparent
plan of destruction is carried into effect. The company's
lodges are now fairly built up in every part of their interior
with straw, barrels of gunpowder and hand grenades, and
the 'Armazen de Hesketh' may be literally said to be full
of combustibles. Indeed, in consequence of events, Villa
Nova is in such a state of anarchy and confusion that
I find I cannot remain in the lodges, nor go to them with
any degree of safety. Officers have no longer command
over their soldiers, and soldiers have no command over
themselves. My life has been twice threatened…[1]

Baron James Forrester

THE WITHDRAWAL OF THE Miguelites from Porto and
the lifting of the siege was a messy affair, accompanied by
continued musket and artillery fire, vengeance, and score
settling by the departing forces. At the start of August, local residents
noted the dismantlement of some of the artillery positions held by
the Miguelites.[2] Some of the Miguelites departed, heading towards
Lisbon to challenge the Pedroites' hegemony of the capital city.
Before the major part of the withdrawal took place however, there
was the thorny issue to be resolved over the fate of the Port wine,
and the numerous lodges in Gaia where it was stored. Unfruitful
negotiations took place between the Miguelites who controlled the
area, the Pedroites led by Saldanha, and the British led by Consul

Colonel Sorell. While the talks continued the Wine stores were mined by the Miguelite French officer Count d'Almar and his team. Efforts were made to move out some of the wines. Baron Forrester reported that much looting of Port wine took place with near-total breakdown in discipline among the soldiers that were charged with guarding the wine lodges.

Reports indicated that it would only be the Portuguese-owned lodges that would be burned. In response, Portuguese properties put Union Jack flags above their doors in the hope that their stores would be spared. This did not work, and only drew the British lodges deeper into the plot. Forrester reported that he was instructed to hand over the keys to his company's lodges on 15 August. Everybody in Gaia waited in anxious expectation of whether the plan of destruction would be carried out.[3] Tensions were heightened by the heavy stormy weather, which brought torrential rains. Ships anchored at the bar moved out to sea for protection.[4] A final effort to save the stores failed in the evening of 15 August. Baron de Haber, the Miguelites' negotiator, offered to allow the British to place a British seal on the wine in order to save it. Saldanha refused the proposal, believing that any deal would be linked to the granting of an orderly retreat from Porto of the Miguelites.[5] In his heart, Saldanha did not believe that the Miguelites would blow up the stores rather than allow them to fall into the hands of the enemy. The majority of the people of Porto did not believed the threat either. At 11.30 am on 16 August, Saldanha told a British officer:

Don't you believe that they will dare to destroy a drop. Tis all talk. I know my countrymen better than you. It will all end in smoke.[6]

The officer, a Captain Glascock, told Saldanha that the destruction of the wines had been assigned to a Frenchman and that they would go ahead with it as planned. Other witnesses added, 'No Portuguese general officer could be found reckless enough to execute this barbarous mandate'.[7] With negotiations at an end, people waited to see if the threat of blowing up the stores would be acted upon. At 1.30 pm, the question was answered. A hollow rumbling and a pop, pop sound were followed by a thick black mass of debris rising into the sky and coming to rest all over riverfront. Baron de Haber and the Miguelites had carried out their threat. Later, the Baron claimed that the order was given to destroy only one wine store to show Saldanha that their threat was serious. The reality however, was that all the companies' wine stores were blown up or set on fire. Estimates of the damage vary from 13,000 to 27,000 pipes of wine destroyed. On top of this there was the value of the buildings. If 27,000 pipes were destroyed at £20 per pipe which equalled £540,000, plus £400,000 for the premises meaning that more than one million pounds of damage had been done in one fiery afternoon.[8]

Captain Glascock witnessed the resulting destressing scenes:

Wine and brandy in boiling and flaming torrents were running in rapid streams down the different lanes leading to the destroyed lodges. It was impossible to approach the scalding vapour floating in the air. We were, therefore, compelled to walk, or rather run, a round of nearly three miles to get in the rear, as well as to windward of the fire. Fortunately, there was a well of water in the rear of the wines, for the boiling flood prevented any approach to the river's side. It was near four o'clock before we got well to work.[9]

Another eyewitness described the fires, 'The hissing steams of wine were like rivulets pouring out of the smoking ruins into the Douro, whose waters were tinged to a deep red'.[10] The witnesses to the terrible fires praise the bravery of Captain Glascock for landing the ship's crew and a few armed marines into Gaia to fight the fires and prevent them from spreading further and endangering British properties. As Britain was officially neutral in the war, Miguelite commanders were furious that Captain Glascock had arrived in Gaia with an armed force. Heated exchanges took place and threats made against the captain and his men, but 'Captain Glascock was too cool, too determined in the just object he had in view to be moved in the execution of his duty'.[11]

Baron Forrester could not match Captain Glascock's coolness under duress. His mood was one of being highly agitated; mixed with anger towards the Miguelites for the fires, and fear that if the flames spread his company would lose everything. He sprang into action later recording his fire-fighting experiences in a letter to his uncle.

I directed the men I found there to remove the wooden hoops and shavings that were lying about the Pateo, immediately adjoining the burning lodges: they remained idly looking on and refused to obey. Half-an-hour afterwards the whole of the square was in flames. Our danger became imminent, the wine as it streamed from the company's lodge was set on fire by the burning hoops, so that in a very short time the flames of the burning wine communicated with the door of Christovão's Lodge and threatened the destruction of the whole property. At that moment I collected all the men I could meet with in the neighbourhood, entered the Pateo where the fire was raging, and, after two, or three, hours incessant application of water, fortunately succeeded in preventing the further progress of the flames.[12]

Perhaps the hardest part to understand about the decision of the Miguelites to set fire to the wine stores was that the Portuguese people it hurt the most were Miguelites. The fires ruined hundreds of Miguelite families, as the main part of the Portuguese shares in these wine companies were owned by the families who were part of that camp. So much damage, hardship, and destruction just to prove a point to Saldanha. The sorry events of the day the River Douro turned red were best summed up by Elizabeth Noble writing about the loss of the wine in her diary: 'So much work for no purpose'.[13]

A few days later, there was better news for the inhabitants of Porto, still reeling from the last major offensive of the Miguelites with its waves of artillery and musket fire, plus the siege which had prevented food from entering the city. On 18 August 1833,

Saldanha still smarting from his miscalculation over the wine lodges, extracted his revenge on the Miguelites. An officer who witnessed Saldanha's brilliant attack described the scene:

> Saldanha aware that the Miguelites to the North had thrown back their right, abandoning their batteries on the flank, moved out to force their retreat, covering as they did the main road to Valongo. He maneuvered well, and concentrated his three columns on the destined point, the Valongo heights, with great precision as to time, and in good military style. The enemy made a demonstration of resistance, but when he threatened their flanks, they retreated. He had completely surprised them at daybreak... Some hundreds of prisoners, and large quantities of ammunition, all marked 'For Riflemen', were the results of this day's parting kick to the Miguelites – by far the best executed sortie during the siege.[14]

The casualty figures for the Pedroites were, compared to past efforts to break out of Porto, relatively light with 118 lost, including twelve officers. Among the approximately 250 captured Miguelites, there was bemusement at the flimsy nature of the defences of the Pedroites when they were escorted past them into the city.[15] Many failed to understand why their commanders had not adopted a more aggressive approach to overrunning the city. Had they known the state of the defences they would have pressed home their advantage more clinically during the early days of the siege. The operation came to be known by the Pedroites as 'our battle outside the lines, which obliged the enemy to raise the lengthened of Porto'.[16] Revenge was sweet for Saldanha. His relatively poor showing during the campaign was soon forgotten and the Pedroites were quick to laud his leadership in breaking the siege, sending the Miguelites into full retreat towards Lisbon.

The ending of the painful siege of the city was met by massive celebrations by the citizens of Porto. Amidst all the jubilations there was surprise at how quickly and easily the Pedroites had been victorious. Elizabeth Noble summarised the events of the day from the perspective of a British civilian.

> Charles woke me at 4.30 am to tell me there was much musketry and all the bells were ringing for the troops to get under arms. Sir John Stubbs went out immediately and headed the advance, but the fighting was nearly over... They (the Miguelites) made the only serious resistance afterwards, it was a pursuit. Our troops went over the hills onto Valongo, the Miguelites still retreating. The Lancers had a charge, our troops were returning by night.[17]

The Siege of Porto had lasted for eleven months and twenty-two days. The battle of 18 August 1833 moved into the folklore of the history of the city. Critics might well ask, given the ease of the battle, why didn't the Pedroites launch such a daring offensive attack earlier in the campaign? The answer to that question, in all probability, lies in the first such attack by the Pedroites at the outset, which proved to be so unsuccessful and costly to their cause. In the evening of the battle, a streamer ship, the *Echo*, set sail from Porto, headed for Lisbon, carrying the news for Pedro of the blowing up of the wine stores and the subsequent revenge of Saldanha and the Pedroites over Miguel and his forces.[18]

Amidst all the celebrations and relief at the ending of the siege of the city, a brief tribute to the robustness of the people of Porto was recorded by a British officer in Porto which says much about how the city survived:

> Scourged by hunger, cholera morbus, shot and shell, the spirits of those poor inhabitants, a volatile people with few resources, were only kept up by the news of the day. 'How many shells have fallen?' 'Where and what damage?' 'How many were wounded in the last assault?' 'What was the loss of the enemy?' These were the everlasting topics of the morning and kept up their animation. Tales and anecdotes of personal valour warmed the blood and created emulous ambition. Scenes of blood and

carnage nurtured the direst spirit of revenge, still more excited by
the knowledge that, if the enemy entered, children in the arms of
their dying parents would be murdered. This was what defended
Oporto during the memorable siege.[19]

The joy in Porto proved to be short-lived. Following the departure
of Pedro for Lisbon, and soon after the end of the siege that of
the Duke of Saldanha as well, the city was emptied of Pedroite
troops that were needed elsewhere. The discontent that prevailed
across Porto was based on fear and traditional Portuguese
jealousies. The former centred upon the news that the Miguelites
continued to arm their traditional supporters in the countryside.
The latter was based on the feeling that Pedro felt the defence
of Lisbon to be more important than that of Porto, which had
first supported his cause, making great sacrifices in doing so.[20]
At this juncture, the visitor should be reminded of the historical
jealousies between the populations of Portugal's two major cities.
The war between the Pedroites and Miguelites, their ideologies
of liberalism versus absolutism, did not end the rivalries between
Porto and Lisbon.

The breaking of the Siege of Porto did not bring the curtain
down on the war. There followed a period of stalemate, lasting
nearly nine months. The Pedroites controlled the two major
cities: Lisbon and Porto, in which they enjoyed strong support
among the middle classes. The Miguelites continued to control
rural areas, supported by the aristocracy and the local peasants.
There was much debate in British political circles as to whether it
should try to impose an agreement on the two brothers. At first,
the government in London was reluctant to do so.[21] Fearing
political strife in Spain, and a major Spanish intervention
in Portugal, Britain changed its mind. On 22 April 1834, the
constitutional governments in the west formed what was known
as the Quadruple Alliance. On 23 May, a month later, the war
in Portugal ended. Miguel, facing the dual threats of attacks
by Portuguese and Spanish forces held his last council meeting.
He refused an unconditional surrender, but seventy hours later

his forces capitulated at the Battle of Évoramonte.[22] Miguel demanded an assurance that his officers could keep their ranks, and a general amnesty for political crimes was acceded to in the negotiations. The key part of the agreement was that Miguel would leave the Peninsula within two weeks, and never return. At the start of June, he departed Portugal onboard a British frigate. He had been guaranteed an annual pension and eventually settled in Austria, playing no further role in Portuguese politics.[23] Pedro moved swiftly to purge the armed forces, the church, and the civil service of Miguelites.

The War of the Brothers had placed a vast burden of debt on the state. This was made all the more serious, coming so soon after the economic damage inflicted upon the country by the Peninsular War. The struggle between Britain and France had proved to be a catalyst for the industrialisation of the two countries. Not so for Portugal, which became the battleground for the competing armies. The result of the two wars was that Portugal experienced economic difficulties at a time when much of the rest of Europe was rapidly expanding. Public finances remained in a mess for much of the nineteenth century with the country running large budget deficits. The wars had coincided with the loss of the trading monopoly with Brazil, putting a further dent into the public finances.[24] The cost to the city of Porto was more severe than the cost to Lisbon. Consecutive governments continued to maintain a bloated state sector based in the capital city, whereas the financial impact to the industrial sector, largely based in Porto, was much more damaging. Porto, as a result, needed to overcome these challenges in order to become an elegant industrial city with all the trappings of international trade and wealth.

Pedro did not live long enough to have to deal with the consequences of the wars. He died of consumption on 24 September 1834, less than three months after his victory. His legacy in Brazil and Portugal has been much debated. In Porto, the visitor can look at the impressive statue of Pedro on his horse and know that he will forever be known as the leader that withstood the siege of the city by his brother and the Miguelites. In his will, he stated his wish for his heart to remain in Porto. On his last trip to the city he had paid tribute to the Portonians:

> The royal family attended at the balls given to them by the British and Portuguese associations, where they danced... Oporto was in its glory. Dom Pedro's pallid countenance betrayed his inward decay, and many an aching heart foreboded the early loss of his guardian arm over the tranquillity of Portugal, as he waved his handkerchief to thousands who cheered him crossing the Baron his return; when, with evident marks of emotion he said to his fair companions, – 'Did I deceive you; are they not my faithful Portonians?' 'Adieu, Oporto, I shall never see thee more!' He turned aside and shed tears.[25]

Upon his death, the guns in Lisbon fired every fifteen minutes for three days and three nights.[26] The Portugal that Pedro left behind was a very different country to the one he had inherited. The pathway of constitutionalism had been fought over, the battle won, and its implementation seemingly assured. This was not the end of the story for there followed much debate as to which form this liberalism should take, with Porto, once again, in the forefront of the political battles that dominated the rest of the nineteenth century in Portugal. The linkage between the city and the liberal cause remained strong as did its position at the forefront of Portuguese politics.

PART THREE

Day Two – Morning

10

Liberal versus Liberal

The heroic and ever unconquered city of Oporto, as is now designated, is one of the most irregularly built towns with which I am acquainted. Few of its streets are level, and fewer still run at right angles with each other; indeed, its inhabitants seem to have an abhorrence of right angles; it is, however, a very interesting place. It well earned the title of heroic from the gallant defence it made against the army of Dom Miguel, in 1832, when every military man declared that, according to all the rules of military tactics, it ought to have been taken. The armed inhabitants, the few regular troops, and the foreign auxiliaries, thought otherwise, or, being ignorant of the art of war did not know when to yield! So the city was preserved, to prove the nucleus whence genial beams of true liberty and enlightened education may radiate over the fair surface of Lusitania.[1]

William Kingston

T HE VISITOR SHOULD WALK up the Avenida dos Aliados towards the Câmara Municial do Porto building (City Hall) that dominates the square. The austere building, home to the rulers of the city, was built in 1920 and only finished into its present-day form in 1955. The centrepiece is a seventy-metre-high clock tower that looks straight down the Avenida. Built by the Portuguese architect António Correia da Silva, it divides opinion on its beauty and merit. Inside its more glamorous corridors, sit the decision-makers who shape the past, present, and future narratives of the city. Local officials scurry between its rooms legislating and implementing the decisions of the elected officials to keep the city moving forward. The outside of the building resembles similar functionary buildings of the north of Europe, and casts a long shadow over the top of the Avenida. It offers some nice framing, and Instagram opportunities, to the central Avenida in Porto that draws comparisons with the Avenida da Liberdade in Lisbon. Arguably it lacks the style and panache of the previous building, which stood on the same ground, but functionality has become the key necessity in modern city hall planning rather than efforts to create architectural objects of beauty.

Of greater interest than the building is the statue that sits proudly in front of it. It is of Almeida Garrett, the Porto-born great poet, novelist, orator, and liberal politician. The statue, which was sculpted by Salvador Barata Feyo, was inaugurated on 11 November 1954 to commemorate the 100th anniversary of Garrett's death. Rarely has there been a more important inhabitant of Porto, one whose literary and political legacy remain closely linked to the city that saw the origins and development of liberalism in Portugal. As previously mentioned, Garrett, after a period of exile, landed back in Portugal with Pedro and his armed forces in 1832. He saw action during the Siege of Porto, but it is during the post-War of the Brothers era that his literary and political influence becomes more important. Like many Porto-born men of letters and politics he moved to Lisbon, the seat of government, in order to seek influence and power. He eventually died in the capital city having established himself as one of the great writers and orators of his generation. Despite his detour to Lisbon, Porto still regards him as one of its most important sons, a figurehead for the city's historical rejection of absolutism and connection to the liberal movement.

Perhaps one of the greatest disappointments for Garrett, and his fellow liberals who fought so valiantly during the Siege of Porto was that the defeat of the absolutists, in the form of Miguelites, did not lead to an era of political stability and strong economic development. Instead, the victorious liberals morphed into two distinct camps: 'moderates' and 'radicals', creating a dispute that came to lead the country into another brief round of fighting. The moderates supported the principles of the constitution framed and implemented by Pedro. The radicals wished to return the country to the constitution of 1822. At first, the moderates held the upper hand. The first government of the era of Queen Maria II (Maria de Glória) was comprised of moderates, led by the Duke of Palmela. The duke represented the slightly more conservative faction of the moderates, but his ministers were divided and clashed with the *Cortes*.[2] The economic situation was dire and Palmela's government collapsed in May 1835 unable to pass a budget. The old government was replaced by a new one led by the hero of the Siege of Porto, and political rival, Palmela, the Duke of Saldanha. This government proved to be short-lived, lasting only a year until May 1836.[3] It collapsed over repeated attempts to reduce the debt burden by selling off key fertile lands in the valleys of the rivers Tagus and Sado, as well as some military estates owned by the state. A further two governments came and went in rapid succession before the idea of selling the lands was raised once more and agreed upon. Despite the sale, the state of Portugal's finances remained perilous. State debts had reached £24,000,000.[4]

Elections held in July 1836 saw the radicals, rebranded as the Patriotic Front, emerge victorious in Porto. Their campaign focussed on a return to the first liberal constitution as a means for dealing with the high unemployment and the wider economic crisis. The upheavals did not stop there. When the deputies arrived in Lisbon to take up their seats in the assembly, they were greeted by demonstrations of support calling for a return to the 1822 constitution.[5] Soon after, the National Guard joined in support of the radicals and the liberal government collapsed. The September Revolution led in turn to the establishment of a radical dominated government on 10 September, led by the Porto activist Manuel da Silva Passos and the Visconde de Sá da Bandeira.[6] Passos, a charismatic idealist, believed that the ills of the country were essentially economic but offered predominately political solutions centred upon constitutional reform.

The government announced plans to abolish the Constitutional Charter and temporarily reinstate the constitution of 1822 until it could be rewritten by a Constituent *Cortes* to reflect the economic and social challenges facing the country. The decision was met by widespread opposition from the moderates, fearing that the charter was to be consigned to the history books. The British argued that the hidden hand of France was behind much of the agitation for a new radical constitution, and moved to defend the queen who sought temporary shelter aboard a British warship. The threat of a foreign intervention in Portugal at the request of the queen was discussed. The King of Belgium selflessly offered to send a rescue expedition, in exchange for the transfer of some of Portugal's African possessions to his country.[7]

Eventually a compromise was reached, the queen returning to Lisbon with the realisation that the seeming threats against the royal family had been not as serious as first presumed. A new constitution was framed and approved in April 1838. The document reflected an attempt at bridging the two previous constitutions.[8] The radicals (now rebranded as Septemberists after the revolution of September 1836) held power until a coup in June 1841 led to the return to government of the moderates. Most of the liberals of 1820 and 1832 had shifted towards the centre. Palmela had become elder statesman and Porto's son Almeida Garrett was also much changed.

(He) had left behind his youthful and romantic anti-clericalism and was now a viscount and a supporter of reconciliation with Rome: his energies were largely directed towards the establishment of the National Theatre in 1842.[9]

The most important personal conversion to the moderates was that of António Bernado da Costa Cabral. By 1844, with the current of political and social opinion increasingly behind a return to the Charter, Costa Cabral was the man controlling the political developments of the day. Such was his control over events that the era came to be known as *Cabralismo*. The list of this dynamic leader's achievements remains highly impressive. He almost single-handedly reformed the judiciary, introduced new fiscal reforms, created the national printing house, reorganised the national archives at Torre do Tombo in Lisbon, and introduced new forms of state education. He also developed a new road infrastructure, spanned the River Douro with a new suspension bridge, created a register of rural properties. and banned burials in churchyards.[10] This last reform might appear as the least important, but it was the one that led to Costa Cabral's fall from grace and eventual exile from Portugal.

In the Minho (the furthest northern district in Portugal), women complained of their loss of the right to have their family members buried in the grounds of the village church. A rebellion started, involving mainly women from the area. It was given the name Maria da Fonte, although it is not clear if she was a mythical figure to help shield the names of those individuals responsible from the small hamlet of Fonte.[11] Their protests quickly gathered momentum and support. Marches of armed peasants in the villages and towns were soon organised, during which the demonstrators destroyed the local registers and documents.[12] The hidden hand behind this were the rural nobility and clergymen who still held Miguelite sympathies. The governor of the Minho region refused to intervene to restore order so it was left to Costa Cabral to resolve. His first move was to send his brother to Porto with instructions to end, with strong force, what had become a fully-fledged challenge to his policies. The officers of the units sent into end the rebellion, however, refused orders to take action against the uprising.[13] Soldiers from the countryside often crossed sides to support the insurgents, making the use of meaningful force all the more complicated for government.[14] Other opposition figures to Costa Cabral, who had quietly been waiting in the wings, attempted to seize the moment. By the start of May 1846 Cabral's position appeared to be untenable. The queen was left with little choice, but to fire the minister on 20 May and to form a new government. Cabral and his brother went to Spain, where they continued to try to influence events though the Spanish Ambassador in Lisbon.[15]

On 20 May 1846, the queen tasked a new government consisting of what appeared on paper to be a sensible mixture of moderates and radicals led by the Prime Minister, the Duke of Palmela. Terceira became Minister of War and Maritime with Saldanha as Minister of Foreign Affairs. They were later joined by Sá da Bandeira. Among its first actions was the decision to rescind the unpopular church burial regulations imposed by Costa Cabral as well as the road tax system that he had introduced under his administration. Despite containing an impressive who's who of the constitutionalist leadership of the past two decades, the government soon started to unravel. Palmela's following by this late stage in his career was relatively small, Terceira was fired for being too close to the previous government and Sá da Bandeira was no longer trusted by his original more radical supporters.[16]

A few months later in October the government collapsed when Palmela decided to call for new elections. His aim had been to try to unify the moderates that were divided into two camps. The decision, however, inflamed the Septemberites and put Porto, once again, at the forefront of Portuguese political events. Slowly but surely Portugal was sleepwalking into a potential new civil war at the very time its economy needed reforms to help kick start its process of industrialisation. The Septemberists set up a provisional junta in Porto and were able to resist the attempts of Saldanha, who had replaced Palmela, to suppress the rebellion, which had now spread to other parts of Portugal.

What followed was a curious, potentially devastating, return to civil war. Thankfully, it lasted a short 10 months and was known as the *patuleia* (rabble) – the name given to the Porto Junta. As the troops of the rebellion approached Lisbon the British decided that their strategic interests were coming under threat and intervened on behalf of the queen, whose throne London argued was in danger, as well as her own life. British warships blockaded the mouth of the River Douro, in effect placing Porto under a sea siege. On the ground, a Spanish division was sent to restore the authority of the queen in the city. Faced with the robust intervention of the foreign powers, the Porto Junta were forced to enter into peace negotiations.

On 29 June 1847, an agreement known as the Convention of Gramido was signed by representatives of Britain, Spain, the queen, and the Porto Junta. In exchange for the dismantling of the Junta a general amnesty was declared, bringing the ten-month conflict to an end.[17] With the agreement signed, Saldanha resigned, leaving his friends to lead a transitional government to prepare for free elections.[18] The agreement appeared to bode well for political stability in the country, but the decade of the 1850s was characterised by a number of deaths and power struggles that presented further serious challenges for the country.

Saldanha was able to form a new government in December 1847 but Costa Cabral returned from exile in Spain to take up his seat in the House of Peers and to prepare to challenge Saldanha's hegemony. What followed was a bitter power struggle wrapped in ideological clothing between the two dominant foes of the era. Initially, relations were quite cordial between the two men although not among their respective supporters. Cabral in particular made efforts to get along with Saldanha but their relationship slowly, but steadily, declined. In June 1849, Saldanha's government collapsed, and Costa Cabral was able to return to power.

To rub salt into his wounds, Costa Cabral demanded that the queen dismiss Saldanha from his position as chamberlain. This was a step too far for a furious Saldanha, who joined the opposition to the government. The main issue that he chose to fight Costa Cabral on was the government's concerted attempts to control the press. In April 1851 Saldanha and his supporters attempted a revolt against Costa Cabral.[19] It got off to a bad start when Saldanha's initial proclamation, given in the town of Sintra, did not attract much support. Even in the traditional hotbeds of rebellion in Porto and the north of Portugal, there was unease about supporting a man they barely trusted. With the revolt stalling, Saldanha prepared himself to go into exile when news reached him that the hugely important garrison in Porto had given him their support.[20] This turned things around for Saldanha, and it was not him, but rather Costa Cabral who was forced to go into exile once again. In May 1851, Saldanha formed an administration and returned to power.

The Duke of Palmela had died in 1850. His voice of moderation had been a dominant force in Portuguese politics for decades and his close connections with London had done much for Anglo-Portuguese relations. Following Palmela's death Saldanha's hands were freer to navigate a more modernist approach to liberalism, particularly with his other great rival Costa Cabral weakened and forced into exile. Saldanha moved quickly to create a new political party, the Regenerators, with the intention of attempting to broaden the support base by including conservative ex-Septemberists and by further modifying the charter. Central to the changes was the introduction of direct elections, but still with limited suffrage. Moves were made to try to reduce the influence of the military in political life, as well as limiting some of the actions of the political press, and the death penalty was abolished for civil crimes. The thinking behind these measures was to try to make government more stable, allowing it greater time to deal with pressing national issues of the day. The opposition, old style Septemberists also rebranded themselves, becoming known as Progressives or 'Historicals'.

The Regenerators and Progressives were not political parties in the modern sense of the word. At the time, the Portuguese electorate was only comprised of around one per cent of the population. There were no mass memberships of these factions, rather loose groups of local notables; important citizens that centred upon personal patron-client ties and local, not national, issues. Elections were held to legitimise one faction over the other by providing it with a majority in the legislature. One faction would govern for as long it felt it could before handing over power to the other faction. This policy of *rotativismo* (rotation) became institutionalised, helping to provide a degree of political stability in the second half of the nineteenth century that had been severely lacking during its first half.[21]

A number of royal deaths complicated the political situation, the first of which occurred when Queen Maria II died in childbirth in November 1853. She was 34 years old and was survived by five sons and three daughters. She was succeeded by her eldest son, the sixteen-year-old Pedro V. Saldanha and the Regenerators continued to rule, placing Fontes Pereira de Melo, who later succeeded Saldanha as leader of the party, as Minister of the Treasury. At this late stage in his career, Saldanha was running out of political friends and ideas. Good at ideas, not so good at implementing them was a frequently made charge made against him. The old marshal's skills were starting to desert him. This was brought into sharp focus when he overplayed his hand during a spat with the new young king.

In 1856, he lost his majority in the House of Peers, and in the country. He requested that the king help him by *fornada* (baking) some new peers. The king's refusal to comply with the request, left the huffy Saldanha with little choice other than to resign. He was given a consolation job of ambassador to Rome. This served the purpose of getting him out of the country, preventing him from rallying any internal opposition. Eventually returning to Portugal in 1865, he attempted to make another political comeback. His sell-by date, however, had expired and to the relief of much of the country he failed to make an impact.

In October 1861, Pedro V and his two youngest brothers were taken ill with typhoid fever while on a hunting trip. The king did not recover and died the following month. His twenty-three-year old brother Luís succeeded him as king, largely staying out of politics. King Luís I left the two political factions to continue their policy of rotation. The factions continued to morph into new groupings, but the system remained unchanged. When the king sensed that his government was running out of ideas and energy, he would dissolve parliament and appoint a new one. As a matter of course, the new government was widely expected to win the resulting election.[22] In October 1889 Carlos I succeeded his father and continued to rule with the same basic principles that had been present for decades. All in all, there was a much stronger degree of political cohesion and stability during the latter decades of the nineteenth century up until 1890. This not only brought political calm, but allowed the country to move forward with dramatic and much needed improvements to its infrastructure, national economy, and social advancement.

While it is natural to concentrate on the important political developments in the country during much of the second part of the nineteenth century up until 1890, these do not tell the whole story of the development of Porto and the country during this time. The visitor needs to be reminded of the great success stories that defined this era, the resulting growth in Porto's population – notably in the middle classes – and the rise of a more interconnected nation. Although many men were involved in the development of Porto as an elegant industrial city, one name stands out head and shoulders above the rest.

11

Birth of an Elegant Industrial City

Country of villages that do not communicate, inhabitants who do not live, products that do not circulate, manufacturers that do not move and even riches and wonders that are not known.[1]

Fontes Pereira De Melo

IT TURNED OUT TO be an inspired decision by the Duke of Saldanha in 1851 to appoint Fontes Pereira de Melo as Minister of Finance (1851-1852). Later, Fontes was made Minister of Public Works (1852-56) and served as Prime Minister on three separate occasions (1871-77, 1878-79 and 1881-86). Under Fontes, a centrally controlled public works programme was developed and implemented leading to major changes in Portugal, most notably in Porto. The modernisation of the country's infrastructure and industries was long overdue. Successive invasions by the French and the resulting Peninsular War, followed by the War of the Brothers, along with the political instability had cast a long shadow over the first half of the nineteenth century. This had postponed or slowed efforts to undertake such ambitious programmes. The programme of public works came to be known as *Fontismo* (after Fontes); its main objective was to modernise Portugal by making material improvements, especially in the transportation and communication sectors.[2]

Fontes got to work right away; consolidating foreign debt at 3 per cent, he raised a new loan and created a new and more effective Ministry of Public Works. The access to continued foreign investment was extremely important for the development of the Portuguese economy.[3] Fontes used the Ministry to launch one of the most ambitious programmes of economic expansion.[4] He authorised the construction of new roads, finished the first national telegraphs, and in 1856 opened the first part of the Porto to Lisbon railway line. Fontes also pushed for plans to lay underwater cable services to link Portugal with the Azores, and later the United States. In order to pay for these extensive programmes, he raised taxes on properties and imposed higher customs duties.[5] It is worth looking at the statistics of the key changes. Starting with roads when Fontes was first appointed as the Minister of Public Works in 1852, Portugal only had 218 kilometres (135.5 miles) of modern all-weather roads.[6] By the time he left the ministry four years later, there were 678 kilometres (411 miles), along with an additional 120 kilometres (75 miles) under construction. By 1884, the figures had increased tenfold with 9,155 kilometres (5,667 miles) of roads in the country.[7] The increase in the number of roads told only part of the story; the quality improved markedly as well, reducing journey times between the major urban centres. Porto did well out of this expansion with improved road infrastructure north to south and east to west. This encouraged better communication with Lisbon in the centre of the country, and the Minho in the north as well as parts of the Douro in the north-east of the country. The sum of all this was to help cement the city as the leading place of commerce and industry in the north of Portugal.

The railways experienced a similar transformation. Work on the rail infrastructure had started under Costa Cabral with an effort to build a track from Lisbon to the Spanish border.[8] Cabral had previously founded the *Companhia das Obras Públicas* (public works company), partly to develop this project. In the end, the project failed, so Fontes is left with the credit as the pioneer of the Portuguese railways. Between 1851 and 1856, the contracts were signed (many with foreign companies) and construction of the lines and rolling stock started. The pace of the expansion of the lines was highly impressive. The statistics indicate an increase from the initial line in 1864 of 36 kilometres (22.3 miles), 1,500 kilometres (932 miles) by mid-1880, 2,288 kilometres (1,421 miles) in 1892, 2,381 kilometres (1,479 miles) in 1902 and during 1912 just over 2,900 kilometres (1,802 miles). At the end of the nineteenth century, Portugal was ranked in an impressive tenth place in the world for the amount of rail track for each 100 miles of territory. This placed it above neighbouring Spain, as well as several other European countries. The ranking was maintained, remaining roughly in the same position for the next twenty years.[9]

Along with the railroads came an ambitious engineering works programme that transformed Porto and the rest of the country.[10] The construction of bridges and tunnels was at the centre of these efforts. The construction costs were enormous; Fonte travelled around Europe to raise the required foreign capital. During his first period in office, he oversaw the building of seventeen bridges with an additional twenty-eight planned for construction.[11] Among these was the train bridge over the River Douro, which, as we have mentioned, was to complete the Porto to Lisbon trainline. Another major railway bridge in the Minho linked northern Portugal with Galicia in Spain for the first time. Within four decades all the major population centres in Portugal had been connected by the train network, making movement around the country for an increasingly mobile population all the more easy.[12] Arguably the most impressive engineering feats were the construction of tunnels allowing trains to reach the city centres. In Porto a tunnel that allowed trains to arrive right into the heart of the city was constructed.[13] São Bento station remains one of the best, and most beautiful, reminders of this golden era of engineering.

The age of advancement was not restricted to the roads and railways. Infrastructure at the ports also underwent something of a revolution. Entrances to harbours were greatly improved as were lighthouses. In the Porto region the most important maritime development of the period was the construction of a new deep-water port at Leixões; built between 1884 and 1892, it served the city and the northern region.

Prior to the port at Leixões, ships were faced with the dicey prospect of trying to dock at Foz. As the size of fleets increased, this became too risky and the new port helped maintain the Porto region's ability to trade with the rest of the world. Business was also helped by the liberal ideology that prevented the state from interfering. 'Free trade' was the buzzword: a free exchange both inside and outside the country. Historian A.H. de Oliveira Marques summed up the opportunities:

> ...Hence all the measures abolishing local tolls, permits of circulation, municipal monopolies, exclusives and privileges for certain companies, sales taxes, the corporations and the like. It was, however, possible for the state to endow commerce with a framework that could regulate, organise and also simplify the free circulation and distribution of products.[14]

How businesses in the twenty-first century must dream about the existence of such liberal trading laws.

The better transportation and communications contributed to the rapid population growth of Porto during this era. Porto increased from 50,000 inhabitants in around 1820 to 60,000 in 1838, 86,000 in 1864, 105,000 in 1878, 138,000 in 1890 and 160,000 at the start of the twentieth century.[15] When taken together with Lisbon the two cities accounted for eleven per cent of the total population of Portugal, up from eight per cent some eighty years earlier. It was not all plain sailing; the country was hit by a number of economic crises, perhaps most severely in 1890. The crisis in 1890 was caused by a range of internal and external events and developments that simultaneously damaged the economy. A decline in wine exports coincided with the abolition of Brazilian slavery, the loss of two important trading bases in Africa, and the revolution that overthrew the Brazilian wing of the Braganzas.[16]

The years of growth, while extremely impressive, left a number of crucial economic issues unresolved. The two major cities appeared prosperous, but there were not many clusters of wealth. Banking and communications were the two main sectors of the economy where a select few made their fortunes. Others, such as lawyers, administrators, and politicians remained dependent on the increasingly large state. For all his good work, Fontes had placed an emphasis on developing communications infrastructure rather than on much-needed production.[17] The presence of a chronic budget deficit was not considered a serious enough issue by the Portuguese to do something about it. Fontes believed that the deficit would, in time, be reduced as the expansion of the economy gathered pace. This proved to be a tad over-optimistic; the economy with its linkage to foreign investment continued to be highly susceptible to external events. The importance of customs duties as revenue for the government further entrenched the economy's links to those of the outside world.

The resignation of Fontes in 1885, and his death two years later, removed the central figure who had dominated the politics and finance of the state for decades. It also led to a shift in power, a decline in support for the Regenerators he had led, and the rise of the Progressives. Using the good old tried-and-tested formula of manipulating elections, the Progressives were able to secure a large parliamentary majority. The economic crisis of 1890 was matched by a political turning point, bringing to an end the period of relative political stability of the era of *rotativismo*. The impact on Porto of these important shifts was a return to major political agitation, a slowing down in the pace of the economic development of the city, and eventually political revolution.

At the time of the crisis in 1890, and after, there was and still is much debate as to why it happened. Much of the focus remains on the dominating and extended role of Britain in economic underdevelopment and the establishment of strong dependency ties to London. In a memorandum written by a disaffected Portuguese noble to the British Foreign Office, some of these frustrations are clearly vented. Although written after World War I, its content reflected on a critical approach to the impact of Portugal's relationship with Britain. Direct, wounding, and powerful, the memorandum strikes at the core of what its author sees as the British historic sacrifice of Portuguese interests and its consequences:

Great Britain is practically unknown to Portugal, yet Great Britain has never tried to correct this. Notwithstanding that

Portugal was for a long time the only nation with whom Great Britain maintained a political alliance, she was one of the few nations with whom they could not have a commercial treaty... How could Portugal love Great Britain, when everything tends to show that Great Britain distained Portugal and in the arrogance of her great pride and power, treated Portugal as if she was little more than one of her dominions. This opinion has long been in the mind of the Portuguese lower classes, and finally gained the more educated.[18]

The reply to the letter by the British Ambassador to Portugal was equally to the point and scathing. It reflected the deep stuffiness, arrogance, and nationalist self-interest of the Foreign Office towards Portugal.

The first pages of the memorandum, dealing with various questions of past history which contributed to the unpopularity of Great Britain in Portugal, do not call for remark. Everyone acquainted with Portugal knows very well that in spite of the ancient alliance between the two countries the Portuguese have always disliked the English and still do, not only for the reasons given in the memorandum but because it is natural that a weak and conceited people should secretly detest a great nation to whose protection not given because of any special love of Portugal, they owe their independence and existence as an important colonial power.[19]

At the centre of the tensions between Britain and Portugal at the end of the nineteenth century were serious disputes over African colonial possessions. During the second half of the century until the crisis of 1890, with political stability at home, Portugal looked towards Africa and its colonial possessions on the continent. For much of the nineteenth century, it was widely presumed that the loss of Brazil could be made up for with the development of Portugal's colonial possessions in Africa. The two perquisites were an expansion of the state sector (administrators, lawyers etc.) and an influx of capital.[20]

Central to the African policy was the sending of expeditions to explore, chart, and make claim to previously unnavigated areas. Separate trips visited the interior of Angola, heading to present-day Zimbabwe and South Africa. Other explorers went from Angola to Mozambique. The Portuguese, however, were not the only colonial power attempting to develop their position on the African continent. Britain, France, and Germany were also busy carving out spheres of influence, and it was only a matter of time before a clash occurred between Portugal and one of the major European powers of the day. The problem which came to snowball into a major crisis started with the Congo.

Portugal claimed the Congo region, but there was opposition, reflecting the competing interests of Britain, Germany, and France in the region. A Franco-German decision to hold an international conference to settle the various issues was accepted by the European powers. The representatives met in Berlin in 1884-85 and decided to award the Congo to the King of Belgium. The key ruling was that in order for any claim on African territory to be upheld, the claimant had to be able to demonstrate 'effective occupation' and not 'historical rights'.[21] The Berlin Conference led to the partition of Africa by the European powers with Portugal being awarded Angola, Guinea, and Mozambique. Naturally this all came as a major disappointment to the Portuguese who regarded the 'effective occupation' doctrine as essentially seizures of lands which Portugal believed it had strong 'historical rights' to owning. What followed was both complex and simple to understand. Portugal, feeling more than a little miffed by the new definition, organised successive expeditions to the lands between Angola and Mozambique in order to stake its claim. This brought it into direct conflict with British expeditions running south to north aimed at the construction of a railroad linking Cape Town and Cairo via central Africa.

In the meantime the Portuguese had been proactive; the Minister of Foreign Affairs, Barros Gomes, proposed that Portugal claim the lands between Angola and Mozambique, producing a document known as the 'Rose-Coloured Map'.[22] In 1886, Portugal had seemingly secured treaties of support from France and Germany for its claims but closer inspection of the documents reveals that Paris and Berlin had inserted plenty of constructive ambiguity in the treaties, committing them to nothing. After the publication of the 'Rose-Coloured Map', Portugal waited for the British reaction. The British prime minister, Lord Salisbury led the protests from London. At first, these were rather muted. In June 1887, however, Salisbury became clearer, stating that Britain could not recognise any Portuguese claims in areas where there was not sufficient force in place to impose order in the lands. From a British perspective, it was a clever tactic but, as Barros Gomes responded, more than a little hypocritical. He pointed to previous instances of both France and Germany obtaining recognition of lands without either historic claims or high enough levels of occupation to be able to secure order.[23]

The British challenge to Portugal was clear; it needed to throw as much of its limited resources into developing as deep an occupation of the lands as quickly as possible. This posed an enormous burden on an economy whose growth was already coming under severe strain. Portugal was not alone in sending rapid-fire expeditions to the lands to win the favour of local tribal chiefs. Britain did likewise, signing treaties with local kings, some with rather dubious claims over the lands they ruled. Salisbury tried a softly, softly approach with the Portuguese, dispatching an envoy to Lisbon in 1889 to warn Barros Gomes to stop the Portuguese expeditions and refrain making claims over the lands. The vaguely worded message and implied threat was misunderstood by the minister, lost in translation between London and Lisbon.

Portugal proposed resolving the issue of disputed claims by arbitration, as it had in several previous cases. Britain refused point blank. While officials looked for a way forward, events on the ground in the disputed territories in Africa were becoming more toxic. Following a skirmish in one area, Salisbury delivered an ultimatum on 11 January 1890 demanding that Portugal withdraw all its forces from the disputed lands. The issuing of the stark warning shook Anglo-Portuguese relations to the core. Faced by the military power of Britain, Portugal had little choice, agreeing to withdraw its forces with immediate effect.[24] Portugal was stunned by the action of the British. The ancient alliance appeared to count for little. The issuing of the ultimatum came to have a profound impact on the royal family in Portugal, the political direction of the country over the subsequent two decades, and the orientation of Portugal's foreign policy.[25]

Reaction in Portugal was highly emotional leading to demonstrations, riots in Porto, attacks on British properties, the creation of nationalistic societies, and even fundraising efforts to buy warships. The anti-British sentiment, present across the social classes, soon turned into a blame game as people sought out those Portuguese most responsible for the national embarrassment.[26] The pro-British, Portuguese royal family was an obvious target.[27] There were increased demands for the removal of the royal family, particularly from the growing number of Republicans based in Porto, keen to use the frustration and anger over the ultimatum to further their political agenda. The first casualty was not the royal family, rather the progressive government which fell to be replaced by a non-party administration.[28] The change of government was just the start of a process that would eventually lead to a major upheaval at the start of the twentieth century. Once again the city of Porto would be centre stage in the dramatic events that shaped the destiny and direction of the country.

12

The Cradle of the Republic

The first fire produced an extraordinary panic. Many of the insurgents, throwing away their arms, ran headlong down the steep street again to Praça Dom Pedro *[now called Praça da Liberdade, located below Avenida dos Aliados]*. Some of them, however, fought bravely, and, obtaining a little shelter in by-ways, fought for a long time before they were dislodged. The shutters and large panes of glass of the handsome shops in this street are completely riddled with bullet holes from one bend of the street to the other. The insurgents from Praça Dom Pedro made another attempt to ascent the Rua Santo Antonio, with the intention of seizing the palace of the civil governor, getting possession of the telegraph office, and cutting the wires in Praça de Batalha, but were driven back again. There were many victims on both sides in this encounter.[1]

The Times of London

THE ANTI-MONARCHY SENTIMENTS, LACED with populist anti-British rhetoric, found a home with the newly-formed Republican Party. The Republicans enjoyed greatest support in urban areas, Porto and Lisbon being its major strongholds, and among middle class professionals such as journalists, businessmen, junior military officers, and low to mid-ranking civil servants. Using great political skills, the Republicans positioned themselves as the cheerleaders of the popular reaction to the events of 1890 that had culminated in what they viewed as the national humiliation of caving into the British ultimatum over Africa.[2] The Porto branch of the Republican Party was particularly militant, so it came as little surprise when the political fallout from 1890 took place in the city at the end of January, 1891.

As the visitor stands in Avenida dos Aliados, looking down from the wide boulevard, it is difficult to imagine the violent events that happened in 1891. The Porto Revolt took place on 31 January, and for much of the previous evening rumours had been circulating in the city's theatres of possible action by the Republicans. Few people, however, had taken the threat very seriously. The local authorities made no special provision to mobilise any forces. Early the next morning the rebels, numbering about 400, made their move. Gathering their supporters, they marched to the Câmara Municipal do Porto (City Hall), accompanied by a band.[3] Church bells were rung to warn the city and to try to get its inhabitants to come out in support of the rebellion. At precisely 8.00 am the rebels entered the City Hall and took possession of the building. Despite support from some of the garrison in Porto, the vast majority of the population did not join the march. Soon afterwards, the civilian leader of the revolt, Alves do Veiga, appeared at the balcony of the building and addressed the Republican supporters below declaring a new government. He spoke about the need for the emancipation of the people, the rights of man, and outlined in detail the programme of the Republican government.[4] Prior to his speech a red flag with blue borders had been raised over City Hall.

At the end of Alves do Veiga's speech the watching rebel troops shouted 'Death to the monarchy'. Soon after the first shots could be heard as the Municipal Guard, who had remained loyal, moved to prevent rebel reinforcements from reaching the City Hall. Several people were killed during these initial exchanges of fire, shopkeepers pulled down their shutters and the civilian population largely remained indoors.[5]

The fighting escalated. The Municipal Guard moved two cannons into Praça Dom Pedro and started bombarding the city hall, where the rebels were still encamped. The intensity of the firing grew greater, the noise of the guns could be heard in Gaia across the river. The shells exploded off the building, making giant holes in the walls. The guard backed up the artillery with small-arms fire. It was poorly directed, but the sounds of the bullets ricocheting off the building must have still terrified the Republicans inside who returned fire whenever the opportunity arose. The exchanges continued without pause for two hours as the building started to crumble under the severe onslaught of the attack. Thereafter, the soldiers of the Municipal Guard launched a swift and brutal bayonet charge into the building. The rebels fought bravely, but by this stage were heavily outnumbered and outgunned.

The outcome was quickly assured in favour of the loyalist forces. Finally, the defiant rebels surrendered; they started coming out of the building to be taken prisoner. There occurred one final twist to the fighting: as the loyalist troops arrived back at their barracks they found themselves locked out by troops supporting the revolt. After a brief negotiation, the rebel forces in the barracks surrendered. By 4.00 pm, just prior to sunset on a chilly winter's day in January the revolt was over. Order was quickly restored. The Republicans had staggeringly overplayed their hand. While there was widespread sympathy for the Republican cause and plight from the population of the city, few civilians took any active part in the events of the day. The casualty figures were estimated by the foreign press to have been around fifty dead.[6]

There was much excitement in Lisbon as news of the revolt started to reach the capital. The government promised a swift and severe response against all of those who took part in it. Tight press censorship meant that the coverage was highly diluted, the seriousness of the revolt under-played, and the continuation of the rule of the royal family emphasised. The leaders of the military rebels who took part in the revolt were cast as predominantly dissatisfied junior officers, disappointed at being passed over for promotion, and not overtly politically motivated.[7]

In the subsequent days, the authorities were quick to round up the usual Republican suspects in the city and further afield. Military Law was imposed, remaining in place for a month after the revolt.[8] Some Republicans tried to flee to Spain, but most were apprehended before they reached the border in a big security sweep by forces loyal to the king. Several of the captured rebels, fearing a military trial and execution (capital punishment had only been abolished for civilian crimes), tried to claim foreign citizenship. One of the rebels, Joaquim Thomas de Brito, stated that he was an American citizen and demanded the protection of the US consular agent in Porto.[9] American diplomats were present during the legal process for Brito and other countries did likewise for rebels claiming foreign citizenship. On 5 February, *The Times of London* reported that over 500 rebels had been captured and more than 100 killed.[10] There was also speculation about the participation of the Portuguese navy and Spanish Republicans in the revolt.[11] The king was quick to thank the people of Porto for their seeming indifference to the revolt.[12] Punishments for the participants included exile or lengthy prison terms. Many of the leaders found themselves heading for Africa. Of those who escaped capture by leaving Portugal in the days following the revolt Paris was the favoured destination, where they continued contact with Republicans still based in Portugal. Supporters of the Monarchists wanted to make an example of the prisoners captured on 31 January and in the subsequent days but while the sentences were not light, in many cases they were not as bad as feared by the apprehended men.

The 1891 Revolt failed, but did not in the end derail the rise in support for the Republican cause and agenda. Between 1895 and 1905 the Republicans would attract between one quarter to a third of the votes in Lisbon. Their organisation methods however changed to a network of underground secret societies; necessary given the control of the Monarchists over a large number of masonic lodges in the country. Although some Republicans were freemasons, many of their leaders were members of the highly disciplined secret society known as *Carbonária*. The group acted as both a recruiter for the Republicans and as the main organiser of its military activities after 1907. It did not only contain Republicans, also drawing in anarchists and socialists. Such was its power that it became a state within a state with the common purpose of overthrowing the monarchy. Its members took part in highly ritualistic ceremonies and as political repression in Portugal increased, so did the membership of this underground group grow, along with its influence.[13] It became a central tool of the Republican leadership to devise and implement some of its most violent acts.

The Republicans' use of public mass rallies to disseminate their message was particularly clever, bypassing the problems of press censorship and illiteracy among the population.[14] The Republicans were one of the few political parties to consider it worthwhile to address the electorate directly. The ruling Monarchists made little effort to match the Republicans in trying to win support. Republican strategies included the use of political violence to seek political advantage: bomb-throwing attacks and street riots were the *modus operandi* of the party.[15] On the political stage, they continued to stir up anti-clerical feeling and blamed the extravagance of the king and the royal court for the poor state of Portugal's finances.[16] The attacks on the state financing of the king had a major effect on public opinion, which was turning increasingly anti-royalist.[17] The use of high taxes on 'essential commodities', leading to high prices for the poor, was also heavily attacked by the Republicans. Continued efforts to muzzle the Republican press were also condemned, as were increasingly desperate efforts by the Monarchists to fix electoral law (especially in Lisbon) to damage Republican numbers.[18]

Good old-fashioned methods of gerrymandering were employed to reduce the power of the major cities (more pro-Republican) and increase rural influence (mainly pro-Monarchist). Soon the Republican Party of the intellectuals was excluded from parliament and then disbanded. Many however would rush to the Republican cause at the start of the second decade of the twentieth century. Arguably, the major miscalculation of the Monarchists (and there were quite a few to choose from) was to misunderstand one of the basic concepts of politics in Portugal: despite efforts to redress the balance, power remained strongly in the hands of the major cities, not in the countryside.[19] It was in the cities, with all their industrial workers, doctors, teachers, and accountants that Republican support was at its strongest. It was at this time that the centre of the Republican struggle shifted from Porto to Lisbon, which had a literacy rate twice as high as that of the second city. There were other factors in this geographical shift: the increased pace of industrialisation in Lisbon plus its satellite towns, the increase in petit-bourgeois businesses, and political volatility in the capital city that became much more politically radical and unsettled.

Perhaps the major appeal of republicanism was the collapse of the previous system of *rotativismo*, which stopped the political system operating in an effective manner. Arguments between the two factions, Regenerators and Historicals, previously settled privately in smoke-filled rooms became public in order to try to create the impression of debate and help increase public support for the political system.[20] These efforts, however, did not prove fruitful, and the introduction of essentially party politics proved to be a rather destabilising influence on Portugal's nascent political system. By 1906, there was stalemate. None of the factions were able to win a parliamentary majority and the system entered a period of protracted crisis. Prospects appeared rosier for the Republicans who were able to get four deputies elected from Lisbon. Their arrival in parliament added to the already heightened political tension in the country. Given the political stalemate between the parties and resulting paralysis, King Carlos I had little choice other than to suspend parliament. The king's major aim was to try to stop what was increasingly looking like an inevitable slide towards a republic.[21] He chose to install a conservative reformist, João Franco, to govern by decree. The decision, which caused uproar, was opposed by all political parties. It soon backfired with an increasing number of Monarchists joining the Republicans in protest, frustration, or opportunism.[22] In retrospect, the appointment of Franco marked the beginning of the end for the monarchy.

The Republicans attempted to launch another revolt, but were, once again, unsuccessful.[23] Franco's police had got wind of the plot on 28 January 1908 and launched a wave of arrests of Republican supporters across the country. Several of the leaders escaped to Spain. The punishments for those that were caught in Portugal were harsh. Franco insisted that many of the Republicans were sent to the colonies as indicted political detainees.[24] For Republican leaders Franco's action was the final straw, and they planned to seek their revenge on him.[25] In the meantime, King Carlos I had one last secret plan to save the monarchy. In private he had been organising a trip to Brazil, where he planned to try to win support and funds from the large monarchist community in the country.[26] The king was never to make the trip.

An alleged secret *Carbonária* plot was hatched to murder Franco, but the assassins could not find him at his home. They turned their attention, as a result, to the king. The royal party had been in Vila Viçosa and were returning to Lisbon. On the afternoon of 1 February 1908, as the royal party crossed the Terreiro do Paço in the centre of Lisbon in an open coach, the king and his heir were murdered. Local police shot the two killers (a teacher and a clerk), but their accomplices were never caught. To add to the mystery surrounding the events, no crime report on the killing was published.[27] Speculation was rife that leading members of the *Carbonária* were behind the killing. The funeral of the king brought a large following of Monarchists from the countryside in a show of support for the crown, a reminder of the continued divisions in the country between the cities and the countryside.

Carlos I was succeeded by his second son, Manuel II, who had survived the attack that killed his father and elder brother with only minor injuries. He had just turned eighteen and was faced with an uphill struggle to save the monarchy. His first decision was warmly welcomed; he sacked Franco, who went into exile. However, Manuel II was not a natural leader. Permanently marked by the attack on his family he lacked his father's decisiveness, was ill-prepared for the job, and sought the advice of the wrong people.[28] On the day of his father's murder he addressed his councillors and said:

> I am without knowledge or experience. I place myself in your hands, counting upon your patriotism and wisdom.[29]

An already difficult task was made all the harder for the king by the fact that the opposition did not want to deal with him, regarding him as something of a joke. Support for the Republicans was not overtly damaged by the death of Carlos I. The publication in June 1908 of a long list of non-authorised advances to the royal family from past finance ministers further helped the Republican cause. On 1 November, the Republicans won the municipal (local) elections in Lisbon. By this stage, it was clear to all that Manuel II, through his inexperience, had lost the ability to shape events.[30] Governments came and went (seven in total during the thirty months of his reign).[31] The king was well intentioned, brought some modern ideas and fostered national reconciliation, but nothing appeared to work.

The end, when it came, was swift and dramatic. The timing of the intended Republican revolution in 1910 has been much debated. The government's security forces believed that the Republicans would make their move on 13 October 1910 – this date coincided with the anniversary of the death of a leading Spanish martyr of the cause. Some suggest that the intended date was at the end of the month.[32] This is important as when violence did break out on 3 October, it came as much of a surprise to the Republican leadership as it did to the Monarchists.

The catalyst for the revolution came in a most unusual manner. The assassination in Lisbon of one of the Republican leaders, Dr. Miguel Bombarda, by a patient from an asylum on 3 October led to a speedy reaction from *populares* (Republican protestors). Following the death of Bombarda, rumours swept across the city that his killer was actually a reactionary Monarchist, and that the killing had been of a political nature, not simply the actions of a madman. Rumours about his death were not confined to Portugal. *The Times of London* summarised the various theories:

Attempts to obtain further information from Lisbon regarding the reported assassination of Professor Bombarda, a prominent Republican, have proved unavailing. According to telegrams published yesterday by the Daily Mail and the Daily News he was shot in his own drawing-room by a military officer who had been admitted as a visitor. The only further news received last night was contained in a telegram to Reuter's Agency, dated Lisbon, October 3, which simply announced that 'Professor Bombarda died this evening.' Professor Bombarda is stated to have been Director of the Lisbon Lunatic Asylum, and the officer a previous patient of his. It is therefore possible that the crime had no political bearing. But a different interpretation is suggested by the fact that the Professor had lately joined the Republican Party, and had been returned at the recent election as one of the Deputies for Lisbon.[33]

During the evening of 3 October, Republicans attacked symbols linked to the Monarchy including priests, the Catholic newspaper, and individuals. The government had little choice but to respond. By 8.00 pm, all the government's security personnel were mobilised in readiness for what they now expected to be a full-scale attack by the Republicans. The final decision to launch the revolution was taken by the Republican leadership, also at 8.00 pm. The signal for the start of the uprising was to be shell fire from naval boats moored in the River Tagus at 1.00 am on the morning of 4 October.[34]

Events got off to a shaky start for the Republicans. There was some fire at 1.00 am but many of the insurgents, scattered all over Lisbon, failed to hear the shots and thought something had gone wrong. The head of the rebellion, Rear Admiral Cândido dos Reis, committed suicide believing the revolution had failed when his launch did not arrive to take him out to his ship.[35] Despite the slow, slightly chaotic, start the Republicans soon made headway on the ground, quickly seizing key parts of the city centre. Two rebel warships started shelling the Palácio das Necessidades, the king's living quarters, at 11.00 am on the morning of 4 October.[36] Two hours later the king, poorly defended by his Monarchist leaders, left by car for the town of Mafra some 20 miles to the north-west of the capital. The Republican forces were outnumbered by loyalists, but, crucially, could count on the support of armed *populares*. It was clear that the working classes in Lisbon were pro-Republican and many were willing to risk life and limb to support the cause. Monarchist supporters appeared much less willing to do likewise.[37]

By the late afternoon of 4 October it was clear to all that the Republicans could not be defeated. A large section of the armed forces in Lisbon wished to remain neutral and, for a variety of reasons, were unwilling or unable to attack the revolutionaries. The last hope of the Monarchists, the arrival of major reinforcements from outside the city, did not materialise. Following an offensive against the Monarchist forces in Rossio Square there was little left but to surrender. At 8.45 am on the morning of 5 October 1910 the government commanders surrendered. Fifteen minutes later the Republic was proclaimed from the balcony of the Câmara Municipal (City Hall) in Lisbon and a provisional government set up. The British Ambassador in Portugal reported the news back to London:

> Serious disturbances broke out Monday night, when some troops of the garrison declared themselves Republican. Fighting took place throughout yesterday and last night. This morning troops hitherto loyal went over, and the Republic has been proclaimed. Great excitement prevails, and proclamation has been enthusiastically received by people.[38]

American diplomats reported the same news, 'Enthusiasm is indescribable' wrote Henry Gage, the American Representative in Portugal. Later, in the afternoon he wrote, 'City unusually quiet. People apprehensive but orderly'.[39] The Americans in Portugal appeared rather impressed by the revolution: 'the revolution was perfectly planned and carried to success in every detail with great celerity'.[40] He added more details:

> There has been no pillaging, and good order has prevailed... The Republican Provisional Government is supreme in Portugal, and the people have acquiesced in the change. I believe that the newly organised power is capable of maintaining itself, and that it will continue to keep a place as a nation.[41]

The tone of the American diplomatic correspondence differed greatly from that of the British. The formation of the Republic did not present a threat to American bilateral relations with Portugal as it did to Anglo-Portuguese ties. As well as concern for the personal safety of the king, there were worries about the Republic's attitude to Britain and its trading relationship with Portugal. Despite the seemingly overwhelming loss of the Monarchists, there were still some people in London hoping for a last stand that might overturn the events of 4 and 5 October. Put simply, Britain believed that its interests, those of the Port wine producers in Porto as a whole, were better served by Monarchists, not the members of the Republican Provisional Government.

At the same time as the proclamation of the Republic, King Manuel II and some of his family were on their way to the small fishing port of Ericeira, where they boarded the royal yacht. At first the king wanted to sail to Porto, where he hoped to rally Monarchist forces to continue the resistance to the Republicans. *The Times of London* summed up the king's situation in a reminder of the warm relations between the British and the monarchy in Portugal:

> If the King were able to rally round him the loyal support of his people throughout the country districts, and of those regiments which are still true to his uniform, it might very well prove that Lisbon is not Portugal, and that the kingdom as a whole still bears allegiance to its King. Without further knowledge such speculations are vain to pursue; but whatever the King's situation may be, he is assured in his own person of the warmest sympathy from the people of this country, who have welcomed him so recently as their guest. Such trials as he has had to face have seldom fallen to the lot of so young a man.[42]

A last stand by the king in Porto was eventually thought impractical, so the ship sailed for Gibraltar, and eventual exile in Britain. Manuel settled in Twickenham, near London, where he focused his efforts on developing his extensive book collection. He died in 1932.[43]

At 12.00 pm on 6 October 1910 Porto followed Lisbon's lead in declaring the Republic. Most of the rest of the country made similar proclamations. The demise of the Monarchists had been brutal, quick, and, above everything else, remarkably easy. An uprising that had started in Porto nearly twenty years earlier came to its conclusion in a dramatic manner in Lisbon. Today, both the major cities in Portugal are full of symbols to the events that led to the creation of the republic. Streets named after key members of the Republican leadership can be found in Porto, such as Rua de Miguel Bombarda, the main street in the city's art district, and Rua de Cândido dos Reis, in the city centre near the bookshop called Livraria Lello. There is also a Rua de Cândido dos Reis across the river in Vila Nova de Gaia by WoW.

PART FOUR

Day Two – Afternoon

13

Where the River Meets the Ocean

I was born in Porto. The city, its outskirts, the beaches nearby, remained for me, when I moved to the south, a country within a country, my maternal homeland, the primordial place that created me. That's where they are, enormous trees, mornings of fog, beaches saturated with the smell of the sea, rocks covered in seaweed and anemones, Botticelli spring-times, plane trees, cherry trees, camellias… Because I was born in Porto, I know the names of flowers and trees and I cannot shake off a certain local bias. But I escaped the provincialism of the capital.[1]

Sophia De Mello Breyner Andresen

FOR THE VISITOR, A worthy starting point for day two is the Museu Nacional Soares dos Reis, located in one of Porto's most historic buildings, the Palácio dos Carrancas. The museum houses a first-class range of Portuguese art and sculpture, jewellery, and pottery from the Portuguese royal family. It is, however, the palace itself that houses the collection that links the visitor to the historical narratives of the city during the years of war, siege, and upheaval in the nineteenth century. It was originally constructed between 1795 and 1809, in a neo-classical style by wealthy local merchants, the Morais e Castro family. The intention was to build a family home along with a small factory in this much sought-after location.

The architect, Joaquim da Costa Lima Sampaio, was one of Portugal's leading figures of the day, working on both Portuguese and British sponsored projects in Porto. He had recently worked with the British Consul in Porto, John Whitehead, on the design and plans for the British Factory House in the city, built between 1785 and 1790.[2] There is evidence that Lima Sampaio was also the main architect of the Sandeman wine lodge in Vila Nova de Gaia; although the exact date of the building of the lodge is unclear, it is believed to be 1797. The same architect was also involved in the project to build the British chapel in Porto in 1815.[3] Town planning and improvement in Porto were at the forefront of debate in the eighteenth and early nineteenth centuries.[4] Architects, engineers, planners, and visionaries dreamed of creating a beautiful Porto, making the city's architecture a proud reflection of the its prominent place in the world.

The buildings constructed in Porto during the early nineteenth century, reflected a change in style away from the Italian baroque favoured by the Italian architect Nicolau Nasoni towards the Palladian style first introduced to the city by the British architect John Carr. The Palácio da Bolsa and Porto University building are perhaps the most prominent examples.[5] The strong British influence on the architecture of the city reflected the importance of British merchants on the affairs of the city, and led to the famous phrase 'Port Wine architecture'.[6]

Within the story of nineteenth and early twentieth century Porto, the Palácio dos Carrancas brings together under one roof many of the key individuals that were mentioned in the previous section. The *palácio* served as the headquarters of Marshal Soult during the French occupation of Porto and the north of Portugal. It is not difficult to imagine his staff scurrying about the rooms, bringing news of developments in Porto and the wider Peninsular War. Soult eating with his officers in the grandiose dining room. Later on, the shouts and confused panic as news reached the headquarters that the British had crossed the River Douro upstream, out of sight of French forces, and were breaking out of their bridgehead on the north bank of the river. The rooms contain the ghosts of the officers ordered to make a swift and unplanned retreat by Soult. The fate that awaited them as the British pursued them, cutting off their exit, as the unseasonal rains arrived to turn roads and tracks to mud. Rumour has it that they departed the building in such a hurry that their lunch, prepared by the local chefs, was left uneaten.

The British arrived soon after, taking over the building, becoming Arthur Wellesley's (Duke of Wellington) headquarters and residence. One army exchanged for another as Wellesley sat down for dinner in the same room in which the French had been forced to abandon their luncheon plans. As the visitor walks around the *palácio*, we can imagine the tension following the arrival of the British, mixed with the joyous response of local dignitaries who visited to offer their thanks and good will towards the British forces, and think of Wellesley sitting in his room dictating his dispatch to London, bringing together all the details of the battles of the day, while waiting for news from his generals giving chase to Soult and his men. After Wellesley, the building was occupied as one of his residences, by William Beresford, the less than popular British commander of the Portuguese army, at the conclusion of the Peninsular campaign.

The next famous inhabitant was Dom Pedro IV. After he marched into Porto from Mindelo, launching the military campaign against his brother Miguel and the Miguelites, Pedro chose the *palácio* to be his residence and the headquarters of the Pedroites. From the perspective of comfort, Pedro's choice appeared very sensible. The visitor, however, can well imagine the sounds of incoming artillery fire from the batteries of the Miguelites, positioned in Vila Nova de Gaia. The building was in easy range of the Miguelites, who pounded its walls after discovering it to be the headquarters of Pedro and his senior military officers.[7] Shells fell on it day and night, as the Miguelites hoped to land a terminal blow against the Pedroites. After four months' residency, Pedro decided to move out to spare the building any additional damage. He relocated to a less luxurious residence in Rua de Cedofeita, which provided better cover from shrapnel of the shells from being sent over by the Miguelites.[8]

In 1861 the building was sold to the royal family, who were keen to find a suitable residence in Porto for their excursions to the city. It was used by Manuel II during the time he succeeded his murdered father. After the Republic was declared in 1910 the building was closed while a solution was sought regarding the ownership of royal buildings. Living in exile in England, Manuel II decreed in his will that the palace should be given upon his death to the *Santa Casa da Misericórdia,* the charity of the church. In recognition of the king's gesture, the local council changed the name of the road the building sits on from Rua do Triunfo, named after the victory of the Pedroites over the Miguelites during the Siege of Porto, to Rua de D. Manuel II. During 1937, the building was acquired by the state in order to house the Museu Nacional Soares dos Reis.

From the Palácio dos Carrancas, head in a westerly direction down Rua de D. Manuel II towards the Jardins do Palácio do Cristal. The walk is little more than a couple of minutes, passing the former Quinta da Torre da Marca army barracks, subsequently the Rectory of the University of Porto (1976–2007), now the Faculty of Pharmacy (FFUP) and the Abel Salazar Institute of Biomedical Sciences (ICBAS). Entering the park gardens, the noise of the city recedes into the background, allowing a more tranquil state of mind and a slower pace with which to explore the gardens. It is a pleasant setting, with elevated views to the river and the ocean, as well as to riverfront areas of both Porto and Gaia. In the early mornings, the river mist often hangs in the valley between the two banks, making the ocean invisible and partially hiding the city behind an eerie damp blanket of greyness. Wandering through the wide pathways, exploring the lower, shaded reaches of the gardens is particularly enjoyable on a hot summer day. There is much to take in with miniature gardens, statues, a chapel, and a small sculptured lake.

While pleasing on the eye, the park is not simply a well-maintained local beauty spot. The history of the Jardins do Palácio do Cristal tells us much about the importance of Porto to the outside world. It also highlights the city's complex relationship with the authoritarian state, *Estado Novo,* that dominated Portugal for over forty years during the twentieth century (1933-1974). The *Estado Novo* came as the Republic, so proudly proclaimed on 5 October 1910, collapsed in disarray, to be replaced by a brief period of military dictatorship. A severe financial crisis, mixed with poor political leadership by the dictatorship, led to an agreed takeover by one man, António de Oliveira Salazar, on 5 July 1932. The *Estado Novo* was introduced the following year. Porto proved to be both a willing participant in the authoritarian state, but also home to some of the biggest moments of opposition to it. The Jardins do Palácio do Cristal was chosen as the venue to host the first major exhibition to sell the Portugal of Salazar to the outside world.

The original Palácio do Cristal was built to host the Porto International Exhibition of 1865. Based on the Crystal Palace of the Great Exhibition of 1851 in London, its planners hoped that the publicity of the fair would bring European companies to Porto. Its lengthy corridors, high glass ceilings, and elegant façade hosted over 3,000 exhibitors, mainly from Europe. French, German, and British companies took up most of the stands while non-European representatives included the United States, Brazil, and Japan. The Exhibition fitted with the previously described policy of pushing forward the economic development of the city, especially of transportation and communications, with the help of foreign capital. While it was successful in terms of attracting people to the city, its longer-term goal of acting as a catalyst to a new wave of foreign trade with Porto remained unrealised.

The building was also chosen to host the Colonial Exhibition in 1934, a key part of the propaganda drive of Salazar to convince the Portuguese that Portugal was not a small country but rather that it still enjoyed important colonial possessions with whom it traded. To mark the event a map was produced entitled, 'Portugal is not a small country'.

To the outside world, it served as a reminder of the new values of the *Estado Novo*, focussing on nationalism, corporatism, and conservatism. The exhibits were highly ambitious, including the construction of villages from the colonies and a cable car over the gardens. The blueprint for the exhibition was used in the planning for *Exposição do Mundo Português* (Portuguese World Exhibition) held in Lisbon in 1940.

Following the 1934 exhibition, there was much debate about the future viability of the building. Local, and a few international, fairs were held but not enough to justify its upkeep. Its use as a concert venue helped prolong its usefulness, but in 1951 the building was demolished. In its place a new circular green-roofed domelike building was constructed in order to host the Roller Hockey World Cup in Porto (this sport is taken very seriously in Portugal, who have been traditionally amongst the strongest teams competing in such competitions). The new construction soon became known as the 'UFO building' and continues today to tower over the gardens to the rear of the complex. After a lengthy refit the building was rebranded as the Pavilhão Rosa Mota (Super Bock Arena) in 2019 and serves as a concert and conference venue.

Before leaving the gardens, it is rewarding to take a few minutes to pause and look at the Almeida Garrett Library which dominates the main pathway. We have already encountered this writer, liberal, and veteran of the march from Mindelo with Dom Pedro, the Siege of Porto, and the political disputes that followed the victory of the Pedroites. The library was inaugurated in April 2001 as part of the city's role as one of the European Cities of Culture in the same year. It includes an auditorium that holds nearly two hundred people and forms the central location of the Porto Annual Literary Festival, held each autumn. The strange structure combines elements of tradition and modernity, blending with the nature of its leafy surroundings. It is a worthy tribute to one of Porto's most important sons, a reminder of the great quality of his writing and of his carefully honed oratory skills that graced the national assembly.

Porto's selection as one of the Cities of Culture, the other that year being the Dutch city of Rotterdam, provided it with a golden opportunity to transform the city. Its programme was entitled 'Bridges to the Future', with the aim not only of improving culture in the city, but to use the title to help environmental renovation, along with economic and housing development. During the course of the year the city put on 452 events, attracting over 1.25 million visitors.[9] It was the urban renovation programme that took the major share of the budget, helping the city start the twenty-first century with much needed improvements to its infrastructure. This was reinforced when the city hosted part of the Euro 2004 Football championship, including the opening ceremony and first match. The colourful ceremony focused on the exploits of the Portuguese explorers, offering a reminder to people of the past glories of the country and the long list of countries that once belonged to its empire. Improvements to the city's infrastructure included extensions to the Porto Metro system to link the city centre with the home of FC Porto at the Estádio do Dragão.

After leaving the Jardins do Palácio do Cristal heading towards Rua da Boa Nova immediately in front of the main gate to the gardens, and walking up the modest hill in the direction of the city's maternity hospital, the road runs into Largo do Maternidade de Júlio Dinis. On the left, set slightly back from the street, behind a rather imposing high wall, we find a modest church, which is, nevertheless, one of the most important historical connections between the city and its British residents. St James's Anglican Church of Porto and the British Cemetery have served the community for centuries. The cemetery, originally known as the Burial Ground, predates the church and is the only Protestant burial ground in northern Portugal. The British Consul John Whitehead was, once again, the driving force behind another British-led project in the city. Prior to the acquisition of the land in 1787 Protestant burials had to take place on the banks of the River Douro. No Protestants were allowed to be buried in Catholic cemeteries and, thanks to the strong influence of the Catholic Church, no Protestant burial grounds were permitted. Whitehead changed this situation and soon after work was started on creating a place of worship that over the years has developed into the church we can see today. Planning permission has proved to be an issue with no church bell, spire, or cross allowed. The church, as a result, can be mistaken by the unprepared visitor as a meeting hall not a place of worship.

While the church still fulfils a practical and active role in British life in the city, its official links to London and the Foreign Office have long since been cut. During the nineteenth century, the British government sponsored a Consular Chaplain in Porto after the passing of the Consular Act of 1825. By this act, chaplains were able to raise from public funds a sum equal to that raised by voluntary subscriptions for 'inter-alia, the Chaplain's salaries'.[10] The act also changed the process of appointment:

> Under the Consular Act Chaplains were appointed by His Majesty, though one of his Principal Secretaries of State and were to hold their offices for and during His Majesty's pleasure and no longer. It was customary for the Bishop of London, or from 1848-1852 the Archbishop of Canterbury, to give the Secretary of State an assurance as to the suitability of a clergyman before appointing him.[11]

The office of the Consular Chaplain was abolished in 1874, the withdrawal of state funds making the maintenance of the role and the church much more difficult. The history of the position pre-dates the involvement of the British government. There is evidence that the first Chaplain was appointed in 1660 (other records suggest 1671) and faced expulsion from Portugal if caught providing spiritual services to the British community.[12] The survival of the church owes much to the raising of finance by the British merchants based in the city.

It is, however, the British Cemetery that contains the most moving and interesting stories linking the British community to Porto. A prominent monument is dedicated to John Whitehead, whose energy and negotiation abilities were needed in abundance in order to buy the land, win planning permission against the judgement of the all-powerful Catholic Church, and to create the vision of a Protestant church in the city. There is also a memorial headstone to Baron Forrester. We came across Forrester, the man of many trades – expert on viticulture, cartographer, painter, and Port wine activist – as he was running around trying to put out the fires in his wine lodges during the Siege of Porto. Forrester was one of the most important men in the history of the Port wine trade. Controversial and, during his disputes with winemakers over the addition of brandy in the process of Port production, accused of going native, Forrester was a remarkable character. His legacy of the precise mapping of the River Douro and the Port wine areas was important and ahead of its times.

It is necessary to point out to the visitor that Baron Forrester is not actually buried in the British Cemetery. The story of the death of Forrester was just as dramatic as his life. On 12 May 1861, he was returning down the River Douro, accompanied by two prominent ladies of the wine industry, Baroness Fladgate and Dona Antónia Adelaide Ferreira, following a lengthy lunch at Quinta de Vargellas. In those days, the river was not dammed and there were parts of it that were considered most difficult to navigate. The most dreaded area were the rapids at Cachão da Valeira. On that fateful day, as Forrester's boat entered the rapids, he commented that the rudder had been lashed the wrong way, to prevent it from moving in the fast-running waters. The boat capsized in the rapids. The two ladies were kept afloat by their crinolines and were soon washed up to safety on a little beach at the far end of the gorge.[13] Forester's body was never found. He was presumed drowned.

His death remains shrouded in mystery with rumours of foul play. At the time of the incident, Forrester was wearing a money belt containing gold sovereigns, the normal method of payment for Douro farmers who deeply distrusted hard currency.[14] The gold sovereigns were never found. Forrester's son was reportedly informed that his father's body had been discovered very early the next morning down-stream near Pinhão and had been robbed of the gold, and then sunk.[15] There is no documentary evidence to confirm any foul play. When news of the death of Forrester reached Porto, public buildings in the city and ships in the harbour lowered their flags to half-mast in tribute for one of the most colourful characters in the Port wine trade.

A small part of the British Cemetery is dedicated to the graves of eleven Allied airmen, lost over Portuguese airspace during World War II. At the front of the church there is a memorial cross to the members of the British community of Porto who were killed in action during both world wars. The monument serves as the focus of the annual remembrance service held in November. A large number of the local British community served in both wars, especially those from families related to the Port wine trade who had spent their teenage and university years based in Britain. As we shall see later Portugal, although originally neutral, joined World War I on the side of the Allies in 1916 at a great cost to its people and political system. The slightly quaint, understated and hidden nature of St James's Church and the British Cemetery makes it an appealing place for a visit. There is an air of belonging to a bygone era, one in which British traditions and culture were important, and in which the Foreign Office footed at least half of the bills.

After leaving the church, retracing steps slowly back along Largo da Maternidade de Júlio Dinis onto Rua da Boa Nova, before entering the Rua de Miguel Bombarda, the shift in style could not be greater away from the old world of yesterday Britain as you step into the buzzling main street of the 'Arts District' of Porto. This long straight road is home to the contemporary art scene with galleries that fill almost every building. It is very much a shop window for local artists to exhibit and sell their works. The city of Porto has a proud traditional of art and artists, as does the north of Portugal. The Arts District is full of energy, urban regeneration projects, and opportunities for casual and professional collectors. Perhaps the most internationally known Porto-born artist is Júlio Resende, a graduate of the city's world-class School of Fine Arts. Upon his death in 2011, Resende was described by President Cavaco Silva as 'the great master of Portuguese art of the last century'. A representation of Resende's work can be seen in the Museu Nacional Soares dos Reis where he is one of several key local artists on display.[16]

As Rua de Miguel Bombarda comes to an end it runs into the historic street known as Rua de Cedofeita. It was here that Dom Pedro lived at number 395, during the Siege of Porto. The street became important in the eighteenth century with the economic expansion of the city in the middle part of the century. Today it is a busy pedestrian shopping street with cafes and two small shopping malls. A large number of its elegant buildings have been renovated into apartments, bringing life back to the street. At the end of the street enter Praça Carlos Alberto, a smart square which on Saturdays often hosts a local market. There are two important monuments and statues in the *praça*. One is the statue of Humberto Delgado, whose opposition to the *Estado Novo* and links to Porto we have already talked about. The other is the monument to the Portuguese soldiers who died in World War I.

The monument serves as a stark reminder of the local losses taken at the front in France, and to the even higher number of Portuguese civilians who died at home as a result of food shortages and the lethal virus known as 'Spanish flu'. Portuguese participation in the World War I had profound consequences for the Republic and for the long-term direction of the country. In simple terms, the war was an important, although not sole, factor in explaining the eventual failure of the Republic in Portugal and the country's subsequent slide into military dictatorship and authoritarian rule under Salazar.

14

Republican Misadventures

Senhor Sidónio Pais was strongly urged to postpone his journey north and was warned of the danger that he would incur if he persisted in it. Being absolutely fearless he disregarded all advice and consequently lost his life. In any case, had he escaped the assassin in Lisbon others were waiting for him at Oporto.[1]

Lancelot D. Carnegie

STANDING IN FRONT OF the impressive monument of remembrance to the Portuguese dead in Praça Carlos Alberto, the visitor might well wonder how a country on the western edge of Europe, deeply split, politically unstable and with little interest in either the Allied or German cause, came to become involved in World War I. The answer was simple: Africa. Fear of losing its African colonial possessions to Germany encouraged a Portuguese miscalculation of enormous proportions. With the benefit of hindsight, the decision to join the Allied war effort in France was arguably the single biggest mistake made in twentieth-century Portuguese history. Germany provoked Portugal to join the conflict, but the eagerness of the leadership of the Republic to join the fray in 1916 remains difficult to fully comprehend.

The horrors of the price of the war; the cost to human lives, the damage to various economies of the belligerents, were all clearly established by this point so Portugal could not claim ignorance of what it was exposing itself and its people to in France. Nevertheless, in 1917 it dispatched an expeditionary force of 40,000 men to fight for the Allies. The poorly trained and badly armed soldiers suffered terrible losses in the fighting in Flanders.[2] The slaughter of the Portuguese at the front was not the only disaster to befall the nation. At home food shortages led to thousands of deaths, in addition to the victims of the Spanish flu outbreak.

Even prior to its participation in the war, there had been plenty of political instability in Portugal. Splits, mergers, personality clashes, and military interventions characterised the period of the Republic. Basic political statistics serve as the best example of the instability. For the fifteen years and eight months existence of the Republic there were as follows: seven elections for the Congress, eight for presidency and a staggering forty-five governments. The impact of the country's participation in the war made an already bad situation all the worse. The fallout from the war and the food shortages led to a military intervention on 5 November 1917, the second one since the start of the Republic. It brought to power the autocratic General Sidónio Pais, whose position was confirmed in an election soon after.[3] Pais instigated dramatic change, altering the constitution to give more power to the president, making it, in effect, a combination of the president and prime minister into a 'presidentialist regime'.[4]

Pais had originally taught mathematics at Coimbra, Europe's oldest university, and had served in the army and the Portuguese diplomatic service. For his supporters he was the man that the country had been waiting for; strong, forceful, charismatic, and decisive to point of authoritarian. His policies focused on law and order, social justice, and the independence of Portugal (political and economic). He drew support from the lower middle classes, elements from the military that had opposed entry into the war, conservative Catholics, and some former Monarchists.[5] The central thrust of his philosophy was to create a New Republic, a smart attempt at reinvention. Events did not go well for Pais and his New Republic. During the course of 1918, Portuguese troops fighting in Flanders suffered heavy losses, leading to increased debates about their participation and a controversial Allied military decision to remove them from the front line.

The economy came close to collapse, with the government having to print *escudos* (the Portuguese currency) to pay its way. The *escudo* soon lost almost fifty per cent of its value.[6] The regime started to fall apart, despite attempts to form local military committees to help preserve it. The original supporters of Pais began to turn against him and prepare for a revolution that most people felt was inevitable. Law and order had broken down on the streets, instances of political violence were high, and the jails were crammed full of political prisoners. A deputy addressing the Chamber of Deputies suggested that 'the streets were so dangerous that insurance companies refused to insure people against assault'.[7]

A failed assassination attempt on Pais on 5 December 1918 further heightened tensions. The assassin's pistol failed to fire three times. Pais was advised to increase his security but chose to carry on as if nothing had happened. The president continued with his daily schedule in Lisbon, but he had an eye on potentially damaging developments in Porto. As Pais had become more and more dependent on the support of the Monarchists to keep him in power, they organised themselves in Porto into a military party, and later into a strong Junta. Once organised, they proceeded to 'ill-treat and insult all Republicans'.[8] All of this was not reported in the press, but Pais learnt of it from his sources in the north. He decided as a result to travel to Porto to find out more about the situation and to dissolve the party in the city. Naturally, the party in Porto objected to this possibility and was also worried about the power of the president, which they feared would impede its Monarchist ambitions. The president was warned not make his proposed journey to Porto and of the dangers involved if he persisted in going.[9] He decided that the stakes were too high not to go as the military Junta were stirring and making worrying noises.

On a chilly winter's night, at around midnight on 12 December, as the president was starting out on his trip to Porto at Rossio station in Lisbon, he was assassinated. Pais had sensed the presence of the assassin and reached for the pistol he carried, but it was too late. Two shots fired rapidly, one after the other, into the president's chest mortally wounding him. A young military aide tried to protect the president but his actions were in vain. President Pais died soon after.[10] The assassin, José Júlio da Costa, was a long-time supporter of the Republicans and ardent democrat. He was an admirer of Afonso Costa, one of the most important leaders of the Republican era (who had essentially been replaced by Pais). His aim, was straightforward: kill President Pais to restore freedom and end absolutism.[11] There has been much speculation as to whether he was a lone assassin, or acted on the instructions of one group, party, or junta.[12]

In London, King Manuel II was keen to stir the pot of conspiracy theories in meetings at the Foreign Office which incensed his opponents back in Portugal, giving hope to his supporters that there would be a return to the monarchy.[13] The king remained convinced that the assassin had not operated alone. The Foreign Office noted the king's accusations:

King Manuel pointed out that Portugal was at this moment in the throes of a revolution, and that this condition of affairs had become chronic during the past years. The assassination of Senhor Pais, who was a strong and able man, had been a misfortune for the country. It had been arranged in Paris, and was the work of the Democratic Party in Portugal, who were supported by German gold from Spain and by funds from French Masonic Lodges.[14]

The king's meeting in London also covered the major political issue of the day: the poor treatment of Portugal at the Peace Conference that followed World War I. Appearing well informed about British plans to essentially belittle the Portuguese and ensure that they gained little from the conference, the king outlined his opposition to the policy, indicating the destabilising impact it would have on Portugal:

He declared with a good deal of emotion, that if the arrangement was actually decided, the effect in Portugal would be catastrophic. That Portugal, our oldest ally, who had given her best in the war even if that were not much, should be placed far below her old colony (Brazil) and lower than Greece which had almost been an enemy in the earlier stages of the war and only became an eleventh-hour ally, was the worst of insults and would be so regarded by all the Portuguese.[15]

On this point, the king's warning proved to be correct. Portugal was poorly treated at the conference. In a separate issue that heightened Portuguese discontent, its soldiers were accused of cowardice in the war by British officers. The tone of British reports on the alleged actions of the Portuguese forces verged on racist, and the charges were largely unsubstantiated. The damage to Portugal from World War I was also economic. In the decade following the end of the war Portugal had one of the highest rates of inflation in Europe.[16] The cause of the long list of problems: inflation, high levels of external debt, reduction in workers' remittances from Brazil, and decline in industrial and agricultural exports were not solely war related. The continued political uncertainty added to the dire economic situation, making it near-impossible for 'here today-gone tomorrow' governments to impose meaningful fiscal policy and implement much-needed economic reforms.

The political instability following the death of President Pais continued unabated. In Porto, a violent conflict broke out as the Monarchists, led by Henrique Paiva Couciero, attempted to reintroduce the monarchy. The uprising went as far as declaring the return of the monarch.[17] Intense efforts to seek international recognition, especially from Britain, were undertaken in Porto. These proved unsuccessful, partly based on the situation on the ground in Portugal. Supporters of the Democratic Party were mobilised and retained control over much of the rest of the country. It was only a matter of time before the Porto leaders were forced to offer terms:

Representative of the Oporto Royalist Government here has approached me through minister of state, who has refused assistance to it, with the view of going to England obtaining authority from King Manuel to come to terms with the Lisbon government. He may have difficulty in getting through France: can this be arranged, or could you obtain and send me a message from King Manuel authorising him, if necessary, to treat? Although Royalists are not doing badly their resistance in view of (anti) Spanish attitude has not much chance of ultimate success and some of its leaders are inclined to give it up in order to avoid further bloodshed.[18]

Despite the efforts of the monarchists in Porto, they failed to bring back the king to Portugal; reintroducing the monarchy to the country as a means of stability did not enjoy enough support outside of the Porto region. In retrospect there was a feeling of the regret of a missed opportunity – that the monarchists had not proclaimed its return in Porto on the same day as the death of Pais. Many believe that had they done so they would have prevailed and Manuel would have returned to Portugal.[19] Instead the Democrats returned to power but no government, whatever it tried, could find a way to survive. There were four reshuffles in 1919, seven in 1920 and five in 1921.[20] At a time when the country was crying out for leadership and stability none was forthcoming. Afonso Costa, having had enough of the petty bickering, disunity, and bitchiness in his own party decided to leave Portugal, robbing the country of arguably the man best placed to resolve the political and economic crisis.[21] Meantime, the army remained, rustling in the background, starting to make more hostile noises about pay and the lack of investment in new weapons. Senior officers with long memories of previous interventions were just about able to restrain younger officers, keen to make a point and take over the running of the country. This did not prove to be the case for much longer.

As in the past, developments in Porto, and the rest of Portugal, were not immune from events in the Iberian neighbour. Spain had remained just about neutral in World War I, hoping for an economic boom at the end of the war. This had not materialised. Instead Spain entered a major economic crisis, eventually leading to a military intervention that helped bring a degree of economic and political stability back to the country.[22] The question in Portugal remained how far the military would let the situation deteriorate before intervening. The army were not the only people considering intervening in Portugal at the time.

So bad were the state of affairs of the country that United States officials considered taking it over during the 1919 mini civil war by declaring it a protectorate. One US official in Lisbon believed that the country was becoming largely ungovernable. The major sources for this belief appear to have been Monarchists trying to use the Americans, and possibly the British, to prevent the return of the Democrats to power. In an attempt to get the US State Department interested in the scheme, the embassy in Lisbon talked up a Bolshevik takeover in Portugal. While this appeared highly unlikely at this juncture, it did reflect American concerns about the spread of the 'red menace' in Europe. The United States rejected the proposal, as did Portuguese leaders. British influence remained, despite the Portuguese sense of betrayal over Africa and the Peace Conference, much stronger than that of the Americans.[23]

As the crisis in Portugal deepened so the very people who had originally supported the Republic started to turn against it. The urban middle class in cities such as Porto came to reject liberalism and republicanism, which were both increasingly discredited in favour of more traditional policies. By the middle of the decade, the Republic had ceased to be a vehicle for governing, instead becoming something of a cynical joke. Corruption was rife and for many years was an accepted part of the political and economic process. People, and especially the armed forces, were becoming increasingly tired of this 'creaming off' of much-needed funds. The Republic had still not resolved one of the core issues at the centre of its original platform: anti-clericalism and the resulting clash with the Catholic Church.[24] This allowed the Catholic intelligentsia to develop as a viable opposition force to the Republic from outside of the system. For all its efforts to downgrade the Catholic Church, the Republic had failed to totally remove it from everyday life, most notably in rural Portugal. In 1917 three shepherd children at Cova da Ira in Fátima recounted how the Virgin Mary (our Lady of

Fátima) had appeared to them, and thousands of people flocked to the area. The events became known as 'The Miracle of Fátima'.

In Porto people were looking beyond the Republic. Some disillusioned people started to be attracted by the concept of authoritarian government in order to put the house in order. The authoritarian takeovers in Italy in 1922 and in Spain in 1923, heightened interest in, and support for, such regimes. For many Portuguese this appeared the best opportunity to bring political stability and to find a way to address economic issues in a more structured and less populist manner. These feelings were not lost on the military, which made two unsuccessful attempts to seize power in the final months of the Republic. It was a case of third time lucky, when, on 26 May 1926, they succeeded with a *coup d'état* led by General Manuel Gomes da Costa, Portugal's best known officer from World War I.[25]

The origins of the coup took place in Braga, with the young officers who had prepared it announcing their intentions to march to Lisbon. Soon after, there were similar military uprisings across Portugal; none of them met by any meaningful resistance. Two days later, on 28 May, General Gomes da Costa entered Lisbon and on the following the day the prime minister António Maria da Silva resigned. This brought an end to the Republican era that had been in place since 5 October 1910. Unlike previous changes of power in the country, the coup was relatively bloodless due in large part to the fact that the military was united in the need for change, but less so in who should takeover. Tellingly, no units came out in support of the government.

The takeover proved to be the easy part. The fight for control of the new government divided the armed forces along existing and new political lines. On 30 May 1926 the outgoing president, Bernardinho Machado, controversially handed over power to Commander José Mendes Cabeçadas, a naval officer and strong republican, rather than to Gomes de Costa. The result of this decision was a period of infighting within the armed forces that lasted for some time after the initial takeover. The split ran along the lines of those officers that only wanted to end the period of rule by the Democratic Party, and those also wanted to get rid of the existing system of parliamentary democracy in favour of a national non-party government, 'A National Revolution', as they described themselves.[26] The military had no real programme of government above and beyond a hard-line approach to law and order, and were deeply divided along ideological, geographic, personal, and generational lines.

The rule of Cabeçadas did not last long; a naval officer who lacked support in the army which controlled the revolution, he was unwilling to risk a return to violence to protect his position. He was replaced by Gomes da Costa, who favoured a return to parliamentary freedom but he did not last long either. Following a brief power struggle between himself and General Óscar Carmona, Costa Gomes, who was said to be in poor health, was forced into exile in the Azores but was awarded the rank of marshal; the highest in the army.[27] On 9 July General Carmona was made the acting president: he was eventually elected as such in 1928 and then re-elected in 1935, 1942 and 1949.[28] The conservative dictatorship had now well and truly arrived.

15

Porto Revolts and Salazar Arrives

> I know quite well what I want and where I am going but
> let no one insist that the goal should be reached in a few
> months. For the rest, let the country study, let it suggest, let
> it object, and let it discuss, but when the times come for me
> to give orders, I shall expect it to obey.[1]
>
> António De Oliveira Salazar

TWO QUESTIONS MIGHT OCCUR to the visitor regarding the shift towards authoritarian military rule in Portugal. Why did Republican leaders and their supporters not do more to prevent the initial military takeover? And why did they not make a strong concerted challenge when it became crystal clear that the military meant to dismantle all that had gone before? The answer to the first lies in the false belief that the military engagement with the civilian political sector would be temporary. Put simply, the military officers, who favoured a return to the monarchy with the retention of a parliamentary system, would win out in the power struggle over the ultra-conservative elements. Instead quite the opposite occurred. The response to the second question is that there were uprisings against the military in 1927 in both Porto and Lisbon.

The Revolt of February 1927 by military rebels started at 4.30 am on 3 February. It was led by General Gastão de Sousa Dias and aimed to overthrow the military dictatorship. *The Times of London* described the scene as 'some, not all, troops in Porto came out against the government'. Loyalist forces were able to retain control over the once more strategically important Serra do Pilar monastery on the south bank of the River Douro. The government responded with a carefully worded communique promising reinforcements to arrive soon:

> The Minister of War has arrived in Aveiro from Lisbon, where there is being concentrated a strong nucleus of loyal troops, who will tonight march and join the troops at Serra do Pilar opposite Porto.[2]

Martial law, which had already been in place, was tightened with all restaurants and theatres closed until further notice. The movement of traffic in the city was suspended, with people warned to be in their houses by 10.00 pm.[3] At the start of day two, with Lisbon also engaged in a revolt, the leaders in Porto appealed to the civilian population to join them. Very few did. It was to remain an essentially inter-military dispute, albeit with casualties among the local population, mainly from the shelling of the city from the Serra do Pilar monastery. Much of the artillery fire was directed against the rebel stronghold in Praça da Batalha, many of the shells landing in the surrounding area. By day three of the revolt the promised arrival of the cavalry had taken place and they immediately entered the city to engage the rebels. Foreign journalists reported that the rebels did not have much chance of holding out for long.[4] Reports circulating that the leaders of the rebellion had already surrendered turned out to be false. The situation for the government was complicated a little by a strike of the train workers, forcing loyalist troops to take over stations to ensure that further reinforcements could be moved into place by rail.

The artillery fire into the city started in earnest on 6 February, killing and wounding a number of civilians. Negotiations took place under a white flag of truce, but without success. The government informed the leaders of the revolt that it would only accept an unconditional surrender. Perhaps fearing the worst, discipline among the forces of the revolt began to break down. Some tried to escape to the northeast along the Douro railway line, but were captured by government forces that had surrounded the city.[5] The morning of 7 February, saw the heaviest bombardment of Porto by government troops. The firing began at 10.30 am. It was temporarily halted to issue a communique warning the civilian population to leave the city. Most did not, choosing to pull down their shutters and hide in their basements.[6] Premature reports of the surrender of the rebels were circulated for a second time on 8 February, but by the morning of 9 February it appeared that the negotiations were complete for the unconditional surrender of the forces of the revolt.[7] Eighty people were killed in Porto with 360 injured.[8]

The leaders of the revolt managed to arrange an amnesty for non-officers who they argued were only following orders. This plea was eventually accepted by the government. The rest were not so lucky. The revolt in the capital collapsed soon after, allowing the government to re-establish control over the whole country. Justice was swiftly and robustly issued. From this point onwards the repression grew much stronger and more ruthless. No activity from politicians was permitted, some 600 were arrested and eventually deported to the Azores or one of Portugal's colonies.[9] Many others fled the country before their arrest, setting up dissident groups abroad in cities such as Paris and London. The military dictatorship did not stop there. A political police department entitled the PVDE (Polícia de Vigilância e Defesa do Estado) was set up to help control any dissension and opposition forces. The force was the forerunner to the much feared PIDE (Polícia Internacional e de Defesa do Estado) secret police of the post-World War II *Estado Novo* era. The dictatorship remained in place until the creation of the *Estado Novo*.

The military dictatorship was not without its supporters. Many Portuguese continued to view it as a source of stability, and were not interested in the efforts of the politicians to return the country back to civilian rule. Most were too busy dealing with the effects of the economic crisis on their jobs and daily lives to devote much attention to political dramas in Porto. In the countryside, with its staggeringly low rate of literacy, the peasants continued working as normal and the landowners largely kept quiet. Portugal had still not escaped the financial costs of its participation in World War I. The leaders of the military dictatorship, in particular the wily and politically astute President Óscar Carmona, understood that if the dictatorship was to survive it would have to successfully deal with the economic crisis and introduce fiscal responsibility to the country's accounts.

It was largely on the basis of necessity that the government turned to António de Oliveira Salazar, a professor of political economy at Coimbra University. The dictatorship had first spoken to him in 1926 about the job of Minister of Finance, but were alarmed by his demands to have control over all government spending departments. Two years on, and the economy had not improved. In the meantime, Salazar had produced a number of scholarly articles on the management of public accounts that had impressed key leaders in the dictatorship. An envoy was dispatched to Coimbra to approach Salazar, who hesitated before agreeing to take over the position.

In the first year in office, he managed to achieve a budget surplus, something that he had only promised for the second year.[10] Public debt was also steadily reduced as Salazar won both national and international recognition for his work.[11] Governments came and went under the military dictatorship, but Salazar remained firmly in control of its finances. In 1932 President Carmona invited Salazar to become prime minister (president of the council). The decision reflected the realisation of the president, and other members of the dictatorship, that Salazar was head and shoulders above anybody else in the administration in terms of intellect and political ability. On this occasion Salazar did not hesitate and he became prime minister on 5 July 1932, holding the position until the autumn of 1968.[12]

Perhaps rather wisely, one of Salazar's first moves was to put some distance between himself and the increasingly discredited military dictatorship. He drafted a new constitution, known as the *Estado Novo* (New State), which was approved by a national vote in

March 1933. Prior to the vote, Salazar had allowed public debate about its merits with republicans, socialists, the Catholic Church and the army all weighing in with various criticisms. The result in favour of the new constitution was clear cut, albeit with charges of the manipulation of numbers by opposition figures. There was a curiously high amount of abstentions, as well as complaints about the process of voter registration.[13]

The constitution set out the philosophy, ideology, and political direction for the state and the country. The complex document reflected the times in which it was framed, containing typical right-wing ideas: anti-communist, anti-parliamentary, and pro-nationalistic. In politics, power was concentrated in the executive: in economic management the market economy was to be subjected to state control; and in philosophy, state and society were to become one corporation.[14] Much has been written about the philosophies and *modus operandi* of the regime, centring upon questions as to whether it was authoritarian or fascist, and there is also great deal of work on the personality of Salazar and his professional and private lives.

Decades after his death in 1970, Salazar remains a highly divisive figure in Portugal. Despised by the left and far-left, denounced in universities, he still enjoys widespread support from the Portuguese keen on the nostalgia of the past when Portugal still retained its empire. Among a small minority of far-right wing youth, there remains a certain attraction towards the style of political leadership of Salazar, and interest in him from all walks of society continues to produce a large number of books about him each year. Indeed, should the visitor walk into a bookshop such as *Livraria Lello* in Porto they will no doubt browse the shelves and see the pictures of Salazar on the covers of countless books.

As the visitor moves on from the World War I monument in Praça Carlos Alberto we come across the statue to General Humberto Delgado in the same *praça*, some fifty metres to the front and to the right. We introduced Delgado earlier with a description of his life and end at the hands of PIDE, the much-feared secret police of the *Estado Novo*. The death of Delgado and Salazar's potential involvement in it still casts the biggest shadow on the regime, more than any other person that the regime might have been involved in killing.[15] The post-1974 Revolution political leaders have continued to investigate without a conclusive result either way. Like most leaders Salazar had a complex personality, a deep explanation of which, while fascinating, must be saved for another book. A good introductory summary was provided by Cardinal Manuel Gonçalves Cerejeira, who headed the Catholic Church during the era of the *Estado Novo*. Cerejeira roomed with Salazar at Coimbra University for a number of years and probably knew him better than almost anybody else. He said of Salazar:

Salazar walked on a straight road, oblivious of side turnings. He was a man for great issues, also for small detail. In his youth he had already developed his tenacity of will, his high intelligence and his absolute calm. Those of us who knew him recall his rare capacity for objectivity in discussion. He had the art of outlining a theme with fine irony, but was scornful of eloquence. Now, as then, he starts a thing with a timid gesture, hesitates before committing himself, needs to feel he is supported.

But then he throws himself into action. I have never observed such contrasts in a man. He appreciates the company of women and their beauty, yet leads the life of a monk. Scepticism and zest, pride and modesty, distrust and confidence, the most disarming kindness and at other times the most unexpected hardness of heart – all are in constant conflict within him.[16]

Cerejeira and the rest of the Catholic establishment were generally supportive of Salazar. He placed the church firmly back into the centre of Portuguese society following years of the anti-clericalism of the Republican era. The values of the *Estado Novo* mirrored those of the church, and it appeared to be a return to normal with church and state closely aligned. Towards the latter period of Salazar's rule however, points of friction started to appear, mainly related to the increased repression in both Portugal and in its colonies. Cerejeira was careful to temper any criticism he voiced with continued praise for the work of the government.

The Bishop of Porto, António Ferreira Gomes was less discreet and offered stronger reproach, but still attempted to wrap it in faint praise for Salazar's achievements. The tensions between Salazar and the church became much worse when in 1958 the Bishop of Porto wrote a sixteen-page private letter to Salazar. In parts of the letter he criticised Salazar's regime, calling for the Catholic Church to adopt a more politically independent line. The letter was a curious mixture of support for Salazar and his regime mixed with charges that his policies were helping to fuel the radical opposition groups in the country (communists). If the letter was meant to provoke the prime minister it proved to be successful. A furious Salazar responded by effectively exiling the Bishop (he was not allowed to re-enter Portugal following an overseas trip). Despite concerted efforts from the Vatican to resolve the crisis, Salazar refused to give any ground. Instead, he applied pressure on the church to try to get the Bishop to resign, and for the Catholic Church to appoint a new bishop. In a letter to the Portuguese Ambassador to the Vatican, Salazar vented his anger and called Gomes 'a sick person' and that 'the greatest evil was having made him a bishop'. There was no way back for Gomes, or other figures that Salazar deemed to be a threat to his leadership and the *Estado Novo*.

Despite the best efforts of Salazar's secret police (the PIDE) to keep the Bishop's letter private it was widely disseminated in Portuguese society and became a catalyst for opposition figures to more forcibly challenge Salazar's legitimacy to rule. To his dying day, Salazar believed that Gomes had crossed a red line in state-church relations and viewed it as a personal slight. In truth, the letter reflected the thinking of several leading figures in the church who supported calls for greater democratisation in the country and independence for the church from the *Estado Novo*. Close links subsequently developed between key members of the church and leading moderate opposition figures. These people increasingly challenged Salazar to return Portugal to a democratic state.

Gomes was only able to return to Portugal following Salazar's death in 1970.

Opposition to Salazar and the *Estado Novo* was largely muted and confined to areas where the Communists enjoyed their greatest support: satellite towns from Lisbon such as Barreiro, and in the Alentejo region. In Porto the armed forces from time to time threatened rebellions, mainly due to poor living conditions as well as for ideological reasons. One such revolt took place on 10 October 1946. The numbers involved were small and the action was immediately suppressed by the government. British diplomats believed that a *coup d'état* had been intended but that the leaders 'lost their nerve at the last moment'.[17] The officers involved were quickly arrested in the north of Portugal and were most displeased to learn that their senior officers had informed the authorities of the details of their plot.[18] Among the residents of Porto there was not much appetite for a revolt. The British Consul summed up the situation in the city:

> Discontent is increasing among the working classes at this state of affairs (high food prices and shortages), and if the situation ever arose in which the police were unable to control the masses in think that in Oporto at least there would be a good deal of looting and violence. However, there seems at present to be no fear of a popular rising, as the people have no leaders and organisation. The Movimento União Democrats, which consists chiefly of unsuccessful lawyers, doctors etc., is not taken seriously, and it is agreed that the armed forces are the only ones who can bring about a change of regime.[19]

One factor that any plotters from the armed forces needed to take into account was the lack of foreign appetite for political change in Portugal at this time. The Spanish leader General Francisco Franco was generally sympathetic to Salazar's government, and the Americans, keen to maintain a presence in the strategically important Azores airbase, did not want to rock the boat. The British attitude was most enlightening as the Foreign Office wrote:

From the purely material and strategic point of view I expect he (the Ambassador) is right in saying that a firm efficient government even though based on authoritarian principles (i.e. one like the present regime) would suit British interests better than a weak hesitant government based on more democratic principles.[20]

The British clearly preferred the devil they knew, believing that any change in regime would most likely be violent, reflecting what the Foreign Office, somewhat condescendingly referred to as the political immaturity of the Portuguese.[21] Porto, as a result, remained relatively politically quiet until much nearer the end of the *Estado Novo*. Away from the masses, discontented junior officers in the armed forces, and some democratic groups, there were strong conservative elements at play in the city. Much of the Catholic Church, except the Bishop of Porto (who prior to his criticism of Salazar had been sympathetic to the regime), landowners in the north, and business, all preferred the continuation of the regime. The alternative, as Salazar was fond of highlighting, was the Communists, rather than any likely return to democratic government.

Salazar carefully rode out the international wave of democratisation that occurred at the end of World War II. Portugal's former colony Brazil was one such country where the results of post-war democratisation were far from perfect. Salazar believed that given the low rate of literacy and general lack of education, Portugal was not suited to parliamentary politics. He was extremely cynical about the Portuguese people he led, arguing that they were 'easy prey for demagogues'.[22] He encouraged political apathy, rather than participation, and was duly successful in achieving this goal. In Porto and in the north, the regime was much more successful in subduing the population than in other parts of the country.

Much of this changed during the 1958 presidential campaign when thousands of the inhabitants of Porto connected with a charismatic alternative leader to Salazar in Humberto Delgado.

When Delgado was asked what he would do if elected as president with Salazar as prime minister, he was reported to have said 'sack him.' Looking at the statue of Delgado in Praça Carlos Alberto, we are reminded of the influence of the general in establishing a connection with the masses of the city of Porto that would outlast his own death. Supporters of the *Estado Novo* in Porto pointed to the fact in their defence that despite the police repression, poverty, lack of advancement in education, literacy, and medical treatment, the city was subjected to far fewer upheavals than at almost any other point in history.

The city remained divided in its attitude towards the *Estado Novo* up until its end. During the 25 April 1974 Revolution, Porto saw perhaps the greatest levels of violence as pro- and anti-*Estado Novo* supporters clashed, most bloodily within the ranks of the armed forces. The fighting in Porto continued long after Lisbon had been pacified by the armed forces which had led the revolution. All of this reflected the complexities of political, economic, and social structures in Porto and the surrounding region.

During the twentieth century, Porto developed in different ways from Lisbon. By its own definition, the *Estado Novo* was a highly centralised administration, based in Lisbon. Its leadership was comprised of a small, closed, political and commercial elite. Decisions were made among these groups on a personal rather than formal manner. Access to Salazar was hugely important, and thus much sought after. He allowed a small number of economically elite families to prosper, nearly all of whom were from the Lisbon area. Families such as Champalimaud, Espírito Santo, and Mello, all Lisbon based, were allowed to prosper during the *Estado Novo*, partly as a result of their winning key government contracts in Portugal and in the colonies. There were also similarities with a quickening in the speed of industrialisation, and under-investment in the agricultural sector, leading to greater migration from the countryside into Porto and Lisbon. In Porto, this led to a major increase in the population of the city, many of whom were living in very poor circumstances.[23] The regime was widely blamed for the slow development of the agricultural sector, by not introducing much-needed reforms and investment. While this state of affairs was partly to blame, there were other factors present that subdued the pace of development.[24]

Emigration to the city of Porto was not the only option open to those seeking to leave the countryside. Many of those went on to seek a better life in a northern European country, Paris being the most-favoured destination. The emigrants did not only come from the countryside. In Porto low salaries, limited opportunities of advancement, and high prices for basic foodstuffs and utilities encouraged many people to leave the country. As Portuguese networks were established in other European cities this became even more attractive for mainly young people looking to earn higher salaries in the service industries. Workers' remittances became a more important aspect of the Portuguese economy as the emigrants sent back money to their families in Porto and the rest of Portugal.

The start of the colonial wars, in which Portugal was drawn into bloody conflicts, added a new dimension to the waves of emigration. It is important to offer some context on the uprisings which were largely unexpected, certainly in Portuguese circles, and had massive political consequences in the colonies and in Portugal. Following World War II, the world entered the era of decolonisation with the ending of the British Empire being perhaps the most significant symbol. Portugal chose to ignore the process, instead tightening its political and economic control over what it reclassified as Overseas Territories. Its policy drew near-universal condemnation at the United Nations; often the Apartheid regime in South Africa was the only country to cast its vote in favour of Portugal. Salazar had walked a careful tightrope since World War II, with Portugal becoming one of the original members of NATO and he tried to convince the western powers of the need for Portuguese survival in Africa.[25] Portugal, with the Azores air base, became an important ally of the American-led alliance against the Soviet Union. Careful diplomacy, especially in the negotiations to renew American access to the Azores, appeared to have paid off. While the United Nations made hostile noises and proposed numerous, mainly Soviet or Third

World-sponsored resolutions, consecutive American presidents did little to try to force Portugal to allow the right of determination in its colonies. President Dwight Eisenhower's visit to Portugal in May 1960 was a reflection of the strong shared strategic links between the United States and Portugal.

The election of President John F. Kennedy in November 1960, and his inauguration in January 1961, signalled a new phase in the international debate. During his inauguration speech the president had welcomed newly decolonised states to the world order. In communications with Portugal the president and his brother Robert Kennedy made it clear that they would not accept a continuation of Portugal's polices towards its colonies.[26] In February of the same year, the first signs of armed rebellion in the colonies started with the bombings of police stations and prisons in Luanda, the Angolan capital. These were followed in March by outbreaks of serious rioting, along with a massacre of settlers on the border with Congo. Salazar and the regime were taken by surprise by events; a sign perhaps of poor intelligence and the lack of Portuguese soldiers on the ground. Salazar moved to dispatch troops to Angola, and they were able to restore order, but only for a short time.[27] Much worse followed and Portugal found itself drawn into a protracted anti-guerrilla war until 1974. The guerrilla warfare soon spread to other colonies. In 1963, a rebellion started in Guinea, and subsequently there was an outbreak of violence in northern Mozambique in 1964.[28]

The effects of the wars on the regime, and the country as a whole, were complicated. There is a clear line between the costs to Portugal waging the wars and the eventual fall of the *Estado Novo*.[29] By 1968 over 100,000 Portuguese troops were deployed in the three countries. Portuguese casualty figures were relatively light with 1,653 dead up until 31 December 1968. Added to a number of friendly fire deaths, along with other accidents however the figure is approximately 5,000. These casualty figures, although serious, were spread over eight years and were approximate to the losses from fewer than two years fighting in World War I.[30] Among the serving non-officers the wars proved, if not popular, at least acceptable. Awarded higher army pay than in their civilian jobs back in Portugal, the soldiers were subjected to a carefully controlled nationalist propaganda campaign in their barracks in Africa. This prevented a lot of potential political agitation from the lower classes during their compulsory army service.

For the young urban middle classes in cities like Porto it was a different story. Amongst this group there was a sense that the wars were not worth it. University students became very vocal in their opposition to the wars. They believed that the compulsory conscription into the officer's school was not good for their education.[31] Many of those with money chose to undertake their university studies abroad, causing another wave of emigration. Upon the completion of their studies, many chose not to return, choosing instead to start their careers away from Portugal. To make matters worse for the government, there was a general feeling among the young educated men of the country that the wars could not be won. Eventually Portugal would have to agree to a negotiated settlement, making the continuation of its armed campaign seemingly irrelevant and not worth making any sacrifice towards. This feeling was also present among many of the junior officers serving in Africa, who were becoming extremely disillusioned by both the fighting as well as the lack of political debate back in Portugal about how best to seek a resolution to the conflicts.

When the regime did eventually fall in April 1974, two of the principal factors were the wars in Africa and calls for decolonisation.[32] Marcelo Caetano, who had succeeded Salazar after the latter suffered a stroke in 1968, proved unable to find a resolution to the wars which continued to drain public funds away from mainland Portugal and into the cost of fighting the protracted campaign in Africa. Taken together with a range of interrelated additional factors including failure to satisfy either the hardliners or those in the regime calling for reform. There was also the question of the decline in economic standards, due in part to both internal

175

and international factors, as well as a failure to satisfy the demands of the lower ranks of the officer classes in the armed forces. Soon after the fall of the regime, the country's new leaders moved controversially towards immediate decolonisation of Portugal's colonies. In many instances, Angola being the prime example, this did not lead to peace, rather to a prolonged and bloody civil war over control of the country and its rich resources.

PART FIVE

Day Three – Morning

16

Henry the Navigator

Among those princes was the Infante D. Henrique, known
to us and to the whole world as Prince Henry the Navigator.
It was at the inspiration of this astonishing man that
Portugal began the accomplishment of what he conceived
to be her mission in the world, the discovery of new lands
that might be brought to Christ, and the exploration of
the Atlantic Ocean. It was, of course, impossible to get
him to foresee how far this great enterprise would take his
country, or the incalculable consequences which would
result from it.[1]

F. C. C. Egerton

THE BRITISH HISTORIAN COLONEL F. C. C. Egerton
was asked to write a biography of Salazar in the middle
of World War II by Armindo Monteiro, the Portuguese
Ambassador in London.[2] Egerton was widely viewed as a supporter
of the Portuguese leader and an admirer of the stability that he had
brought to the country's economy and political life during his first
decade in office. The aim of the populist book was to encourage
pro-regime sentiment in Britain, where Salazar was still widely,
but incorrectly, perceived as being more pro-Axis than Allied. Not
everything went to plan; Monteiro, despite his best efforts to find a
publisher for the book in London, struggled to get it placed. There
was not much sympathy or interest in Britain for a book on a man
whom most Brits perceived as just another European dictator.
Eventually a publisher was found and the book was released in 1943.

Egerton provided an extremely sympathetic account of Salazar and Portugal, one which was certainly in his brief from Monteiro to write. The author was allowed access to Salazar, as well as the support of the extremely efficient propaganda machine of the *Estado Novo*. Later, Egerton was to become one of the few foreign defenders of the colonial polices of the *Estado Novo*, arguing that Portugal should be allowed to retain her territories, and resist efforts from the outside world and the colonies for self-determination. Most other foreign historians and commentators shunned Portugal at this juncture, and a few chose to produce highly critical papers on the regime's policies.

One of the more interesting curiosities in Egerton's book is the author's attempt to compare Salazar with one of Porto's most famous sons, the Infante Dom Henrique (Henry the Navigator). The comparison is made not in achievements, but in character and *modus operandi*. He sums up his belief about what he terms as the heroes of the fifteenth and sixteenth centuries:

> What they did was to carry over from the ages of faith, and to devote to the service of their country, the spirit which had formerly found only individual channels in which to express itself. This they could do because they believed their county had a mission, that their nation was not an arbitrary association of individuals, loosely bound together by common economic interests or even by a community of ideas, but a living positive force, in whose service they might best serve God. So faith combined with genius to produce a state of mind which the modern age would doubtless regard as folly. The Portuguese sometimes call it *'loucara'* and this word expresses a conception in which folly madness, and something which redeems both folly and madness are combined.[3]

For the most part the Portuguese, Egerton argued, retain a degree of *loucara* below the surface, but in times of national emergencies it appears, enabling them to essentially raise their game to new-found levels that surprise foreigners. The idea was that Henry the Navigator invoked this sense in starting the missions of the early explorers and discoverers, while Salazar utilised it to help resolve the economic national emergency during the latter years of the 1920s.

For the start of the second afternoon, we find the visitor in the Jardim do Infante Dom Henrique. In the middle of the gardens stands the huge statue to Henry the Navigator, facing the river. It sits with the Palácio da Bolsa to its side. Both are reminders of a theme that is common to Porto through the ages: trade, both domestic and international. We should not forget that this has been the rationale for the development of the city from its origins through to the Golden Age of the Empire and into the industrialisation of the nineteenth and twentieth centuries. No longer the stock exchange, the Bolsa today serves as a wonderful monument to Porto's great successes in trade.

It is worth spending some time admiring the statue of Henry the Navigator and considering the enormous achievements of this quiet, scholarly, visionary man, and how they changed Portugal. The sizeable statue reflects more than an effort merely to remember the catalyst for the era of overseas expansion, it stakes Porto's claim to the man who was born in the city on 4 March 1394. The small garden is a peaceful place to reflect upon the changes that the empire brought to the city. Situated behind the front lines to the river, it acts as a buffer between the bustle of the city centre and the crowded steep roads that fall towards the river.

The era of the empire is generally regarded as running from 1415 to 1825.[4] There is some deviation in the latter year with other historians suggest a finishing point of either 1807 or 1808.[5] There is a serious point to all this in that this era of expansion is most probably the most widely written-about period of Portuguese history: scholars, non-scholars, literary figures from across the Portuguese-speaking world and beyond, have added to the debates and the body of knowledge on the topic. Hitherto, Porto's role in these exploits have been overshadowed by that of Lisbon, from where many of the voyages originated. This representation has been a little simplistic, and a tad unfair, to Porto. In reality, both of

Portugal's major cities played significant roles in helping to build an empire, which in terms of trade was one of the most impressive in the history of global empire building.

Looking at the outstretched arm of Henry the Navigator, pointing towards the New World from the statue dedicated to his memory, it is important to remember that while one man does not make an empire, sometimes, in history, the fate and development of whole nations were driven by individuals. Particularly those individuals who enjoyed significant influence, title, and wealth to be able to transform their visions into reality. In history, it is important to ask the right questions, and in the case of the development of the Portuguese empire this is most relevant. From the start of the fifteenth century onwards, Portugal went to East Africa, India, China, Japan, and South America. Why did this small country, with a limited population, develop such a strong passion to discover and to colonise?[6] Why did it succeed when others with seamen and boats as good as the Portuguese did not? What were the aims that drove the people behind the expansion? Was Infante Dom Henrique the sole visionary behind the project or were there others?[7] If not, who was really the leader of the discoveries and, equally problematically, what was the criteria for holding this position: wealth, title, influence, or some mixture of all three?[8] It will come as little surprise that there is not agreement on any of these complex questions.

The answer to the first question lies in part that it was, to borrow an expression from American football, an 'offensive defence'. After the expulsion of the Moors from the lands that formed the boundary of modern Portugal, the Portuguese went on the offensive at sea against the Arabs to prevent attacks on Portuguese ports and ships.[9] In order to help deal with this seaborne threat, two important decisions with far-reaching consequences were made: to build a royal fleet and to appoint Infante Dom Henrique as the Grand Master of the Military Order of Christ, the Portuguese successor to the Knights Templar.

In the first instance, Dom Henrique chose to devote the Order's vast resources into the area of maritime development. His decision reflected the wider motivations that lay behind the 'Age of Discovery' which can be summarised into economic, political, and strategic considerations.[10] This proved to be an extremely important decision; during the first decades of the voyages the exploratory trips made large losses and would not have been able to continue without the great wealth and investment of the Military Order of Christ.[11] In terms of Dom Henrique personally it was said that while he was geographically curious and wanted to pursue the conflict with the Muslims, he was also extremely interested in making profit. In some accounts of his life the latter rationale is wrongly underplayed. He wanted to make money from the resulting trade in gold, sugar, and slaves.[12] His need for economic advancement, honour, and power was all the greater as he was not in line for succession to the throne and he wanted to raise his status through the voyages. Dom Henrique, while not poor, was always left short financially, his titles not earning him enough income for his lifestyle.[13] The interest and knowledge of science did partially motivate his commitment to the voyages of discovery, but it would be foolhardy to ignore these slightly more practical considerations.

Dom Henrique made two further initial contributions in addition to helping to organise the bankrolling of the programme: one lay in practicalities, the other in changing the philosophy of Portuguese sailors.

One of Dom Henrique's first inspired decisions involved the art of shipbuilding. Here the developments were quite staggering, leading to a new wave of mass boat construction, including in Porto, and helping to make Portugal one of the leading maritime forces of the era. It was nothing short of a design revolution, a massive step forward for the nation that opened up new possibilities for long-range voyages going much further than the previous raids across the Mediterranean. He helped sponsor the development of the caravel, a new class of ship that was capable of oceanic voyages. The caravel was first developed in about 1451, based on existing fishing boats, and soon became the preferred ship for Portuguese explorers. They were relatively agile and easier to navigate than previous boats. The caravels could sail upriver in shallow coastal waters. Put simply, it was the best sailing ship of its era and helped open up new possibilities for extended voyages to the new world. With the right kind of ship, the missing ingredient was the need to shift the mindset of Portuguese sailors towards the exploration programme in the name of science and discovery, rather than the existing motivation of plunder. This change became Dom Henrique's second contribution to the voyages of discovery. He was able to bring about this change with a synergy of economic and religious interests under the umbrella of sponsorship from the royal family.[14]

What followed was truly spectacular. The Canaries are considered to be the first Portuguese discovery, most probably prior to 1336, predating the age of the empire. Despite claims on the islands by Portugal, the Spanish took possession of the archipelago over a century later in 1479. The island of Madeira became the next discovery of the explorers. The exact date that they landed is not known, most likely around 1425 after a Portuguese fleet headed for the Canaries ended up landing in Madeira instead. Soon afterwards the Portuguese started to colonise the islands and in 1451 two royal charters were issued to settle Funchal and Machico. Although there is no official record, the first settlers were most probably from the Algarve, as Dom Henrique's caravels sailed from the ports in the region.[15] The pace of development was rapid and the islands were cleared and readied for planting. By the end of the century sugarcane plantations were created, vines were planted along the slopes, and the area became used as a supply zone for future Portuguese settlements elsewhere. Sugar was still something of a luxury item at the time, and the sale of it brought in much-needed revenue to the Military Order of Christ.[16] Funchal, today the capital of Madeira, was awarded the status of a town in 1508, leading to additional economic development and the arrival of more settlers.[17]

The aim of Dom Henrique and the explorers was not simply to settle and colonise; they wished to use each of the voyages to learn new information, most probably the wind patterns of the North and South Atlantic. The experience also helped with ship design as new versions of the caravel were produced with new rigging systems that allowed the ships to sail much closer to the wind. It also helped with nautical science allowing Portuguese navigators to calculate their position and, equally importantly, helped with sailing directions.

The successful colonisation of Madeira whetted the appetite for additional explorations into the Atlantic Ocean. The next was more ambitious, riskier, and resulted in the discovery of the Azores Islands. The first date of discovery of the islands was officially 1427, but it was not until 1439 that there is a record of humans being on the islands. Dom Henrique was given the task of settling the seven islands. The colonisation proved to be more difficult than that of Madeira. The volcanic rocky ground was not as fertile, but the importance of the islands lay in their geographic position. They were a useful half-way house between the Old World (Europe) and the New World (the Americas). In recent centuries the islands have been important in both World War I and World War II to all the belligerents. The first main crop grown on the islands was corn and by the time of Dom Henrique's death, the islands were a major supplier of it.[18] Cattle and sheep were introduced, soon multiplying with the excellent pasture lands. It was not long before the islands were providing Portugal with meat, animal hides, cheese, and wool.[19] Not all the settlers were Portuguese nationals. Many were drawn from Flanders, hence the alternative name of the Azores at the time, the Flemish Islands.

Gaining in confidence, the explorers next embarked on voyages of exploration to Africa. The first ships sailed in 1434 with an agenda seemingly dominated by scientific discovery. The leader of the expedition was Gil Eanes, who was drawn from Dom Henrique's company. Eanes took a huge risk by sailing past the dreaded Cape Bojador.[20] This was perhaps the first of the great epic voyages that pushed through dangerous boundaries along the coast of western Africa.[21] Subsequent expeditions pushed further south along the continent's shoreline. They moved from the land of the Moors to Africa. With much excitement, gold dust was discovered and brought back to Portugal in 1442. The promise of further riches encouraged Dom Pedro, the regent of Portugal, to give exclusive rights to the trade from the newly discovered territories in Africa to his brother Dom Henrique. Dom Henrique was seemingly quick to increase the pace of trade, dispatching his caravels from the port of Lagos in the Algarve. It seems possible that his actions were based on securing the economy of the Algarve, where he was based, and which acted as a substitute for Ceuta on the African shore of the Straits of Gibraltar, which had been captured in 1415. Ceuta was heavily fortified by the Portuguese, but the Moors continued to control the hinterland. There was little alternative other than to supply it from the sea, all of which proved highly expensive.[22]

So why keep hold of it when the British thought it most ill advised to continue to do so? The answer was simple: the capture of Ceuta was heavily symbolic. It illustrated a massive reversal of fortunes for Portugal in its wars with the Moors, who had themselves previously occupied much of southern Portugal. It was also seen as a foothold on the African continent; one that could be expanded through further conquest, giving Portugal ample opportunity to use the area as a forward staging post for exploration along the west coast of Africa.

In 1437 an attempt by Dom Henrique to annex Tangier failed. The attempt was surrounded by controversy; the *Cortes* in Evora, fearing the costs and limited chances of success, opposed the expedition but King Duarte gave Dom Henrique his consent to proceed. The younger brother of the king, Infante Dom Ferdinand, was captured during the attempt and held hostage.[23] The members of the expedition to Tangier only escaped after agreeing to the surrender of Ceuta to the Moors; Dom Ferdinand was left behind to make sure the *Cortes* back in Portugal ratified the surrender. They refused to do so, as a result poor Ferdinand was left to die in captivity.[24]

It is said that King Duarte never recovered his health after hearing the news of the Ferdinand's death and he himself died the following year in 1438. The crown passed to his young son, Afonso V. The Portuguese launched further expeditions to North Africa in 1458, 1471, 1508 and 1514. However, in 1515, they suffered another major defeat, this time in Mamora (near Casablanca), losing 4,000 men and 200 ships. This loss brought an end to any further expansion into North Africa. The lands that they had conquered were isolated and easy prey to attack. The empire in North Africa took centuries to finally die, but the Portuguese learnt important lessons that would be put to use during the era of global maritime expansion.[25]

Portugal's efforts along the west coast of Africa proved more successful both during and after the life of Dom Henrique. Trading posts started to be set up in West Africa. Initially, Portugal took in grain and cloth and took back to Portugal gold and slaves. The latter were traded in Lagos to help with the labour shortage in the Algarve.[26] The further discovery of the west African coast became the major aim of the early fifteenth-century voyages. It was not however until around the 1440s that trade with the west African coast became profitable for Portugal.[27] The risks of exploration in the area were high, conditions along the coastline being unpleasant and dangerous:

> From Cape Não on, it is a desolate and dangerous area, with nothing in sight but scarped cliffs and sand dunes. The roaring of the waves against the reefs can be heard from afar. When the west winds blow, the waves on the coast may be more than fifty feet high. From October to April extremely thick fogs are usual. For a medieval sailor, with a long training of listening to all kinds of fabulous tales about the sea of darkness and the end of the world, that dangerous and deserted coastline undoubtedly heralded the limit of all possible navigation.[28]

Dom Henrique died on 13 November 1460. During his lifetime, Portugal had set itself on the road to global expansion through voyages of discovery. Madeira, the Azores, and the west African coast were all important legacies of the time. His contribution to setting Portugal on this pathway was extremely important. He was not the only driving force behind the expeditions, but his was the most important voice of the era in driving the project forward.

Portugal's African adventures did not end when he died. Pushing further south, Portuguese explorers reached present day Sierra Leone and eventually circumnavigated Africa when they reached the southern tip of the continent.

Dom Henrique was only the start. Portugal went on to establish a massive maritime empire in subsequent years. Several of the names of the explorers would become as famous, or even more so, than Infante Dom Henrique. Eleven years after his death, in 1471, Tangier eventually fell to the Portuguese. On the western side of Africa, Diogo Cão reached the River Congo in 1482, while Portugal consolidated its presence on the Gold Coast. Only five years later, Bartolomeu Dias rounded the Cape of Good Hope in 1487–88. By the end of the century, Vasco de Gama had discovered the sea route to India, first navigating it in 1497–98. This opened up massive trading potential for Portugal. In the following year, the expedition of Gaspar and Miguel Corte Real arrived in Newfoundland, Labrador and Nova Scotia, establishing a Portuguese presence in each. Arguably the most important discovery occurred at the onset of the sixteenth century when Pedro Álvares Cabral discovered Brazil. This was a monumental breakthrough that opened up new possibilities for Portugal in South America. Portuguese control over Brazil was consolidated by the appointment of a Governor-General to administer the country in 1549.

From 1510–1515, Goa, Malacca, and Ormuz were taken over and occupied by Afonso de Albuquerque. The Portuguese invested heavily in Goa, so much so that by the middle of the sixteenth century it was sometimes referred to as the second city of Portugal on account of its size of population and the beauty of its buildings.[29] Inter-marriage between Portuguese emigrants and the local population was encouraged, and the Jesuits made it their base in the Orient for the dissemination of their missionary message. The religious zeal of the spreading of the word of God gathered momentum as Goa proved to be a very useful gateway to Asia. Portugal was on the road to becoming a truly global player.

Trade links were soon established with important countries and empires. In 1514 a Portuguese trade mission visited China for the first time. Later, in 1557, a Portuguese trading post was created in Macau. In the meantime, the Portuguese had reached Japan in 1542–43 and 1571, establishing a post in Nagasaki. As Portugal discovered new lands, it moved to try to consolidate its control over its early discoveries: by way of trade, building infrastructure, and settlement. The latter of these had profound implications for Porto and the north of Portugal, as many of the emigrants to the new world were drawn from these areas. It is important to remember that the Portuguese empire was not built in isolation. Other competing empires were being built by nations motivated by the same rationale as Portugal: trade, power, and religious fervour.

Building an empire is a difficult enough challenge; keeping hold of it against rival nations is altogether harder. The Portuguese empire faced challenges at home and abroad. From 1580 until 1640, Portugal found itself effectively taken over by the Spanish in what was known as the 'Castilian usurpation', which was claimed by Spain to be a unification of Iberia. In 1581, the *Cortes* based in Tomar proclaimed Fillipe II of Spain as Fillipe I of Portugal. What followed was a very difficult and complex period in inter-Iberian relations. Two further Spanish kings followed: Fillipe II (III of Spain) from 1598–1621 and Filipe III (IV of Spain) from 1621–1640. Eventually, in 1640, the Spanish Governor in Lisbon was overthrown and the Duke of Braganza took over the throne as João IV. The external challenges to Portugal were just as complex and dangerous. From 1630–1634, the Dutch occupied a large part of north-eastern Brazil. The Dutch also competed for influence in Africa and were not expelled from Angola until 1648. There were additional losses as well: Ceylon and Malabar to the Dutch between 1655–1663.

Losses of territory were also incurred by royal dowry deals. In the case of the marriage of Catherine of Braganza to Charles II of Great Britain, Portugal ceded Tangiers and Bombay to their oldest ally. Catherine proved to be rather controversial in England, especially her strong attachment to Roman Catholicism. The presence of several Catholics in her household staff, the priests that she brought with her from Portugal, and her help in assisting

English Catholics led to charges against her of trying to mount a 'popish plot'. This was all rather unfortunate as she highly valued the Anglo-Portuguese friendship and saw the advantages to Portugal of maintaining close ties with England. Catherine's greatest contribution to England was to make the drinking of tea highly fashionable.[30] Tea had been introduced to England some time before, but it had not been widely drunk until the arrival of Catherine. There are also claims that she introduced marmalade to the English, but this was less likely. More probably, she might have introduced Portuguese 'marmelada' which was made with quinces and sugar. It is possible that at some later stage, when oranges became more widely available in England, that they were added to the boiling process to create marmalade.

Better territorial news for Portugal came in the form of victories against the Spanish in the Battle of Ameixial in May 1663, in the following year at Castelo Rodrigo in 1664, and at Monte Claros in June 1665. A further piece of good news from further afield proved to be very important for the Portuguese finances: alluvial gold was discovered in Minas Gerais in the last decade of the seventeenth century. As a result, the first shipment of Brazilian gold arrived in Portugal in 1699.[31]

As for the city of Porto, while it benefitted from the general upturn in the economy from the middle of the fifteenth century onwards, it was the Algarve, from where Dom Henrique had originally dispatched his ships, and the south of the country, that initially saw the greatest advancement due to trade with Africa. Porto, however, was a city on the up. This growth was officially confirmed in the sixteenth century when Portugal conducted its first ever population census from 1527–1532. The results confirmed that Porto had overtaken Santarém and Évora to become Portugal's second city, a position it holds to the present day. The city, like the rest of Portugal, benefitted economically, physically, and culturally from the trickle-down wealth of the import of the Brazilian gold at the start of the eighteenth century, as well as the development of the British-dominated Port wine trade. The latter came to take on enormous importance in the city, with the dark ruby-coloured wine proving to have a much greater longevity than the golden gifts delivered from Brazil.

Porto and Portugal were left much changed by the empire that had been the vision of a man born in the city. The changes affected all walks of life from the nobility to the rich merchants and the peasants. Trade from the empire helped transform the country from a small nation on the western edge of Europe to a nation founding the first global economy. There would be even greater financial rewards to follow during the eighteenth century. The original reasons outlined by Infante Dom Henrique for sending out the first exploration voyages were largely realised. Economic wealth, scientific and navigation discovery, spreading of religious faith, and the wars with the Muslims were ended on satisfactory terms. This was quite a vison to achieve, albeit mostly after his death. During his lifetime, Dom Henrique was never known by the nickname 'Henry the Navigator'. The myths, the legends, and the name only came centuries later in accounts written on the empire. As for the name Henry the Navigator, this was introduced by German historians and British biographers. In Portugal though, he is still more widely known by his real name, Infante Dom Henrique.

17

British Treaties and Wine

As wine greatly elevates and exhilarates depressed spirits, and remarkably cheers old age, inasmuch as it is frequently termed its milk, relieving the fatigues of human live, for which all countries have, time out of mind, prescribed its use as a most sovereign, beneficial, or genuine cordial, and as such it has stood the test from the earliest antiquity. Indeed, we learn that Noah was the first that planted a vine, and intoxicated himself with the juice of it, if we believe the Old Testament; therefore, out of modesty, shall not dwell on it being so often mentioned or spoken of with rapture in the sacred text, and by the great philosophers as well as physicians, who have all recommended the moderate use of it.[1]

John Croft

A FTER LEAVING THE PALÁCIO da Bolsa, and the garden containing the statue of Infante Dom Henrique, the visitor should make their way the relatively short distance to the British Factory House, located on the appropriately named, Rua do Infante Dom Henrique. From the outside, the building appears much like the other similar, slightly austere granite buildings that dominated the architectural style of the eighteenth-century building programme of Porto city centre. It remains, however, a unique reminder of the establishment, and continuation, of a permanent British merchant presence in the city since the eighteenth century, centred upon the Port wine industry. Its members retain the deeply held customs and rules of the House, established by the founding members. We have already learnt about the establishment of the Anglican Church in the city, and the life of Baron Forrester, but it is important to understand the development of this hugely important international trade, much of which still remains in the hands of the descendants of its founding families.

The Treaty of 1654 between Britain and Portugal, often known as the 'Favoured Nation Treaty', granted special trade and religious privileges to the British in Portugal. It seemingly also coincided with the arrival of the original permanent British communities in Portugal, first in Viana do Castelo and subsequently in Porto.[2] The trade agreement was most controversial in Portugal, with many people believing that it offered too much autonomy to the British in the country. Like most deals however, it reflected the political realities of the day. Signed by Oliver Cromwell and King João IV, the agreement was much needed by Portugal, which was at war with Spain and Holland. The military and naval support of Portugal's oldest ally was therefore required by King João IV and Cromwell was, as a result, largely able to dictate the outcome of the negotiations. Naturally, these were heavily in favour of the British.[3] The treaty proved to be the foundation of British commercial hegemony in Portugal. The main concession João IV had been forced to offer was in the granting of British access to trade with Portugal's colonies.

British merchants in Portugal were effectively granted rights that put them above Portuguese traders. They could not be arrested unless a British judge gave written permission (except in criminal cases), were exempted from any new taxes, and upon their deaths the Portuguese authorities did not have any jurisdiction over their property. Equally important was the capping of customs duties at twenty-three per cent, and this could not be changed without the agreement of the merchants. It was at this time that the authorities, as part of the agreement, started to allow Protestant church services (such as in Porto) and agreed to assign a burial site, ending the process of having to bury Protestants on the riverbanks.[4] It was a wonderful era to be British in Portugal with great legal freedom, generous trading conditions, and a social scene that reflected the customs of protestant England.

Thanks to Cromwell, it was boom time for British merchants in Portugal, and in the north of the country traders arrived from across Britain to settle. The security of the privileges granted by Dom João IV encouraged the merchants to make their permanent homes in Portugal and to develop new trading links between the two countries. Many of the first wave of British traders made their way to Viana do Castelo on the northern coastline at the mouth of the River Lima. There they traded in the export of red wine and other goods. One of the most controversial figures in British history, Cromwell can be considered to be the father of the Port wine trade having created the right conditions for the creation for the establishment of a factory (a body of merchants) in Porto.

The first groups of British merchants in Porto, did not trade in wine, but rather mainly in cloth and cotton and were known as the 'rag merchants'. For decades, the wine trade continued to flourish in Viana do Castelo, where the British merchants would travel up the River Lima in their boats to buy wine from the local Portuguese producers. The quality of the wine was not good, it also did not travel very well and was not well thought of in London. In the city's 'gentleman's clubs' it acquired the reputation of being a poor man's wine. Still, large flagons of it were sold to the British Navy to give to its sailors, who no doubt had few alternatives to drinking it. The wines were also low in alcoholic strength and were said to be fortified with brandy to try help preserve them long enough to stand the voyage to England.[5] No matter what was tried to improve the wine, the results remained disappointing. It was for this reason that the merchants moved south-eastwards to the Alto-Douro to try to discover better quality wines that more resembled the still highly sought-after French wines, most notably Burgundy, which remained a favourite on the tables in London.

The result was an eventual shift away from Viana towards Porto, where the British merchants predominantly chose to settle. The Alto-Douro was considered too remote and underdeveloped for the merchants to consider living; summer temperatures were stiflingly hot and winters cold, wet, and most unpleasant. Porto offered an altogether much more attractive prospect with its cooling Atlantic breeze that kept the summer heat much more manageable. It should be remembered that the British were traders, not pioneers, and were happy to lead and train the local population in growing vines but did not themselves want to undertake labour-intensive tasks. Charles Sellers summarised the differences between the two wine-making areas:

> The wines of Monção and Viana are, when judiciously treated, very similar to those of Burgundy. I have paid 7s. for a quart bottle of sparkling Burgundy which was not as good as what I have obtained for as many pence in Viana. The conditions under which the wines are produced are very different from those prevailing in the Alto-Douro. In the first place, the composition of the soil is not the same, and the next important point is that the geographical formation is as like Tras-os-Montes as the pasture lands of England are unlike the sandy plains in the Sahara. The, again the cultivation of the wine in the two districts differs most materially as well as the making of the wine. The Alto-Douro district is essentially and almost absolutely a wine-producing country. If its vineyards disappeared, its lofty hills would be left bare. The northern part of the province of the Minho is a grain producing country, and the vine is only adjunct to the farmer's principal source of revenue.[6]

Sellers describes the timeline for the shift from Viana to Porto, suggesting that up until 1678 all the red wines that were shipped from Portugal for export came through the port of Viana do Castelo. Even as late as 1730 sizeable amounts of wine were still dispatched from Viana.[7]

The first of the traders to make the move south from Viana to Porto was Peter Bearsley, the son of the founder of the firm that is today know as The Fladgate Partnership (the owners of several brands of Port wine, hotels and World of Wine).[8] In terms of the origins of Port wine there is a fine line between myth, storytelling, and assumed reality. Bearsley clearly moved to Porto to try his hand at developing Douro wines for export.[9] John Croft recalled Bearsley's alleged experience:

> ...On the road to the wine country, at an inn, he met with an Elder tree, whose juice he expressed, and mixed with the ordinary wine, and found it had the effect of heightening and improving its colour.[10]

The idea of adding to, or mixing, the wine with an additional ingredient to change its taste, strength, and longevity was to become an integral part of the Port wine industry. Bearsley soon became the pioneer of the new wine territory: the first man to 'penetrate the Douro'.[11]

Bearsley was not alone in Porto. Soon other merchants started to explore the use of Porto and the Alto-Douro as a wine-making area. According to a report produced by Consul John Crispin for the Foreign Office in 1830, the British traders in the city started to organise themselves into a factory as early as the end of the seventeenth century or at the outset of the eighteenth century.[12] There is evidence to suggest that this process started much earlier, but these formations might well have been of a less formal nature than the process described by Consul Crispin.[13] What is clear is that at the start of the eighteenth century many of the names in addition to Bearsley, who were to become icons of the Port wine industry were already in residence in Porto. These included Phayre and Bradley, the founders of Croft, and the Warre family.[14] In addition to the British merchants, their competitors from Holland and Germany were also established in the city; names such as Kopkes, Burmesters, and van Zellers. The merchants, families, friends, and business associates met in the road in front of what is today the Factory House.[15] The name of the road has undergone change: from Rua Nuova to Rua Nova dos Ingleses (the new street of the English) to the current, Rua do Infante Dom Henrique. Both names continue to be included on the street sign.

Whatever the correct date for the start of the British Factory in Porto, the year of 1703 proved to be a watershed in the development of the wine industry in Porto. The signing of another highly controversial treaty between Britain and Portugal opened the door for the wine traders in Porto to eventually greatly increase their production and export sales to London. The Methuen Treaty of 1703 and its impact on Anglo-Portuguese trade remains a hotly debated topic in Portugal. Once again, it reflected the political situation at the time of its signing. The commercial treaty was preceded by a military one, signed on 16 May 1703 and negotiated by John Methuen with his son, Paul, helping him. The agreement provided English access to Portugal and its ports at a time when its strategic position was being threatened by the alliance of France and Spain.[16] The commercial treaty, which is popularly known as the 'Port Wine Treaty', was also negotiated by John Methuen and was signed on 27 December 1703.

The treaty was unusually brief and was negotiated in a very short period of time.[17] This made it quite a remarkable document in diplomatic history.[18] It essentially allowed a preferential duty for Portuguese wine in England to protect it against foreign competition, in return for the removal of all restrictions on the import of British textiles to Portugal.[19] More specifically, article two of the treaty included the following:

> Her sacred Majesty of Great Britain be obliged in her own Name, and in the Name of her successors, at all times to admit into England, wines gathered from the vineyards belonging to the Portugal Dominions, as that at no time, whether there be Peace or War between the Kingdoms of England and France, any more shall be demanded for such Wines, either directly or indirectly, on account of Customs of Imports, or upon any other Account whatsoever, than what shall, after deducting a third part of the Customs of Impost, be demanded from a like quantity of French Wine, whether such Wines shall be imported in Great Britain in Pipes, Hogsheads or any other vessels; but if at any time this Dominion of Duties, to be made aforesaid, shall in any

manner be attempted, and the same shall be infringed, it shall be right and lawful for his sacred Majesty of Portugal to prohibit again Woollen Cloths and Woollen Manufacturers of England.[20]

At the time, there were questions raised over the issue of the self-interest of the Methuen family. They had connections to the English cloth trade and were said to be looking for access to the Portuguese market.[21] The family also owned a vineyard in Portugal which could have potentially gained advantage from access to the reduction in duties of Portuguese wine into England.[22] These, however, were not the major concerns of the critics of the agreement, who argued that it helped destroy the Portuguese cloth trade and stunted Portuguese industrial development during the eighteenth century.[23]

In Portugal there was a growing sense that the country had been exploited by the British through the Methuen Treaty.[24] This feeling was accompanied by bitterness and envy at the success of British companies in Portugal. Perhaps the most telling statistic of Anglo-Portuguese trade during the post-treaty decades was that by 1736, Portugal accounted for a massive 19.1 per cent of all British trade.[25] It was not long before the personal attacks started on John Methuen and his family. He was accused of bribing key officers of the Portuguese king, and questions were raised over the award to him of £2,000 by the secret service for activities related to political treaties.[26] The Methuens, like many English families, did indeed do rather well out of the treaty, but there is scant evidence to suggest that this had any bearing on the original negotiations.

In retrospect, the criticisms of the treaty itself and its alleged damage to Portuguese economic interests are a little simplistic and partial. In the first instance, the commercial advantages given to the English by the Portuguese were soon expanded to other nations, such as the Dutch starting four years later in 1705.[27] The Portuguese soon allowed the French similar access.[28] Moreover, the Portuguese woollen industry in 1705 was already in trouble as Portugal had moved away from previous protectionist policies aimed at shielding the sector.[29] At the same time, eleven per cent of the exports of British textiles already went to Portugal prior to the signing of the treaty. This figure did drastically increase later in the century when, between 1736 and 1740, British textiles exports to Portugal accounted for fifty per cent of the sector's total exports for those years.[30]

Many argued though that the British dominance in Portugal was based not on the enforcement of the terms of the treaty, rather on the higher quality of the British woollen industry.[31] The quality factor helped the British companies exploit the lucrative Brazilian market through re-exports from Portugal. The rich British merchants in Porto were able to use the wealth of London to be able to offer more generous, and longer, lines of credit to their Portuguese and Brazilian customers than other local or international producers.[32] Put simply, the British woollen industry enjoyed qualitative and financial advantages over its local and international rivals in Portugal.

Although the Methuen Treaty came under attack from local businessmen, economists, and public officials, much of the development of Anglo-Portuguese trade would have materialised without its presence. What the treaty did inadvertently encourage was the separation of the Anglo and Portuguese trade sectors. Most members of the British Factory in Porto were largely isolated from the local community. They employed English-speaking slaves in their home, so had no need to speak Portuguese or develop business cooperation with the Portuguese. In this respect Viana do Castelo was the exception as there is evidence of cooperation between British, Dutch, and Portuguese traders on mutually beneficial matters.[33] In Porto the treaty did not have as much of an immediate effect as many people claimed. It would take two decades before its full impact reached the city.

18

Port Wine and the Factory House

I am a farmer, and a large one, but I am also a merchant, and declare to you that my customers do not desire, as some now present know well, wine full of brandy; on the contrary, they do prefer wines the most pure, and the least inebriative possible... When the taste for strong wines commenced, many farmers were accustomed to graft their vines with different kinds, whose only merit was the great colour which they imparted to the grape, despising in such manner, those kinds formerly preferred, which although they gave less colour, produced wines of high flavour and an especial aroma.[1]

Baron James Forrester

THE METHUEN TREATY PROVED hugely important for the cloth trade, but over time it has become most linked to the development of Port wine and the city of Porto. It did not, however, have an immediate impact. Some fifteen years after the treaty was signed, the phrase Port wine was just starting to be heard.[2] The use of the term was not specific: it implied any Portuguese wine. At the time, the most desirable wines from Porto were its table wines; colourful and full bodied. The birth of what we now know as Port wine, meaning wine fortified with brandy to stop the fermentation, dates to about 1720, although there is some evidence that the process started before this date. During the eighteenth century the wine industry in Porto evolved, with a powerful group of traders, enjoying their privileged access to the much sought-after British market, exporting large amounts of Port wine and making their fortunes. The century also witnessed debates about the composition of the wine, with the addition of brandy increasing the longevity of the wine and its strength. Portuguese attempts to regulate the Alto-Douro later in the century challenged the hegemony of the British traders, as well as offering opportunities to local traders. At the start of this tumultuous century it had been a very different story with Lisbon the dominant wine region and continuous complaints over the quality of the wines from Porto. The trade from Viana do Castelo all but dried up. Disease, emigration of key traders to Porto, and the general poor quality of the wine, compared to those from Lisbon, and later Porto proved too much of a challenge to overcome.

There were a number of reasons why the Methuen Treaty did not have an immediate impact on the wine industry in Porto despite being called the 'Port Wine Treaty', ranging from the availability of cheap table wine from Lisbon to the extended length of time it took newly planted vineyards in the Alto-Douro to reach maturity. From the second decade of the century onwards however, there was a rush to cash in on the opportunity to grow grapes in the region and to make wines. Not everybody was pleased with this state of affairs. Critics argued that the concentration of grapes came at the expense of the growing of foodstuffs, which the country was therefore having to import. John Croft wrote:

In the infancy of the trade the first cost of a pipe of Red Port in Sima de Douro was about 16 l. or 17 l. and the duty in England very inconsiderable to what it is at present, or has been of later year; all which served, as well as the high demand they had, to encourage the Portuguese to attend to their vineyards, and neglect their corn-land; for at any time of day the province of Sima de Douro was chiefly corn-land; and, from the richness of the soil, and the fruitfulness of the country afforded as fine a produce as any in Europe, and so great a plenty as it was never known that the province of Entre-Minho e Douro, or Oporto, wanted grain of any sort; nor was it ever known, at any time, that any corn was imported or wanted from abroad, there being a regular and sufficient supply from that rich and plentiful province.[3]

The situation in parts of the Douro came to resemble a gold rush. Peasant farmers made good money and the owners of the larger estates acquired fortunes as the demand for grapes outstripped the supply. John Croft's concerns had been realised with the Alto-Douro transformed into vineyards, traditional farming for foodstuffs all but ended.

Prior to this, the wines from the Lisbon region had proven to be more successful, largely outselling the Porto wines in London. The figures for the export of Porto wines are very revealing: in 1693, 13,011 pipes of Porto wine were imported into Britain. In the years following the signing of the Methuen Treaty from 1703 to 1710 only around 8,000 pipes arrived in Britain. It was not until 1716 that the 1693 figures were bettered by the Porto exporters.[4] It should be mentioned that the years from 1703 to 1710 were war years, with all that brings in terms of the difficulty of transportation, but it also reflected the important point that the Porto wine producers had not, at this stage, been able to provide a wine of acceptable quality for London society. Through experimentation: trial and error, and the use of new technologies regarding bottling, this was soon to change.

In Porto, the British members of the Factory started to organise themselves and their financial activities more formally. In 1721 the merchants introduced their own detailed rules to organise the Factory.[5] The merchants also started the Contribution Fund, created by a British Act of Parliament of the same year.[6] The Foreign Office described how it worked:

This was money raised by a levy on merchandise carried to Portugal on British ships from British dominions, according to the provisions of the Portugal Contribution Act of 1721. The sums were paid by the 'Masters or other Chief officers or Commanders' of the ships concerned who were in turn to be reimbursed by 'their respective Freighters, or by Persons to whom the said Goods and Merchandises shall be consigned or who shall receive the same'.

Section 4 of the Act laid down that the money should be applied as follows, '… all monies to be raised or received as aforesaid, shall be applied in manner following; that is to say, to the Minister residing in Lisbon, for the time being, for his support and subsistence, to pray, preach and exercise his Ministerial function there, three hundred Mill Reis per Annum, by equal quarterly payments, and the remainder of the said monies should be applied for relief of shipwrecked mariners, and other distressed persons.

His. Majesty's subjects, and to such other pious, charitable and public uses, as shall from time to time be appointed by the majority of the British merchants and factors residing in Lisbon, and other ports and places in Portugal, and Dominions thereof respectively, being assembled with the Consul General for the time being or any of his Deputy Consuls aforesaid.[7]

The fund was to become a very lucrative and successful way of financing the activities of the British merchants in Portugal. Part of the funds which were gathered were used to buy the land for the British Burial Ground in Porto as well as other charitable projects. It also helped ensure the financial viability of the Factory in Porto, allowing it to move to the next stage of development.

Six years later in 1727, the Factory formalised the rules and regulations of the British Factory House relating to the conduct of public meetings, admission of members, and the election of an annual treasurer.[8] The terms of admission were strict, often a point of resentment for semi-permanent British expats in Porto who were not allowed to join.[9] Although never considered as a corporation, the members of the Factory considered themselves to be a body in charge of a public trust and which could enter into public agreements.[10] How exactly the Factory was managed and maintained during this era remains something of mystery owing to the loss of the Factory's documentation for this period.[11] From local archives it is fairly clear that the Factory had residences dating back to 1710, but it was not until the arrival of the Consul John Whitehead that plans were made to build the impressive headquarters that have served the Factory House right up to the present day.[12] Prior to this, the Factory often met in the private residences of the British merchants, or near, Rua Nova dos Ingleses.[13]

In the meantime the Porto wine industry had suffered a number of setbacks: both self-imposed and created by the Portuguese state. While the addition of brandy to the wine was still at the experimental stage, how many gallons of it should be added to one pipe of wine during fermentation remained a controversial and hotly debated topic for much of the century. The quality of the results was not always good and it was not until the middle of the nineteenth century that the amount of brandy was upped from the previous four or five gallons for each pipe to a figure nearer twenty gallons, that the fortification of the wine was considered to be excellent.[14] Until that point, the Port wines were widely inconsistent in quality and despite increases in the number of pipes being exported, the market was susceptible to change and decline. Part of the reason for the fall in demand was not only down to problems with ascertaining the correct amount of brandy to add. Issues arose with the quality of the land as the industry tried to expand too fast to meet the growing demand. The reputation of the wines suffered as farmers, agents, and the merchants tried to cash in on the once-in-a-lifetime gold rush conditions in the Douro.

The temporary decrease in the Port wine market coincided with the traumatic Lisbon earthquake of 1755, which destroyed much of the Portuguese capital. Porto was thankfully spared the horrors of the disaster, but the political and economic fallout from the quake impacted upon the Port wine trade and the wider city. Sebastião José de Carvalho e Melo, better known as the Marquês de Pombal, planned and successfully implemented a hugely successful rebuilding and reconstruction programme for Lisbon. A strong leader with a ruthless streak, whose power had been enhanced by the earthquake, he was not a person with whom to pick a fight. In the wake of the earthquake, Pombal started to implement a number of economic and financial reforms, known as the 'Pombaline Reforms', aimed at making Portugal an economically self-sufficient and politically stronger nation. He was not a fan of the Methuen Treaty, which he felt favoured the English too heavily. One of his key aims was to build up a strong Portuguese manufacturing sector to counter foreign imports into the country. The British merchants in Portugal with their special privileges and rights were a natural target for his reforms. Pombal wanted regulation of the Port wine market, control over it, and for there to be more of a level playing field between its British and Portuguese stakeholders.

It was not long before the British wine merchants in Porto provided Pombal with ample opportunity to move against them and secure state control over the industry. The year of the Lisbon earthquake had also seen the biggest slump in wine sales. Prices reached rock bottom, and demand was still low with pipes being sold for as little as two pounds. Quality was very poor and the English wine merchants did not visit the Alto-Douro area, choosing instead to send a harshly worded letter to the wine growers in the Douro region. It offered a stark warning that the English would not continue to buy their wines unless the quality improved.[15] The message in the letter might well have been fair but the tone and language used was highly condescending and arrogant. The growers soon took their revenge; visiting Lisbon to demonstrate against the British threats, they placed a copy of the letter into the hands of Pombal.[16] It was soon made public with both the *Cortes* and the wider population taking great offence at its contents. It was viewed as an insult towards the Portuguese, and one that needed a response. The Portuguese leader now felt he had ample reason to act against the British merchants in Porto.[17]

A man of action, Pombal did not take long to respond. He announced that the whole Port wine industry would be controlled by a state monopoly company, and that all wines that were for export had to be bought from it – at prices set by its officials.[18] This was not the first state monopoly company set up by Pombal, who was looking to gain control over large sectors of the economy. In retrospect, this made the high-handed actions of the English Port wine traders all the more curious. Surely, given what was going on elsewhere in the economy, and with Pombal's nationalist policies, they must have suspected that he had eyes on their industry.[19] The merchants complained bitterly to Pombal that he had broken the terms of the two commercial treaties that Portugal had signed with Britain.[20] They visited Lisbon in the hope of changing his mind, but Pombal was having none of it. His response was as confrontational as the original letter from the British merchants. John Croft reported its contents:

> ...When they named the British Factory, he (Marquês de Pombal) said that he had never heard of any British Factory but one, and that was on the Coast of Coromandell, and that it was the highest piece of insolence for a handful of English to give themselves such consequence, by printing so dictatorial a letter, with the name of the English Factory at the bottom, which was treating Portugal as scurvily and insignificantly as if it was the most petty Republic imaginable, and not a Kingdom that had an indisputable right to make its own domestic laws.[21]

Pombal also stated that the British should be happy with the establishment of the new company as it would ensure that quality was maintained and monitored. There was little that the merchants could say in reply to this, but their resentment towards Pombal did not recede. In 1756, the *Companhia Geral da Agricultura das Vinhas do Alto Douro* (more simply known as Real Companhia Velha) was created. The company was heavily staffed and bureaucratically centric with enormous and controversial rights. The list was extensive:

1 A monopoly of the wine trade with Britain and Brazil.
2 Exclusive rights to distil and sell brandy in Northern Portugal.
3 A monopoly of selling wines to the inns (bars) of Porto.
4 The vine-growing area of the Alto-Douro was strictly demarcated and divided into two categories: one for export and another for domestic consumption. The former area

was said to produce the finest wines, fetching the highest prices, and were called Factory Wines.

5 Each year, officials of the company would decide on the amount of wine to be designated for export.

6 The wines chosen for exportation were then classified by tasters from the Company, their prices fixed, and the wine growers and shippers had to accept the price.

7 Permits were issued for all the wines selected for export and no pipe could be moved without this paperwork having been completed.

8 A law was passed making it illegal to have an elder tree growing on any property that lay within the demarcation area. The punishment for this crime was exile for life and the confiscation of all properties.[22]

The British merchants argued amongst themselves on how best to respond. When they approached Pombal from time to time, his response was always the same; if they did not like it, they could leave Portugal and return to England. The British government, busy waging the Seven Years' War with France and Spain, chose not to take up the case of the merchants in Porto. London was more concerned about keeping Pombal happy. British geostrategic needs took precedence over bilateral trade disputes. As the protests continued, the position of the Portuguese government hardened. Threats of imprisonment or expulsion were used to try to intimidate the merchants. Pombal openly rejected the 1654 treaty that granted special rights to the British, arguing that it had been signed by the discredited figure of Oliver Cromwell.

The two Portuguese groups that were affected by the changes of 1756 had very different reactions. The wine growers, who had seen their incomes rise with the increase in price that resulted from Pombal's takeover, were extremely pleased with their lot. Not so the innkeepers and winebibbers in Porto. They opposed the mandatory new high prices and protested in the streets of Porto in what became known as the 'Tipplers' Riots'. Pombal's response was brutal, and very much in line with his previous *modus operandi* against dissenters.

He ordered thousands of troops onto the city's streets and the rule of law was restored. In equally swift legal justice, thirteen men and four women were hanged, others sent to the galleys and over fifty exiled. Pombal accused the British merchants of being behind the riots but was not able to bring them before the courts. For the entire remaining period of Pombal's rule, the power of the *Real Companhia Velha* was absolute, mirroring his own political and economic style. It was intensely powerful. This angered the British merchants who could see monies being extracted by it and put to other uses such as the funding of public works programmes in Porto and the north of Portugal.

Politically astute, and not wanting to completely alienate the British merchants in Porto, Pombal offered something of an olive branch in appointing his cousin, João de Almada to be the Governor of Porto in 1757. His mission, as instructed by Pombal, was to try to reduce some of the tension with the British in the city and lessen the opposition to the *Real Companhia Velha*.[23] It was a difficult task, but the Governor found a willing partner with the arrival of John Whitehead as British Consul in 1756. Despite representing the interests of the British wine merchants in Porto, Whitehead was able to strike up a good relationship with João de Almada, who, as well as serving as Governor was also the Minister of Works, overseeing town planning in the city. Whitehead was to become the most important British Consul, whose legacy can still be seen in the architectural style of many of the buildings in central Porto that survive to this day.

We have already mentioned Consul Whitehead with regard to his work in creating the British burial ground in Porto and his work with the local architect Joaquim da Costa Lima Sampaio. The project of the British Factory House came to represent his major legacy to the British community in Porto.[24]

Whitehead's ascent to the post was not planned. When the previous consul, Robert Jackson, died on 6 August 1756, the post was first offered to Jackson's son-in-law, who for reasons which are not wholly clear, turned it down. The Factory then turned to John Whitehead who was duly elected. Whitehead must have been a local appointee to the position; there is no record of him having any previous experience or role with the Foreign Office. On 9 August 1756 he informed the Foreign Office of his election, and started in the position that he would hold until his death on 15 December 1802.[25] Whitehead was different in outlook to the previous consul, whose aims had been much more limited. In the first instance, he started looking for a sensible location for a building to serve as the headquarters for the Factory. There is evidence that a smaller Factory House building had already existed in the city. As a report written for the Foreign Office suggested:

> In 1765 there must have already existed a Factory House, for the Municipality intending to cut a new street contiguous to it, purchased among other houses to be raised, one that is described in the deed for sale, as parting on the northern side with the courtyard and garden of the Factory House.[26]

The process of getting the building constructed was lengthy and involved, in the first instance, the purchase of several smaller premises next to the proposed site. The road on which the Factory House came to be built was one of the busiest thoroughfares in the city, where property prices were extremely high. The street was recut by the Municipality, most probably in 1767, and Whitehead and the members of the Factory purchased the part of the premises that form the current building. Other small houses were given by the Municipality in compensation for the demolition of other properties belonging to the Factory.[27] In 1772, Whitehead and the Factory bought an additional house adjoining the premises that appeared to be the last piece in the jigsaw of creating a continuous area of the street in order to build the Factory House.[28]

Sadly, the detailed architectural plans for the building were lost along with the records of the initial years of the Factory House. A plan of the façade was found in the building in 1984. The document was in bad shape but has since been restored. It was unsigned and undated, but is widely presumed to be the work of Whitehead.[29] It is still not altogether clear who the main architect of the building was or how the plans evolved and were modified. Whitehead was himself a man of considerable architectural talent and was most probably the driving force behind the plans, including those of the façade. The consul also worked with a leading British architect, John Carr, on other projects in the city, most famously the Santo António Hospital. Some claim that Carr was instrumental in the design of the Factory House, but in the absence of any formal plans bearing his name there is little evidence to support this theory.[30] The predominantly English style of the finished building is consistent with other projects in the city centre at the same time suggesting in all likelihood Whitehead being assisted by Joaquim da Costa Lima Sampaio in the drawing up of the plans for the Factory House.

The Factory House was eventually finished in 1790 and since then the outside of the building has changed very little. It remains the centre for the social life of the British Port wine merchants in the city. Over the years it has hosted formal balls in honour of kings and queens and political leaders, including Margaret Thatcher in 1984. The Factory House still has a wonderful library, ballroom, dining room, and a dessert room. Its large cellar contains one of the finest collections of Port wine in the world with vintages dating back many decades. The aromas emanating from the cellar remind one of a bygone era. Strong on custom and tradition it still hosts a weekly lunch, held on Wednesdays, for the Port wine merchants. The building also serves as a tribute to John Whitehead, whose Herculean efforts to transform his dream and vision into reality were eventually realised.

For the visitor whose appetite for Port wine has been whetted by these tales of evolution, success, and triumph what better way to finish the day than to visit one of the Port wine lodges across the river in Gaia. Crossing into Gaia, note the aromas in the streets near the lodges. The slightly sweet smell of Port wine is never far away. It is possible to imagine the hive of activity along the riverbanks with boats being loaded with pipes to sail to England and returning with a cargo of textiles under the Methuen Treaty. Port has a proud and wonderful history and it is well worth visiting one of the best museums dedicated to its history – Taylor's Museum. Here we can find a good range of interesting topography facts, a history of port wine making, and a family tree that shows how the company has evolved for over the three centuries from Bearsley to Bridge. An added bonus for the visitor at Taylor's at the hour of sunset is the beautiful view of Porto as the light in the sky starts to fade and the streets and houses across the river in Porto become illuminated. Standing outside we can note the deep blue and pink tinge to the light as the river sparkles and then darkens into a night-time sleep mode. It is a magical light show that is unique to the western edge of Europe.

PART SIX

Day Three – Afternoon

19

The Golden Age

King John V (João V) avowedly modelled himself in many ways on the 'Sun King' Louis XIV, as he strove to inaugurate a golden age of absolutism in Portugal, as Louis had done in France. To some extent he succeeded, for during his reign Portugal attained a position of international prestige and importance which she had not enjoyed since the reign of King Manuel I and the opening of the sea route to India... Writing towards the end of his long reign, the King's chronicler, Padre António Caetano da Sousa described it as a 'happy reign, which could properly be called the Golden Age, since the mines of Brazil continued to yield an abundance of gold'.[1]

C. R. Boxer

W HAT BETTER PLACE FOR the visitor to start the day than standing in Praça da Ribeira; arguably the most iconic location on the majestic riverfront of Porto. Here it is possible to soak up the atmosphere of the present-day city, watching the restaurants set up for another busy day's trade and looking at the boats carrying their excited human cargoes up and down the river. Standing next to river in this impressive *praça*, we can also imagine the past: the time when the port area was full of ships unloading their cargoes from the Portuguese Empire; other ships anchored in the river waiting their turn to unload, or to be reloaded before heading back down the river bound for England or the colonies. In eighteenth-century Porto, overseas trade was the driving force shaping the development and enlargement of the city. The Lisbon earthquake of 1755, and the massive planning and reconstruction of the city led by Pombal, also came to play a role in shaping the buildings and planning of the roads in Portugal's second city. What worked in Lisbon was transferred to Porto, with the setting up of a public works programme headed by João de Almada e Melo.

The British Consul and architect John Whitehead influenced the design of Praça da Ribeira, and the unfinished construction project provides a backdrop to understanding life in eighteenth-century Porto and Portugal. The era brought major change to the city centre, transforming it from an essentially medieval city to the modern one, which resembles that which the visitor sees today. Construction works require money and the city was able to utilise two vitally important sources of income to support the creation of new buildings and a public works programme to get rid of the old and bring in the new. In the first decades of the century the Brazilian gold rush brought many riches to the Portuguese court and was the financial catalyst for many of the baroque buildings that the Tuscan architect Nicolau Nasoni designed for the city. The second part of the century, which saw the development of the large public works programme, most famously the Almadino Plan, was financed by the tax on the Port wine trade.

The first part of the eighteenth century were the years of the gold rush. The statistics were quite staggering: 856.5 metric tons of gold were mined in Brazil during the 1700s, which was thought to have represented between fifty-three to sixty-one per cent of the world's total production.[2] European powers wanted to trade with Portugal on the basis of it holding so much of the most important commodity that helped underpin the financial system. Portugal was able to develop trade with its colonies, especially with Brazil, which accounted for eighty to ninety per cent of this business.[3] No wonder the docks in Porto were so busy as the ships took linens, olive oils, and wines to Brazil. Among Portuguese historians and economists there remains a fierce debate about the distorting impact of gold on the economy. Suffice to say that the poor remained poor; there was no development of a professional middle class, but the king got richer. While it was certainly the case that the king did very well out the gold rush, the riches accumulated by João V reached almost mythical proportions. The historian, C. R. Boxer summed it up nicely:

> The ostentatious extravagance of King John V [João V], although it was often made possible only by withholding wages or by 'welshing' on his debts, certainly encouraged the general belief in Europe that the Crown of Portugal was much richer than it really was.[4]

There were rumours of a large building filled with diamonds and gold, with the king having more riches than the rest of the European royal houses put together. The British were very much taken in by the illusion of the treasures of the Golden Age during the rule of King João V.[5] Portuguese and Brazilian gold coins enjoyed a wide circulation, rivalling the English sovereign. Perception accounted for a lot, and Portugal with its ample supply of Brazilian gold was firmly established as a global, albeit temporary, power. Helped by the new-found wealth, João V was able to rule as an absolute monarch. A lot of the riches were spent on ceremonies, weddings, gifts and major projects such as the building of the enormous palace in Mafra.

A large part of it was also given to the church who were able to use it to strengthen their financial position, renovate existing church buildings and construct new ones.[6] Evidence of the gold boom can be seen in the 'extravagantly gilded woodwork of numerous baroque churches' of the era'.[7] The wealth of the Portuguese church seemingly became greater than that of the Spanish church, with it owning around one third of the cultivated land in the country.[7] Within Portugal there was a staggering ratio of one cleric for every thirty-six inhabitants, which was the highest in the whole of Europe. There was also an increase in the number of monastic buildings from 396 in 1600 to 477 by 1739.[8] The increase in religious personnel continued to rise until the middle of the century. The church in Portugal was by the eighteenth century responsible for the vast majority of charity in the country, concentrating its efforts on this, instead of work in the cultural and educational sectors.

The king also gave to the arts and books, with huge amounts of money being donated to build impressive libraries.[9] It was not all lightness; the court, like many other European counterparts, was prone to debauchery, often using nuns in convents which had become effectively brothels for the aristocracy rather than being used for religious worship.[10] For the Portuguese elite the idea of seducing a nun was thought to be erotic, and even the king had at least one mistress who was a nun.[11] There was a wider deviation from accepted Catholic practices by large numbers of the upper classes in Portugal. Although this was not viewed as anti-clericalism, it was more simple indifference to the church.[12] The lower classes continued to follow the norms of orthodox Catholic practice. In short, they continued to be devout and highly superstitious followers of the church.

The impact of these new-found riches on the city of Porto was profound. We find examples of the changes to the architecture of the city made during the first part of the century, most notably the construction of a series of buildings designed by Nicolau Nasoni. His works became icons of the Porto landscape, though there remains debate as to which projects were actually undertaken by him and which were undertaken by one of his disciples. From the Praça da Ribeira the visitor can easily see and visit an impressive portfolio of his works comprising many of the most important buildings in the city centre. Collectively the works provided Porto with a distinctive architectural style that defined the city in the era of the gold rush. A list of places he designed illustrates the range and longevity of his work, along with that of his disciples. It is possible to see much of his work in the small geographic area of the city centre. The walk from Praça da Ribeira is short but the steepness of climb, especially during the heat of the summer months, needs to be taken into account.

As the visitor climbs the hill, they soon reach an oasis that is Rua das Flores. The road and the buildings have undergone much renovation in recent years with new shops, cafes, and restaurants springing up all along its narrow pedestrianised walkway. The first example of Nasoni's work can be found here on the façade of the *Igreja da Misericórdia do Porto* (Misericordia Church of Porto), which he completed in 1749. The building is one of the most important for the church in Porto with the *Misericórdia do Porto* essentially being the charity wing of the church, responsible for social assistance to people in need. It deals with issues such as health, housing, poverty, disability, and social exclusion. In recent times it has started to become more involved with the arts and culture in general, establishing museums and hosting exhibitions in its spaces.

Towards the top of Rua das Flores we can choose a number of exits to continue the climb. Either by walking through the elegant Rua de Trindade Coelho, or by continuing to very end of the road that runs into Praça Almeida Garrett and then along Praça da Liberdade. The visitor will arrive at the wide archway of a street called Rua dos Clérigos. Near the top of the hill sits what is widely regarded as Nasoni's masterpiece, the iconic church and granite tower, Igreja Clérigos (Clerigos Church). Nasoni was asked to draw up plans for the project by a Portuguese nobleman in 1731; the construction of the whole project, including the tower, took decades to complete and was not fully finished until 1763. The church is one of the first examples of the style in Portugal. The opening up of the city to the work of foreign architects was highly symbolic and important. Nasoni, Carr, and Whitehead all saw several examples of their works constructed in Porto during the eighteenth century. It was not only construction that the notable architects worked on; several modification projects and refits were also undertaken, often reshaping old buildings into the architectural vogues of the era.

Of all the buildings in Porto, it was the Clérigos Church project which proved to be the gamechanger in reshaping past architectural synergies and providing the city with a clearer identity within Portugal and with the outside world. This was quite an achievement for the first part of the eighteenth century, with the leadership of the church playing an important role in helping to bankroll many of the religious building projects in the city. Essentially a talented artist and a brilliant architect, Nasoni was a man for the design and development of single projects, not town planning or the reshaping of the whole of the city.

There are many other examples of Nasoni's works across Porto, several of which we will visit later. As well as being a talented artist and architect, he was also extremely productive. As previously mentioned, there are doubts, debates, and disputes about the extent of his role in some of the projects listed below, but nonetheless it is an impressive list that demonstrates the range of his abilities. In addition to the ones included here, he was said to have played a role in several others before his death on 30 August 1691. He was buried in an unmarked tomb in the crypt of the Clérigos Church he had designed.

Nasoni's major projects in Porto and Northern Region:

- Loggia of the Porto Cathedral
- Palace of São João Novo (1723–1733) (Porto)
- Cathedral of Lamego (1738–1743): involved in the rebuilding of the cathedral along with painting of the false cupolas on the nave
- Igreja do Bom Jesus (1743), a Baroque church in Matosinhos
- Quinta do Chantre (1743): designed garden walls with fountains along a central axis, leading to the house with a central tower
- Igreja de Santa Marinha (1745), Vila Nova de Gaia
- The Igreja de Santo Ildefonso (1745)

- Plans for the orphanage of Nossa Senhora da Esperança (1746)
- Quinta de Ramalde (1746): designed Neo-Gothic elements such as decorative battlements to the central tower
- The façade of the Misericórdia Church (1749) (Porto)
- Designs for the Palace of Freixo (1750) (Porto)
- The central part of the palace of Mateus (Vila Real)
- Capela Nova (Vila Real)

Much of the works of Nasoni still survive but look a little out of place as a result of what followed in the second part of the eighteenth century. To some extent, the changes that took place during this period were rooted in Lisbon, where the earthquake of 1755 had increased the power of Pombal, centralising the economy and other parts of the state in his hands. As Lisbon lay in ruins, it required a careful set of plans to rebuild the city. Pombal took charge, revolutionising the structure of the city centre. Suddenly urban planning, hitherto a much overlooked profession in Portugal became essential, and Pombal wanted Porto to follow his lead in creating a more unified and interconnected street system. The gold rush was in decline by the middle of the century so the ambitious programme in Porto had to be funded by other means.[13] The tax on Port wine appeared the most lucrative, easily collected, and best guaranteed method of financing the development of the city. The strictly enforced monopolistic nature of the arrangements put in place on the Port wine trade made it possible for the state to accrue large sums of money from the sector and redistribute it towards making the city better. Pombal's attitude remained steadfastly consistent: if the British merchants did not like it, then they were free to leave. Many did complain, but few chose to leave, instead waiting for the fall from grace of Pombal, or a change of heart in his thinking.

Pombal showed little signs of the latter and in 1763 set up the Public Works Board, led by João de Almada e Melo, and subsequently after his death on 30 October 1786, by his son, Francisco de Almada e Mendonça.

The body was essentially entrusted with similar special powers to those used in the rebuilding of Lisbon after the earthquake. At the centre of the ambitious plans, described as an urban revolution, was the concept of expanding the city beyond the city wall, known as the Fernandina Wall. The idea was to get Porto ready for the nineteenth century.[14] The plans centred upon what came to be known as the Almadino Plan, named after its architect. The plan led to the creation of new *praças* and streets, and the realignment of some existing roads. Streets such as Rua de Santa Catarina were extended, and new alleys devised along the banks of the River Douro. The plan was said to be one of the first comprehensive city plans in Europe. The importance of changing the city was summarised by the present-day Porto Municipal:

> Until the second half of the eighteenth-century Porto was practically bordered by the Gothic wall, extending only to small rural parishes and fishing areas along the banks of the Douro. Decisive factors for triggering the new phase of the city's expansion were the rapid growth of the city population, a favourable economic environment linked to commercial activity, as a result of the growing importance of wine production and the creation of the Companhia Geral da Agricultura das Vinhas do Alto Douro.
>
> The 'Public Works Board' was the body responsible for coordinating all the interventions and its financing was obtained through a tax levied on the Wine trade. The Improvement Plan was considered the First General Plan of the City of Porto. Its underlying purpose was subordinate individual interests to the common good. The port of the second half of the 18th century was undoubtedly marked by the introduction of new urban concepts of enlightenment, such as urban regularity, the introduction of new programs, new stylistic currents, the systematization of architectural and aesthetic elements and the constructive system advocated by João de Almada e Melo.

As we have explained, Consul Whitehead was not content to stop with the construction of this impressive house for the British traders. He wished to make a contribution to the architecture of the city of Porto. This he was able to do, serving as an unofficial advisor to the Governor of Porto, João de Almada e Melo on the implementation of his plan. Given the deep resentment of the British traders towards Pombal, it might appear a little strange that Whitehead was able to form a strong working relationship with a man who was, after all, a relative of Pombal and had been appointed by him to restore the fortunes of Porto and the north of Portugal. It was, however, a meeting of similar minds and shared ambitions that drew the men together, becoming friends and the driving forces behind plans that would transform the physical appearance of large parts of the city centre.

Not all the plans were completed. Arguably the most ambitious of the lot, the enlarging of the old Praça da Ribeira, approved by the king in 1763, was never finished.[15] This was disappointing as it would have resembled the impressive Praça do Comercio in the capital city. Whitehead's influence on this project and the many others, appears to have been a stylistic one.[16] The Factory House and subsequent buildings well into the early nineteenth century, such as the previously mentioned Palácio da Bolsa, reflected a shift away from the Italian baroque influence of the Tuscan architect Nicolau Nasoni towards the British style of Whitehead's English friend, John Carr. One of the best examples of this can be found by taking the short walk from the Clérgios Church to Saint Antonio Hospital, now classified as a national monument on Rua Professor Vicente José de Carvalho. Building work started on 15 July 1770 on empty land on what, at the time, was the outskirts of the city. The hospital was designed in the Palladian style by John Carr. Despite being located in Porto, the hospital would not look out of place in an English northern city, where Carr did most of his work.

Although its over-simplistic to suggest that foreign architects totally dominated building projects in Porto during the eighteenth century, the legacy of the works of Nasoni, Whitehead, and Carr remain central features of Porto in the twenty-first century. In deciding to evolve, change, and look to the future, Porto in the eighteenth century was brave enough to allow foreign influences to mix with local trends. As we shall see, Porto was to become a major centre of architecture and was to produce some very fine local grown architects, whose works would help transform not only Porto, but cites outside of Portugal.

20

The Most Beautiful Bookshop in the World

A little over 100 years old, this art nouveau gem in Portugal's second city remains one of the world's most stunning shops – perhaps of any kind. Competing for attention with the books are wrap-around, neo-Gothic shelves, featuring panels carved with Portuguese literary figures. A track, used by the staff for transporting stock in a cart, leads from the entrance to the lolloping red staircase, which winds up to the first floor like an exotic flower. Books are available in English as well as Portuguese, and there's a small cafe upstairs beneath the stained-glass skylight.[1]

Lonely Planet

THE DEVELOPMENT OF THE city was subdued during the first part of the nineteenth century by the French invasions of Portugal and by the War of the Brothers, both of which we have chronicled in detail. The second part of the century saw a much more rapid expansion with several city plans being presented, as well as the development of the great infrastructure projects such as the construction of road and rail bridges. Several additional projects were postponed or cancelled due to economic crisis or political instability. By the start of the twentieth century however, Porto resembled the city we can still see today. The city was essentially planned from the river up with Avenida dos Aliados serving as the dramatic centre piece and seat of power. One relatively small building, constructed at the start of the twentieth century, has become essential viewing for the visitor to Porto.

Its architect and owner never intended for this to be the case but the beauty of its exterior and interior, matched by the high shelves of books from bygone eras and the present, have created an attraction that celebrates stunning architecture and great books.

The walk to Livraria Lello from Saint Antonio Hospital is short and packed with exciting historical sights, that remind us of the importance of the church and the university to the city. On the elegant, carefully preserved, Rua do Carmo we find two churches, quite literally attached to each other. The *Igreja do Carmo* (Carmo Church) and the *Igreja dos Carmelitas* (Carmelitas Church) both contain degrees of the baroque style made famous in the city by Nicolau Nasoni. The interior and exterior of the church buildings are attractive additions to the road, but it is the tiles on the Praça de Carlos Alberto side of the Carmo Church that are the most memorable feature. Designed by Silvestre Silvestri and painted by Carlos Branco they depict scenes from the origins of the Carmelite Order and Mount Carmel. The purpose of the panels of tiles is to disseminate the story of the Carmelite Order, but its most popular use is as an Instagram backdrop.

By simply crossing the road into often partially shaded Praça de Gomes Teixeira, we arrive at the Rectory of the University of Porto. The neo-classical building dominates the area, and today houses not only the rectory, but also the Natural History and Science Museum of the university.[2] The imposing building is also the administration headquarters of the university, which is currently one of the most crucial academic links between the city of Porto and the world. Its research stretches across a wide range of faculties and it attracts large numbers of foreign students each year through the Erasmus programme. Today its position as one of the leading universities in Portugal and Iberia has been established, and its list of famous graduates range from famous politicians and scientists to, more recently, world class architects. Despite the grandeur and size of the rectory building, the origins of the university are more recent than those of the ancient University of Coimbra, founded in 1290.

The University of Porto was created on 22 March 1911, as part of the Republican revolution, which had brought to an end the rule by the monarchy. Several of its institutions predate its classification as a university and can be traced back to 1762 when King José I created the nautical class. Additional schools were added over the years with the aim of training people in Porto in professions that were required locally: the navy, trade, industry, and in the arts.[3] The origins of education in Porto go back much further. Prior to Portugal emerging as an independent country, three types of schools were already established: monastic, cathedral, and parish.[4] The University of Coimbra was founded in 1290 and was based on an educational system dominated by authority, hierarchy, and discipline with teaching and the textbooks reflecting the view of clerics and the church. The period of reform under the Marquês de Pombal in the eighteenth century paved the way for the creation of secular primary and secondary education.[5] New teaching posts were created and a department of mathematics and one in life sciences started at the University of Coimbra. Pombal used taxes for the increase in the government's commitment to the education system.

Still progress was very slow, particularly during the difficult years of upheavals in the nineteenth century. Reforms proposed in 1822, 1835, and 1844 were never fully implemented with the biggest achievement being the establishment of the polytechnic academy in Porto in 1837.[6] In 1841, only around half of school-aged males attended school.[7] Education remained very much for the elite with over eighty per cent illiteracy rates in the country.[8] The rates fell slightly to seventy-six per cent for those aged over seven in 1890 to 74.1 per cent in 1900 and 69.7 per cent in 1911.[9] By the end of the monarchy, the slow pace of industrialisation in Portugal when compared with other European countries was strongly blamed on the lack of education of much of the population.[10] In simple terms, the country needed more experts in the fields of agriculture, industry, and commerce, but progress continued to be slow with an overconcentration on implementing cosmetic reforms.

The arrival of the Republicans in power following the October Revolution in 1910 was meant to change education for the better with their concentration on the need to implement major reforms in the system. Their ambitious plans, however, were somewhat let down by the lack of state funds available to pay for the changes.[11] Arguably more successful at improving primary over secondary schooling, the Republicans did achieve their aim of ending the monopoly of Coimbra over university education. The establishment of the University of Porto was very much part of this effort to wrestle control away from the clerical-dominated university towards more secular and profession orientated faculties.[12] With the fall of the Republic, the formation of the military dictatorship, and the setting up of the *Estado Novo* many of the reforms introduced by the Republicans were abandoned. In Porto, plans for the development of the university were put on hold and the Faculty of Arts was disbanded in 1928, and only restored in 1961.[13] Tellingly, given Salazar's background in economics, the only new faculty established in Porto during the *Estado Novo* was that in that subject in 1953.[14] Only after the 25 April Revolution in 1974 did the university really start to expand its disciplines, faculties, and student numbers to resemble the important international institution that it is today.

As the visitor walks across the *praça* towards 144 Rua das Carmelitas, where we find the beautiful façade of Livraria Lello, we should recall the era in which the bookshop was conceived. It was in 1906, as the monarchy was drawing to an end and the Republicans were gathering support and momentum, that the bookshop was built by Francisco Xavier Esteves, an engineer and graduate of the Polytechnic Academy of Porto.[15] The neo-gothic façade of the shop features paintings of José Bielman which represent the arts and sciences. Inside the shop there is a majestic crimson staircase, which in recent years has become a hotspot for Instagram photographs. The ceiling looks like carved wood but is, in reality, painted plaster. Although the shop is today more of a tourist attraction than a bookstore, its shelves still contain an excellent range of mainly Portuguese authors. Busts of some of the most famous writers such as Eça de Queirós and Camilo Castelo Branco sit in the shop. One of the most attractive aspects of Livraria Lello is the stained-glass window: an eight by three and a half metre structure with the words *Decus in Labore* (Honour in Work). The glass was restored in

2016 and 2017 by the local artist of Atelier Antunes, whose own works bring beauty to several other buildings scattered across the centre of Porto.

The bookshop was founded by José Lello and his brother António, opening on 13 January 1906 with a launch event attended by local writers, artists, and political figures of the day. The opening of the bookshop in Porto was very much in line with the political and social events of the era. Despite the lack of progress in developing education and increasing literacy in the nineteenth century, there had been significant advancements in culture. For those people that could read, the liberal governments of the nineteenth century ended censorship of books and encouraged the publication of new magazines and newspapers. The resulting cultural development among the elite was impressive with new important authors emerging and, with greater communication to the rest of Europe through railways, new influences arose, mainly French.[16] The century as a result became one of the Golden Ages of Portuguese literature with writers such as the Porto-born Almeida Garrett helping to develop theatres and writing successful plays.

Other genres that did well included historical fiction books, with Alexandre Herculano being perhaps the best exponent of this genre. The books appealed to a bourgeois audience and new important authors appeared at the end of the nineteenth century and at the start of the twentieth century. History became a more rigorous discipline with the establishment of archives and the first serious accounts of the history of Portugal produced. In this respect, Alexandre Herculano once more led the way with his epic History of Portugal (written between 1846-1853), which was based on serious methodologic principles.[17] This golden age of literature and the arts remained very much among the elite who enjoyed the opening up of the country to increasing foreign influences. It was an opportune time to open a bookshop in Porto with all the political rumblings as the Republicans schemed and prepared to make their challenge against the liberals and the monarchy.

In recent years, with Livraria Lello attracting approximately one million visits per year, the business model of the owners has changed from that of a bookshop towards tourism. Renovation works were carried out with an aim of ensuring that the historic features of the shop could be retained despite the enormous footfall through its doors. With this in mind an entrance charge was introduced, part of which can be redeemed against the purchase of a book from the shop. Of course it is not only the physical beauty of the store that draws visitors. The links to the Harry Potter books and films act as a tremendous magnet with fans of Potter keen to see the shop which its author JK Rowling was said to have drawn influence from. When writing the opening chapters of the first Harry Potter book, Rowling was living in Porto, teaching English at a local language school. Married to a Portuguese man, she eventually left and moved to another granite-dominated city: Edinburgh, Scotland. Throughout Porto, it is possible for the visitor to see influences for the Potter books, especially in the formal dress uniform of the students of the University of Porto, and in cafés where she most likely spent time drinking coffee and working on her manuscript of the first Potter book.

After leaving Livraria Lello, head along Rua da Galeria de Paris, one of the key streets in Porto for those who enjoy bars, music, and clubs. At the weekends, and in weekdays during the summer months, the street is heaving with revellers enjoying the late opening hours and cheap drinks. Many choose to remain outside in the street, enjoying the balmy temperatures and pavement bars. People come from outside Porto to drink and enjoy themselves before, often, moving on to one of nightclubs in the city centre which remain open until daybreak. During the afternoon the street is quiet, sleeping, and preparing itself for the festivities of night-time. At the end of Rua de Galeria de Paris, we turn right onto the hilly road that runs down to Baixa called Rua de Santa Teresa. The road provides an important link between downtown Porto and Cedofeita. As we walk down it we find at the first intersection the historic Hotel Infante de Sagres, along with the chic and trendy Vogue Café.

The story of the Infante de Sagres marks an early attempt by Porto to match the boom in top-end tourism in the post-World War II era, which led to an increase in luxury hotels in Lisbon and along its picturesque coastline. The hotel first opened its doors in 1951, the result of the vision of its creator Delfim Ferreira, an entrepreneur and philanthropist. The hotel is named after the Porto-born Henry the Navigator, who was also known as the Prince or Infante of Sagres. We have already told the story of Henry; the driving force and catalyst in Portugal's voyages of exploration which led to the creation of its global empire. The hotel opened at a crucial time for Porto in the middle of the era of Salazar and the *Estado Novo*: a time in which Portugal appeared to be very remote from the rest of Europe.[18] It was one of the first architectural examples of a transformation to modernism in Porto and was designed by the Porto architect Rogério dos Santos Azevedo, a graduate of the Porto School of Fine Arts. Azevedo's modernist style was very much in keeping with the ideology of the *Estado Novo* towards buildings.[19] Among his many Porto-based projects was the garage of the newspaper *O Comércio do Porto*, which today serves as the unofficial car park of the hotel.

The Infante de Sagres hotel was a favourite of Mário Soares, the former president and prime minister of Portugal and one of the country's first post-25 April Revolution leaders. Among its other famous guests have been the musicians, Bob Dylan and U2, movie stars Catherine Deneuve and John Malkovich, as well as members of royal families from across Europe. The hotel was purchased by The Fladgate Partnership in 2016 and underwent an upgrade process that lovingly restored it to its original beauty and increased the number of rooms to eighty-five. For visitors not staying at the hotel there are three things that are a must to do and see in the hotel.

The striking stained-glass panels on the staircase, originally from the workshop of Ricardo Leone, were painstakingly restored by Atelier Antunes (who as we mentioned, did the same in Livraria Lello). Like Antunes, much of Leone's work can be found in Porto, but his most famous project was the restoration of the windows at the ancient Monastery of Batalha. The panels in the Infante de Sagres provide an elegant, timeless backdrop to the hallway and staircase. The light emanating from the panels creates a nicely relaxed and intimate atmosphere, unusual in a hotel located in the city centre. In this modern-day age of selfies and Instagram locations, the glass panels also provide a photogenic backdrop for memorable pictures.

The two additional must do's in the hotel are interrelated. As part of the renovation process, the wonderfully hip and stylish Vogue Café was added to the ground floor of the hotel.[20] The Vogue Café in Porto is the first in Iberia. Its interiors were designed by Paulo Lobo, mixing tradition and modernity into a unique fusion of monochrome, colour, vitality, and style. Sitting at the bar feels as if you are on set of a Vogue photoshoot oozing in glamour, with framed prints of past Vogue covers adding to the timeless sense of tasteful and cutting-edge fashion which has made the magazine such an iconic brand across the globe.

The café has become another Instagram hotspot in the city for those looking for a glamorous backdrop and sophisticated elegance. Above all, the café is a cocktail bar which serves a fine Manhattan. It is also a nice place to sample the local cocktail delicacy, the Porto Tonico, a nice modern twist on the gin and tonic using white port. For the afternoon visitor, the Vogue Café's patio is a calm retreat from the noise of the city centre for afternoon tea. The outside space matches the inside of the café giving a feeling of continuity of elegance. You could be sitting in New York or Cannes, and at twilight as the natural light fades the elegant outdoor lamps bathe the areas in a soft glow. The hotel and the café can act as a base camp before we enter the inner ring of the city centre with the famous shops and streets that have been important to the history of Porto.

The café is also a celebration of the importance of the fashion industry to Porto and the city's re-emergence as an important venue on the international circuit. This reconnection with an important aspect of the city's economic history has helped harness local talent, re-invigorating a largely dormant industry that appeared to have left the city forever. Several local designers are achieving international reputations as the industry continues to grow in Porto and the surrounding region. One of the biggest individual success stories has been that of José Neves, a graduate of the University of Porto. Neves founded Farfetch, an online luxury fashion retail platform that sells products from most of the big brands in the industry. In 2018, the company was floated on the New York Stock Market, netting Neves an estimated $1.2 billion from the IPO.[21] In all likelihood, this makes Neves one of the most financially successful graduates from the University of Porto.

Leaving the Hotel Infante de Sagres and the Vogue Café, we head down the hill on Rua Elísio de Melo and across the Avenida dos Aliados into Rua do Dr. Magalhães Lemos and passing the Teatro Municipal Rivoli before climbing the hill up to the main shopping street, Rua de Santa Catarina. As mentioned above, the street was extended with the plan of the master town planner João de Almada e Melo, in the late eighteenth century. Historically, its cafés, shops, houses, and churches tell us much about the cultural and commercial development of the city from the eighteenth century to the present day. Thankfully, the road is largely pedestrianised, allowing the visitor a greater opportunity to wander up and down without due concern, except at intersections, where roads cut across it.

The first place to stop for the visitor is the Majestic Café which, like Livraria Lello, has acquired new importance in recent years. Opened during the Republican era on 17 December 1921 under its original name, Élite Café, it soon became the central meeting point for the aristocracy of the art world, bohemians, and society figures, who flocked to the café from Porto and the surrounding areas. It was, in short, the place to be seen and many VIPs of the era made it their usual haunt when visiting the city. Among them was the actress, Beatriz Costa, the most famous star of the Golden Age of Portuguese cinema. The title of the café, however, did not fit well with the Republican era due to its air of exclusivity, so was changed to the Majestic which it has retained to the present day. Later it was a regular haunt of the artist Júlio Resende, whose work we have discussed earlier. He was accompanied by students from the University of Porto's School of Fine Arts, looking to devise new synergies in art and sculpture. During the latter years of the *Estado Novo*, the café went into decline, its beauty tarnished by years of neglect and its interior in need of revitalisation. After a period of closure, the café reopened its doors to the public on 15 July 1994 with a new purpose of hosting cultural events and exhibitions in addition to its primary role as a café.

As well as the beauty of its architecture and its plush interior, there is an added attraction to the café. Accounts of JK Rowling's time in Porto remain sketchy, but she seemingly spent time in the Majestic Café, perhaps working on her novel. The apparent Potter connection has brought added custom to the café as it now appears on every to-do list for a visit to Porto. Equally importantly, it helps remind people of the historic links of the streets to bygone eras of Porto and its place in the world. Its decorative style with the striking marble façade, floral elements, and curvy shapes provide the café with a degree of originality, while at the same time reflecting the architectural trends of the era of its construction. It remains one of the best examples of an art nouveau building in Porto and oozes luxury and decadence. In recent years it has become something of a national treasure with prime ministers, presidents, and even the odd royal signing its VIP visitor's book.

It is a short walk from the Café Majestic to another important venue for literature and the arts in Porto: the Grande Hotel do Porto, which opened its doors on 27 March 1880. It is not the oldest hotel in Porto; that distinction goes to the Grande Hotel de Paris on Rua da Fábrica which opened three years earlier in November 1877. The Grande Hotel do Porto, however, remains a part of the rich tapestry of the city's history with its list of famous guests who stayed in this most attractive of hotels. The Portuguese writer Eça de Queirós, who was born in Póvoa de Varzim 35 km north of Porto, was a frequent guest in the hotel.[22] Eça de Queirós was one of Portugal's finest writers from the generation of the 1870s. This group of writers were all in their twenties and they came into their own from the late 1870s onwards to the early years of the twentieth century. As A.H. Oliveira Marques suggests:

They were the result of Portugal's total opening up with the development of communication and the maturity of press

234

freedom. They were the exponents of the new Portugal, European-minded, modern, striving to rise from industrial, commercial and political underdevelopment to a new society based upon the industrial revolution, the bourgeois leadership, and the parliamentary system. Although these intellectuals often reacted against and strongly criticised those aspects of society, they were its best and most thoroughly integrated representatives.[23]

Their influences, either directly or indirectly, were drawn from works by French, British, and German writers. Politically speaking the generation of 1870 were anti-clerical and generally anti-monarchist, some had Republican sympathies and a few held some basically formed socialist beliefs.[24] It probably would not come as a surprise that most of these intellectuals, including Eça de Queirós and the poet Antero de Quental, studied at the University of Coimbra, still the dominant educational institution of the era. Eça spent a great deal of time working in the Portuguese consular service, including postings in England. Widely read in English literature, he was not a fan of nineteenth-century English society, nor the weather. It was during his time in Bristol that he drafted much of what was to become his masterpiece, *Os Maias (The Maias)*, which was first published in 1888. His books have been translated into several languages (sadly still quite a rare occurrence for Portuguese literature). In English, he has been beautifully translated by Margaret Jull Costa, who also includes an enlightening introduction providing context and background information.

Eça de Queirós was not the only famous guest to have graced the Grande Hotel do Porto. The last empress of Brazil, Teresa Cristina, died in the hotel on 28 December 1889. The Brazilian royal family had been overthrown by a Republican coup which was supported by Brazilian military officers on 15 November 1889. They went into temporary exile in Portugal but were told on 24 December that they never be allowed to return to Brazil. They had not been welcomed upon their arrival in Lisbon as it coincided with the ascension of Carlos I to the Portuguese throne. The Portuguese government felt it unwise to host a deposed sovereign in the capital at such an important time. The family as a result travelled to Porto, with the daughters leaving Portugal altogether. Teresa Cristina did not get over the shock of learning the news that she would never see Brazil again. She became ill during the royal visit in Porto, her condition rapidly worsened and she died of a heart attack later the same day. The streets of Porto were full of people as her funeral procession made its way through the city before going on to the capital city. She was initially buried in Lisbon, but her remains were repatriated to Brazil years later in 1921.

There was a Republican connection, this time a Portuguese one, with the other famous incident that took place in the hotel. We have mentioned the rise to power of Sidónio Pais and the events of December 1917. His dispute with Afonso Costa's Democratic Party led to the coup with the Democrat leaders eventually surrendering to forces loyal to Pais. It was at the Hotel Grande do Porto that Afonso Costa was arrested. This was seen as a pivotal moment in the Republican era in Portugal. Many of the other leaders of the Democratic Party escaped to exile in England. The dramatic arrest of Costa confirmed the success of the coup that had already taken over the streets in Lisbon.[25] Afonso Costa and Sidónio Pais remain the two heavyweight political personalities of the era. The arrest of Costa marked an important turning point in the country, which for a time fell under the spell of the authoritarian leader, Pais, until his assassination.

Leaving the timelessness of the hotel and its links to local and international history, the visitor can walk up Rua de Santa Catarina towards the Capela das Almas (the Chapel of Santa Catarina). The most striking feature of the church is its tiles or *azulejos*; all 15,947 of them, which were added to the exterior of the church starting in 1929. Designed by Eduardo Leite they represent the story of the lives of Francis of Assisi and St. Catherine. The largest window on the façade has stained glass by the local painter and graduate of the Porto School of Fine Arts, Amândio Silva. An internationally renowned artist, Silva exhibited in Japan and Brazil with Júlio Resende. The exterior of the church underwent restoration work in 1982 which helped maintain the beauty that dominates the section of Rua de Santa Catarina on which it is located. Like other churches in Porto with similar religious-centric decorative tiles, it remains a favourite for visitors to photograph.

No trip to Rua de Santa Catarina and the surrounding streets is complete without visiting its elegant shops. In recent years, Porto, in tune with most other major cities in Portugal, has shifted away from traditional city-centre shopping towards massive shopping centres (malls) on the outskirts of the city. The presence of the headquarters of one of the most successful Portuguese companies in Porto, SONAE has added to the migration. Among its large portfolio are the Continente super/hypermarkets and ownership of shopping malls such as Norte Shopping. Indeed, the still family-owned SONAE is a reflection of the success of the business-centric Porto region in the twenty-first century. Porto remains the home of enterprise, while Lisbon retains its position as the seat of government. There are of course many exceptions to this rule, but the centrality of business to the life and soul of Porto continues to develop the city and act as a bridge between it and the outside world.

One of the most famous sites in the Rua de Santa Catarina area is the Mercado do Bolhão (Bolhão Market). While the age of the shopping malls belongs to the twenty-first century, the elegant and refurbished market is like a time capsule, reminding us of the Porto of a bygone era. The neo-classical building was constructed in 1914, during the Republican era, and was considered to be something of an avant-garde building at the time. The market, however, is more famous for its produce than the building. As the visitor walks around they will notice that it is divided into four distinct trading sections: butchers, fishmongers, florists, and greengrocers. Walking along its narrow lanes with stalls on each side it is possible to buy some of the best local produce.

Over the years, the market has expanded and pushed additional stalls into the already crowded space. The noise of the market in retained in the building, echoing off its walls to multiply in volume. Women stallholders scream out to attract the attention of customers, each trying to outdo one another with the loudness and pitch of their voices. Porto remains very protective of its city centre market. In other cities, these markets, located on prime real estate, have been closed and sold off to build apartment blocks or transformed into food halls; not so in Porto. The market remains an essential part of the life of the city centre: both practical for the local residents and as an attraction for visitors to the city.

There are also many examples of beautifully decorated shops near the market. One of the most famous is A Pérola do Bolhão, located a stone's throw away from the market on Rua da Formosa. Opened on 23 May 1917, the shop's beautiful art nouveau façade, brightly coloured tiles, and window display promises the most exotic of groceries. It has been under the same family's ownership since it opened and has adapted with the times to sell specialist teas, coffees, and spices in addition to its cold meats, sweets, and dried fruit. The aroma reflects all of these goods as well as musky Port wines.[26] The shop has become an attraction for visitors to the city who like to photograph its façade. For those who enter the shop, the staff speak English, French, and Spanish: a sign of internationalisation of the city centre of Porto that has taken place in recent years.

PART SEVEN

DAY FOUR – MORNING

21

From the Highest Point to the River

In the late fourteenth century, Porto's destiny still lay ahead of it. The ingredients of its future greatness were fermenting in the character of its sons, in its location and in the political and industrial changes which later took hold in Portugal...

Those who saw it crowned with its cathedral, half Arab and half Gothic, rather than crenelated fortress, wedded not to a keep, but to two plain, rectangular and massive bell towers, so different from those of other Christian peoples, perhaps because the Moorish architects wished to leave us with the minarets of their Mosques stamped like a sign announcing an ancient right-of-way, on the face of the Nazarene place of worship, those who saw the episcopal borough of Porto, clinging to the sides of the church and defended more by priestly anathemas than by any machinery of war, would hardly imagine that from this submissive town would rise an emporium of trade where, within five centuries, more than any other settlement in the kingdom.[1]

Alexandre Herculano

THE IMPOSING SÉ DO Porto, (Porto Cathedral), stands guard over the city, occupying its highest ground as a reminder to everybody of the importance of the church and religion to Porto and its surroundings. For the early morning visitor to the area, the views from the square towards the river are often shrouded in a mist that adds to the slightly mysterious atmosphere. The building itself is eclectic in style: mainly Baroque with a Romanesque-influenced façade, while its cloister and chapel are Gothic. The reason for this was that since it was first constructed in the twelfth and early part of the thirteenth century, it has been rebuilt, modified, and repaired on several occasions through the ages. The Porto-based Italian architect Nicolau Nasoni added his stylist touch in around 1736 with the design of an attractive *baroque loggia* on the side façade of the cathedral.

Over the centuries, the cathedral has withstood the attention of foreign invaders, civil wars and revolts. Each part of Porto's history is contained within its thick stone walls: from royal marriages such as that of King João I to D. Filipa de Lencastre in 1387, to resisting the efforts of French soldiers during the invasion of Porto to loot the silver altar. The latter was prevented only by the last-minute building of a fake partition wall to hide it from the rampaging troops determined to steal all that they came across in the city. During the War of the Brothers, the sacred nature of the church did not stop the Miguelites from shelling it. As *The Times of London* described the scene of the birthday of Dom Pedro:

On Thursday evening they recommenced throwing shells, and continued the whole of Friday, the Emperor's birthday with a copious allowance of cannon-shot. High mass was sung at the cathedral, and Count Villa Flor, with all his staff, and the heads of departments attended.

The cortege was very splendid and suited well with the gorgeous richness of the old Gothic cathedral. The service was well and orderly performed notwithstanding the bombardment of the enemy, who, aware of what was going forward, sent several shells upon and close to the church, the vaulted roof of which resisted their force, and those within only knew of the kindness intended them by the hollow thump-thump of the shot above them.[2]

The cathedral survived the attentions of the French soldiers, the Miguelites' artillery batteries during the long Siege of Porto, and various civil disturbances and revolts that took place in the city. Today, it serves as reminder of the different periods of history in the city: the journey from its humble origins through to its Golden Age to its present-day role as a proud outward-looking international city that highlights the best elements of tradition and modernity. The era of the church as essentially the ruler of the city has long passed but its relevance has not diminished.

Right next door to Porto Cathedral is a wonderful reminder of the traditional art of the production of stained glass that graces many of the holy buildings in the city of Porto. Having alluded to the beautiful stained glass in Livraria Lello and in select churches, what better location to house a museum in honour of one of its best exponents than next to the cathedral. Museu do Vitral houses works and collections from the Atelier Vidraria Antunes, the oldest stained-glass workshop in the city.[3] The works by João Aquino da Costa Antunes are drawn from his workshop and home at 19 Rua de Vilar, a house he purchased from the Porto-born filmmaker, Manoel de Oliveira. For Antunes stained glass meant a life painting light, a process he describes as the hardest way to paint as it is the only process that allows light to pass through.[4] The museum displays a series of pieces that covers religious themes as well as decorative arts for private homes; these became fashionable when glass became less expensive and more accessible. There are also examples of abstract art stained glass that follow the styles of the 1920s Portuguese modern art movement, literary and artistic, with influences from Fernando Pessoa, Júlio Resende, and the Amarante-born Amadeo de Souza-Cardoso. International influences are also present in pieces that draw inspiration from the works of the famous American glass artist Louis Comfort Tiffany as well as Frank Lloyd Wright. Antunes describes the delicate and near-silent artistic process:

> It is an art made in conventual silence, in an environment of great tranquillity. Glass is a very fragile matter and requires a lot of patience and precision[5]

243

The finished works, originals and restorations, offer glimpses of past stories mixed with an elegance that highlights the beauty of the buildings in which the stained-glass features are housed. Porto has been lucky enough to have benefitted from the work of artists like Antunes who are able to not only create new pieces of art, but to preserve and renew older examples of stained glass thus giving new generations an opportunity to admire the results of this noblest of professions.

The Museu do Vitral is home to an important archaeological find, which is located in its basement. Inside, an ancient staircase leads to one of the oldest streets in Porto, Rua de Dom Hugo. There is a lovely view of the street from a window in the museum which overlooks it. The archaeological excavations that took place between 1984 and 1987 revealed exciting new finds that tells us a little more about the area from the fourth–third century BC to the present day:

> We are talking about architectural ruins and spoils from the 4th–3rd century BC to the present day. Traces of the proto-historical castro, which was at the origin of the urban centre, as well as the occupations that followed it, were identified. The twenty archaeological strata are overlapping layers of lands of different colour, texture and size, each related to a particular moment in the life of the city. This stratigraphic sequence serves as a sample of the evolution of settlement in Morro da Sé, the main nucleus that originates the city of Porto.[6]

From the museum we head out to the square and walk along Terreiro Sé towards Rua de Dom Hugo; the attractive narrow road loops around the Ordem dos Contabilistas and runs towards the Casa-Museu Guerra Junqueiro. This museum is something of a little hidden treasure which the visitor comes across quite unexpectedly while navigating around the old road. An attractive courtyard with a bronze statue of Guerra Junqueiro greets the visitor.

Abílio Manuel Guerra Junqueiro was a multi-gifted man who at various times served as a leading civil servant, a politician, journalist, writer, and poet. There were strong political overtones to much of his work which centred upon his support for the Republican movement in Portugal. From his early years, his opposition to the monarchy was clear. The British ultimatum to Portugal in 1890 over Africa fuelled his artistic and political juices, leading to some of his best and most timely works, including *Pátria (Fatherland)*. He blamed the monarchy and the delusions of the glorious national past as reasons for the country's treatment at the hands of the British. Wounded, looking to restore national pride, Junqueiro envisaged that only the establishment of a Republic could transform Portugal. Junqueiro is viewed as one of Portugal's most important writers in the lead up to the demise of the monarchy with the 5 October 1910 Revolution. He helped set the tone of discontent with the existing political and social structures that proved to be the catalyst for change. In his later years, Junqueiro dropped his strong anti-clerical beliefs, the subject of much of his best work, and embraced Catholicism.

The eighteenth-century Baroque style house in Porto was donated by his family to the Municipal do Porto, along with over six hundred works from his collection, in 1940. Two years later the museum opened and today remains a worthy memorial to one of Portugal's finest poets. A degree of mystery surrounded the identity of the architect. For many years it was attributed to the prolific Nicolau Nasoni, though it is now credited to António Pereira.[7] It is a calm and tranquil setting, away from the crowds that swarm to the cathedral, a place where to imagine the feeling of optimism that greeted the onset of the Republican era. As we know, this was swiftly to fade away to be replaced by the chaos, confusion, and darkness of what followed as Portugal entered the killing fields of World War I and the Republic started to implode. Entering the building and walking around the collection is like exploring a time capsule of Portugal at the end of the nineteenth and the start of the twentieth century. It houses a fine collection of antiques, ceramic figurines, furniture, glass and metal works, jewellery, and sculpture. It is also a reminder of the wave of Portuguese literature that emanated from the 1870s, many of which had close links to Porto and the surrounding region.

The area in front of Sé, known as Morro de Sé (Cathedral Hill) is of great historical importance as it was seemingly here that the original Jewish quarter in the city was located. The relationship between Porto and its Jewish inhabitants is long and complex. It is mixed, with extended periods of peaceful co-existence in which Jews played a prominent role in business and commerce, and the era of the Inquisition. The latter led to the destruction of all things Jewish, forced conversions, and expulsions. The date of the first arrival of Jews into the lands that today constitute Portugal is not completely clear, although when Portugal became independent with the signing of the Treaty of Zamora in 1143, Jews had been living in the peninsula since the Roman Empire. In terms of the documentation which is available today, the earliest records on the Jews in Porto date back to the twelfth century.[8] Even here there are problems with many of the records being incomplete, and little is known of Jewish history in Portugal predating this time.[9]

There had been a synagogue in the centre of Porto on what is currently Rua de Santana, near Sé cathedral. There was an old Jewish Quarter in the area around here, ranging from what is today Rua de São Sebastião to Rua Bainharia. There are also indications of a second synagogue in the current Rua do Comércio do Porto and a lower Jewish Quarter in the area from Largo de São Domingos to Miragaia. As well as synagogues, the Jewish Quarters in Porto included homes, butchers, and a courthouse. These areas were relatively small in size although in some instances did expand downhill in the direction of the riverbank.

By the fourteenth century, the vast majority of Porto's Jews lived in what was effectively a Jewish ghetto, marked by a high wall and two large iron gates that were closed each day at sunset. In today's streets, the ghetto comprised of the central area between Rua de

The Factory House. The strong British influence on the architectural style of the building reflects the importance of its merchants on the affairs of the city.

The view from São Bento train station looking towards the tiled façade of the Igreja de Santo António dos Congregados.

Palácio da Bolsa, the Stock Exchange. A series of impressive halls and lavish rooms, most notably the Moorish revival styled Arab Room.

Approximately 20,000 *azulejos* (tiles) of scenes from Portuguese history painted by Jorge Colaço adorn the ticket hall of São Bento train station.

The imposing façade of the old customs house, Alfândega
do Porto, stands alongside the Douro river.

The futuristic Casa da Música designed by Rem Koolhaas at Rotunda.

The Maria Pia Bridge, designed by Gustave Eiffel and opened in 1877.

Beautiful views over the Douro river from the gardens at Palácio do Cristal over the Arrábida Bridge towards the Atlantic.

A plaque commemorating the end of the occupation of Porto by French forces during the Peninsular War.

The two churches of Igreja do Carmo and Igreja dos Carmelitas in the baroque style made famous in the city by Nicolau Nasoni.

The statue of Dom Henrique (Henry the Navigator) points towards the Atlantic.

The view over the
historic city centre of
Porto, a UNESCO
world heritage site.

Fishing boats in
the harbour.

Igreja Santo Ildefonso façade covered in tiles painted by the artist Jorge Colaço.

Porto's Jewish community lived in the heart of the city centre.

The ocean front promenade on Avenida do Brasil in Foz.

The Kadoorie Synagogue, the largest in Iberia.

Contemporary architecture in Porto, the offices of
Vodafone on Avenida da Boavista.

One of the city's oldest grocery stores at Mercado Bolhão.

Porto's modern metro system links the airport to the heart of the city.

Igreja do Lapa stands at the summit of the Porto skyline.

On Praça Carlos Alberto stands the statue commemorating WWI.

The commemorative statue to General Humberto Delgado on Praça Carlos Alberto.

Humberto Delgado in Porto during his 1958 campaign for President of Portugal.

Investment in infrastructure since joining the EU in 1986 has resulted in a state-of-the-art airport and new motorways linking the country to Europe.

The view over Porto and the riverside of the Douro from
Serra do Pilar monastery.

Sunset over the Atlantic Ocean, with the Arrábida Bridge
in the foreground.

The two-tiered Dom Luis I Bridge is one of Porto's most
iconic monuments.

The interior of the Kadoorie Synagogue in Porto.

The view from the balcony of The Yeatman Hotel towards Serra do Pilar monastery and Dom Luis I Bridge.

São Bento da Vitória, Rua de Vitória, Travessa do Ferraz and at the top, Rua dos Caldeireiros.[10] The ghetto lasted for over a century with Jews holding important roles in the Portuguese state related to finance and medicine as tax collectors and court doctors.[11] Other members of the community worked in moneylending, commerce, and banking, or were traders, shoemakers, and tailors. Collectively, the Jewish minority were far more educated, more advanced, and richer than the rest of the population who continued to lag far behind. Anti-Jewish sentiment occurred from time to time, but this was largely based on economic jealousy about the wealth of the Jews rather than any religious reasons. All of this changed, however with the introduction of the Inquisition in Portugal, the full impact of which was felt in Porto.

The seeds of the Inquisition in Portugal were sown in Spain where the Inquisition had been established in 1478. In 1492, after Spain had successfully completed the conquest of the Moorish area of Granada, the antisemitic Catholic monarchy of Spain expelled the Jews from the country.[12] Initially the Portuguese *Cortes* did not want to allow them to enter the country. King João II, however, reluctantly allowed many of these stateless Jews to take up temporary residence in Portugal in exchange for them paying a tax of eight cruzados per person at the border for the privilege of entering the country.[13] Wealthy Jews were the most fortunate with six hundred leading families agreeing special terms to remain permanently in Portugal. Once inside the country, they settled in existing large cities, including Porto. There are no accurate figures for the total number of Jews that entered Portugal during this period with estimates ranging from 60,000 (plus the six hundred families) to 100,000.

In 1495, when King Manuel I (nicknamed 'the fortunate') came to the throne and married a Spanish princess, he came under strong pressure to align his religious policy with that of Spain. This was a curious paradox for a leader who became known as a builder of connections between the West and East leading to a golden era of arts and literature. Nonetheless, in December 1496, he announced that all observant Jews were to be expelled.[14] In other words, Jews and Muslims refusing to be baptised were to be forced to leave Portugal.[15] Some Jews decided to leave, but most chose to convert, becoming known as New Christians. There were harsh penalties for any New Christians caught trying to observe Jewish practices and traditions. The results of this semi-forced conversion were tragic. The peaceful coexistence that had characterised Christian-Jewish relations soon vanished. In 1503, the advent of food shortages and resulting price increases were blamed on the Jewish converts, along with all other ills in Portugal.[16] There were several other attacks on, and hostility toward, the New Christians. In 1506, there was a massacre of around five hundred New Christians in Lisbon, and several other smaller incidents. Mistrust between the lower classes plus the clergy towards the New Christians became particularly troublesome.

The establishment of the Inquisition in Portugal took place in 1536. In the toxic atmosphere of religious fervour, anti-New Christian sentiment and increasing state persecution of all things Jewish, charges flew back and forth. Whole families were accused of being Jewish, regardless of any racial origin.[17] The major targets of the Inquisition were the New Christians who were accused of continuing to secretly practise the Jewish faith. Formal courts of the Inquisition were set up in six Portuguese cities, including Porto, although at least one *auto-da-fé* (sentence) took place in the city before it was stopped.[18] In 1543 four people were executed and fifty-eight penanced.[19] There is evidence of a second *auto-da-fé* taking place at which it was claimed that one hundred New Christians were punished for continuing with Jewish practices.[20] Overall, the number of victims of the Portuguese Inquisition is estimated at around 40,000, although the documentation in arriving at this figure is far from complete.[21]

On the whole, relations between Old and New Christians in Porto proved to be much better than in most other Portuguese cities. It was not until the era of the authoritarian rule by Marquês de Pombal that the *autos-da-fé* across the country ended as well as the discrimination against the New Christians.[22] The official end of the Inquisition did not happen until the early nineteenth century. A plaque was said to have been placed on Rua da Vitória in memory of the Jewish victims of the Expulsion Act of 1496.[23] It also praises those that remained in Portugal and continued to secretly practise their Jewish faith.

The story of the Jews in Porto during the twentieth and the early part of the twenty-first centuries revolves around one man and two world wars. Captain Artur Carlos de Barros Basto was a Portuguese army officer who fought in France during World War I. Later, he was the founder of the Jewish Community in Porto and the driving force behind the construction of the Kadoorie Mekor Haim Synagogue, the largest in Iberia. He also led the rescue work to help Jewish refugees fleeing the horrors of the Nazi occupation of mainland Europe during World War II. His personal fate at the hands of the *Estado Novo* made him an internationally known figure and his case has led to him often being referred to as the 'Portuguese Dreyfus'.

Born in Amarante, Barros Basto converted to Judaism after hearing about his family's moderate links to the religion. In the era of the *Estado Novo* there was a strict compliance code in terms of religious affiliation and practices and Barros Basto was kicked out of the Portuguese military on essentially religious and political grounds. There was also a whispering campaign about his sexuality and his political leanings towards the opposition Communists, which was most probably used as part of the general campaign to discredit him by the authorities of the *Estado Novo*. Although wounded by his removal from the army, Barros Basto continued to try to build up and organise the Jewish community in Porto and the north of Portugal. His most notable contribution on this score was the building of the synagogue, opened in 1938, a lasting monument to his work.[24]

During World War II Porto, like Lisbon, was a hive of rescue activity helping Jewish refugees escape from Europe and move to safety in North or South America. Barros Basto and the rest of the Porto Jewish community were at the forefront of the rescue effort. Much of this work involved fundraising and helping refugees navigate their way around the complex bureaucracy of the *Estado Novo*. Much of the red tape was implemented and monitored by the Secret Police. Salazar had initially made it difficult for Jewish refugees to enter Portugal, but the events of the war and the work of many Portuguese diplomats in Europe who were issuing visas against his wishes, led to a more pragmatic policy. The offending consuls, particularly the Bordeaux-based Aristides de Sousa Mendes were treated harshly, with Salazar ending their diplomatic careers, but the refugees arriving in Portugal were treated more fairly.[25]

In Porto, as in the rest of the country, the attitude of the authorities towards the refugees was to carefully monitor their movements to make sure they did not contact local opposition groups such as the Communists. They also strictly enforced the temporary nature of the refugees' entry visas into Portugal. As noted by Neill Lochery in his book *Lisbon: War in the Shadows of the City of Light*:

> Once the initial shock of the arrival of the refugees had passed, the PVDE (Secret Police) came to the conclusion that for the most part the refugees posed little or no threat to the *Estado Novo*, and were simply in transit. Refugees, in short, were not allowed to remain in Portugal on a permanent basis unless Salazar gave his personal blessing, which he reserved for several members of Europe's royal families who remained in Lisbon, effectively in permanent exile.[26]

There were exceptions to the rule, a little more frequently in Porto than in Lisbon, whereby attempts were made by local families to adopt refugees, or applications were made to the authorities on various grounds to offer permanent residence. The vast majority, however, remained in Portugal for a couple of months at most, enough time to get their paperwork in order and find a place on a ship or the Pan-Am Clipper out of Europe.[27]

Portugal remained neutral in the war, slightly favouring the Axis powers until the success of Operation Torch in North Africa at the end of 1942, and the Allies from that point onwards until the end of the war. The country, as a result, was spared the horrors of destruction that the war caused to much of Europe and beyond. Salazar skilfully managed to play one side off against the other in the war, while at the same time Portugal got rich from its wartime trade with the belligerents. By far the most lucrative trade was in wolfram (tungsten), a rare ore, much of which was mined in the north of Portugal, not too far from Porto.

Wolfram was a vital ingredient in the hardening of steel and had a wide range of uses in armaments from artillery shells to tanks and bullets. Without a plentiful supply of wolfram, the Germans' weapons-production would have ground to a halt. As the war went on, the Germans became near totally dependent on Portuguese wolfram. This proved to be both a headache and an opportunity for Portugal:

> The sale of wolfram to the Germans became the most important aspect of the economic warfare involving Portugal. As the near constant references to wolfram in Salazar's diary confirm, it was the single biggest issue of the war for Portugal. Over the years Salazar lost more sleep over wolfram than anything else. The negotiations over wolfram also dominated the lives of British, German, and American diplomats based in Lisbon during the war.
>
> Like the British, the Germans used the carrot-and-stick approach to deal with the wolfram issue with Portugal. The stick was German attacks on Portuguese shipping, such as the sinking of the Portuguese ship, Corte Real, in 1941. The carrot was an agreement with Germany, which included an offer to supply Portugal with German weapons and other vitally needed supplies at favourable rates to Lisbon.[28]

It should be stressed that Portugal also sold wolfram to the Allies who were keen to buy up stocks in order to thwart the supply to the Germans. At first, Berlin paid the Portuguese with forged *escudo* notes, printed on captured presses in the low countries. As the quality of the notes deteriorated the Bank of Portugal informed Salazar who demanded that the Germans settle their bills in gold. This was not an unusual demand in wartime, but by 1944 it transpired that most of this gold was of disputed origin. This was a polite way of saying that it had been looted from the central banks of countries occupied by the Nazis and from Jewish victims of the Holocaust: melted-down gold teeth, wedding bands, and other jewellery.

After the war, Portugal's profits from its wolfram trade were considered to be ill-gotten gains, but unlike most of the other European neutrals it refused to hand over the gold to the Allies. Eventually, a quiet deal was struck with the State Department in Washington whereby Portugal was allowed to keep nearly all the gold in exchange for allowing continued American military access to an airbase in the Azores Islands. Salazar chose not to spend the gold, instead saving it for a rainy day which never arrived. It was a curious decision given how hard he had fought to keep the gold, and the under-development and poverty in Portugal during the *Estado Novo*. Today, Portugal still retains the gold from World War II bars of which, still stamped with the Swastika, lie deep in the vaults of the Bank of Portugal headquarters in Lisbon and Porto (next to the Hard Rock Café).

The story of Barros Basto and the Jewish community in Porto has a slightly happier ending. In February 2012 the National Assembly recommended the rehabilitation of Barros Basto and his reinstatement into the army with the rank of captain. The resolution argued that he had been the victim of political-religious segregation and his rehabilitation was completed with this act. Getting reintegration into the army proved to be more bureaucratically difficult to achieve.[29] The relatives of Barros Basto were meant to receive compensation for his loss of salary, but the Ministry of Defence proved very reluctant to carry out the reinstatement and offered settlement terms. Despite these difficulties, the Jewish community in Porto continues to expand, partly as the result of newly arriving members from the outside world, who reflect the growing sense of insecurity of Jews in many other countries. Porto, for all its dark past regarding its own Jews, has become a safe haven for those seeking security and religious tolerance.

22

The Mouth of the River

Tradition does not mean closure, immobility. Quite
the opposite, the value of traditions is in being open to
innovations. Tradition is not the opposite of innovation,
it is complementary. Tradition comes from successive
interchanges. Isolated cultures that try to preserve their
traditions without being open to new ideas collapse. Every
traditional culture is influenced by outside cultures. When
I was growing up there were very few centres of global
culture – Paris, London, New York, and the rest was a
periphery. Portugal was in the periphery and it was closed
until the 1974 revolution, after which the country was
rediscovered.[1]

Álvaro Siza

FROM THE ORIGINAL JEWISH Quarter, we head towards
Rua Mouzinho da Silveira. This elegant wide avenue, which
descends towards the river, remains at the beating heart of
the city centre. It has historically been a trading street and, in recent
years, has undergone a massive programme of urban rejuvenation to
restore it to its past glories. The results have been impressive with new
shops, boutiques, cafés, and restaurants opening on the ground floors
of strikingly tall buildings that radiate elegance and wealth. The road
serves as the link between the city centre to the top of the Ribeira,
running into Rua do Infante Dom Henrique. Its gentle incline makes
it a slightly more pleasurable route to take than many of the narrower
and steeper link roads between the riverfront and the city centre.

Heading along Rua do Infante Dom Henrique in a westerly direction the visitor soon comes across the rather austere and imposing exterior of the Gothic styled Igreja de São Francisco. The church was built in the fourteenth century on the site of a more modest church that seemingly belonged to the order of the Franciscan Friars who had arrived in Porto around 1223. The church was planned and built in traditional Gothic style: three naves, a transept, and a main chapel inside. The interior was decorated much later with gilt-edged woodcarvings and is considered to be one of the most beautiful in Porto, famed for its baroque decoration. It is a strange contrast of styles between the exterior and interior that does not always work, with the baroque gilt work appearing slightly out of place in the Gothic structure of the building. Nonetheless, it does look visually stunning and is considered one of the best examples of gilt work in Portugal. The gentry of Porto used to be buried inside the church's slightly creepy catacombs, and here there is another example of the exquisite sculptural work of Nicolau Nasoni.[2]

We head towards Foz do Douro, where the River Douro runs into the Atlantic Ocean and the mainland of Europe ends in spectacular fashion as giant, powerful waves crash against the sea wall. For the visitor, there are many different routes and modes of transport to travel the few kilometres to reach this once-separate town which, as Porto has grown outwards, now touches the city's boundaries. One of the most enjoyable is to take the tram that runs along the riverfront and which can be caught at various points in the city. The Linha 1 tram leaves from the bottom of the Igreja de São Francisco and hugs the riverbank as it snakes its way out of the city along the marginal road towards the ocean.

The first building of interest on the route is the old customs house, now the Centro de Congressos da Alfândega (conference centre). This attractive, but slightly soulless, building was originally constructed as a customs house for Porto and the region. This was the first port of call for everything being imported into Porto, as well for the luggage of foreigners arriving in the city by boat in the olden days. Mainly due to financial difficulties, the construction of the building took a decade and was not completed until 1869. Nearly twenty years later, a railway link was completed between the customs house and the station at Campanhã with its links to Portugal and Spain.

As Porto expanded, the main docks moved to Leixões and the airport handled more international flights, and so the location of the customs house became problematic. New customs points opened up nearer the international lorry terminal, the Port of Leixões, and the airport. The building, as a result, soon fell into disrepair and was eventually abandoned. Various ideas were discussed as to what to do with it before the decision was made to create a Museum of Transport and Communication. Renovation works were carried out under the leadership of the local architect Eduardo Souto de Moura, but it was soon clear that the best use of the building was as an international congress centre and this has been the case since the start of the twenty-first century.[3] Porto's links with the outside world have grown considerably during this period with international businesses keen to make use of the city to host their conferences and exhibitions.

It is almost impossible to head out to Foz without admiring the Ponte da Arrábida, the arched bridge across the River Douro. At the time of its opening in 1963, the bridge's concrete arch was the longest of its type in the world. At over six hundred metres long it is an impressive sight, today operating as a motorway bridge linking the south and north of the region. The bridge was the first to be built in Porto using solely Portuguese firms for its design and construction. Although considered iconic, the bridge is a reflection of the architecture of the era of the *Estado Novo*. Amongst the thousands of books in Salazar's library there were only a couple on the subject of architecture: most probably gifts to him rather than volumes he had himself purchased.[4]

Salazar's lack of knowledge on the subject did not prevent him from intervening on architectural projects, most usually with negative comments. Central to Salazar's critique of architecture was the influence of foreign architects in Portugal in adding too many decorative motifs to buildings. He wanted a unified architecture style that would highlight an identification with the nationalist values of the *Estado Novo*. The style that emerged, devised by architects working for the state, was simplistic and traditional. Salazar's opposition to a modernist style was aimed at its long horizontal windows, which he believed to be better suited to countries with more shade than Portugal where the bright light entered into all parts of the house.[5] Portugal and Porto are full examples of bridges, housing, schools, universities and monuments. Today Porto's architecture is an eclectic mixture of the foreign-influenced designs previously mentioned in the book, the *Estado Novo*'s authoritarian style (thankfully less prevalent in Porto than in Lisbon) and the work of local architects, led by Álvaro Siza and Eduardo Souto de Moura.

Porto is naturally very proud of its two internationally renowned architects whose award-winning works in the city have helped regenerate it and have also earned it much publicity. The two men share an office complex and live close to one another. Despite early collaborations the architects are now two distinct brands, collecting awards and designing buildings in both the public and private sectors. Striking simplicity successfully mixing tradition and modernity defines their work which includes strong Portuguese elements of neutral and pastel colours with stand-out window features. Siza's work tends to create either white buildings or red brick ones. They have been described as being 'solid-looking, faceted or with curved profiles and convex or concave facades'.[6] Critics often comment on the strong functionality of his buildings, but for Siza architecture is primarily about creating beauty. As he put it:

Of course, I am interested in beauty. Beauty is the peak of functionality! If something is beautiful, it is functional. I don't separate beauty and functionality. Beauty is the key functionality for architects... I wonder how I could say that beauty was not of interest to me... But a search for beauty should be the number one preoccupation of any architect.[7]

Souto de Moura's buildings attract slightly different praise. The 2011 Pritzker Prize jury wrote:

> His buildings have a unique ability to convey seemingly conflicting characteristics — power and modesty, bravado and subtlety, bold public authority and sense of intimacy — at the same time.[8]

The younger of the two architect friends, Moura has been employed in several major projects in his hometown of Porto, in addition to the renovation of the Alfândega building. Perhaps the most important project was his role in the creation of the Metro do Porto for which he was the head architect and designed several of the stations, including the elegantly futuristic Casa da Música and the central station, Trinidade.

Such has been his influence over local architecture that maps have been produced listing all of his buildings and projects in the city. His creative process is different to Siza's, who was once known to casually sketch out his projects while drinking coffee in local cafés. For Souto de Moura the process is slightly more self-conscious and involves a fair degree of trial and error.

> Architecture is all about copying. We copy the things that we see. But when this copying process happens consciously it is a disaster. It should be subconscious, almost unintentional. Let's say I have a library of images in my head. When I am working, these images come up. This is unconscious. I look beyond solution; I look for an expression. I also collect phrases. For example, I like Freud's, 'From error to error one discovers the entire truth'. Another one is by Beckett, 'Ever tried. Ever failed. No matter. Try again. Fail again. Fail better'. So the intention is always the same—to try to find something special and personal.[9]

Like many architects they share a strong passion for their work and frustration at the bureaucracy that often stands in the way of the realisation of their plans. They are both acutely aware of the links between architecture and politics and the continued battles and debates involving the two. Since 1974 Porto has become the central location for architectural talent in Portugal with the University of Porto producing a number of leading architects who have helped to shape the building culture of Portugal and beyond.

The route from the Ponte da Arrábida towards Foz is one of the most scenic in northern Portugal, often made all the more interesting by a beautiful light that changes with the time of day and the seasons. It is sometimes possible to witness four seasons in one day: from morning mist to bright sunlight, rolling rainclouds and windy storms that roll in from the Atlantic Ocean and up the river at lightning-speed. The electrical storm that was mistaken for the start of the French invasion of the city during the Peninsular War in reality is a frequent occurrence in Spring and Autumn. No two trips along the river road to Foz are the same, the light show produces new surprises with the River Douro sparkling against a backdrop of changing skies.

At the end of the river, we find one of the prettiest buildings along the coastline, Farol de São Miguel-o-Anjo, said to be Portugal's oldest existing lighthouse. It was designed by the Italian architect Francesco da Cremona and was finished in 1538. Ten years earlier the Bishop of Viseu had ordered the construction of the Chapel São Miguel-o-Anjo, which would also be used as a lighthouse to help shipping out at sea. Later, in the eighteenth century, the chapel started to be used as a meeting point for pilots helping shipping dock in the area. The lighthouse was eventually decommissioned in the late nineteenth century. The buildings have undergone extensive renovations works which have restored them to their former glory and the surrounding area makes for an attractive place to sit and watch the River Douro run into the Atlantic Ocean.

When the visitor arrives at the mouth of the river, they are naturally drawn to Farolim de Felgueiras, the lighthouse at the end of a long jetty that struts out into the Atlantic Ocean. Built in the late nineteenth century, the lighthouse is no longer operational. The jetty, however, offers one of the best locations to photograph the Atlantic waves breaking and heading towards land. During winter the jetty is often closed to the public as the large waves break over it in spectacular fashion. They provide a stark reminder of power and the historic difficulties of trying to enter the river from the ocean.

In recent years, Foz has become a much sought-after destination for international visitors attracted by its sandy beaches, promenades, and ocean-view properties. It has become the most cosmopolitan district in the Porto region, somewhere Brazilian, French, British, South African, and Chinese voices can be heard in addition to the local Portuguese accents. It has a reputation of being the Estoril of the north: the land of the gentry and the wealthy, who enjoy its fresh Atlantic breezes and breathe in its clean air. Tour guides from the nineteenth century had already marked out the area as worthy of a visit:

There are a great many new and comfortable houses, assembly rooms, a club-house and billiard tables. The bathing here is pretty good. There are patches of fine sand between the rocks, on which are pitched a number of tents intended for dressing rooms for the bathers. Ladies issue forth in a kind of Turkish trousers and very short dress; gentlemen wear the same trousers, and scanty coats, and caps long and hanging down. The ladies are attended by bathing-men, and the gentlemen by bathing-women; and with the crowds of spectators, seated on chairs for their accommodation, the bright dresses of the bathers, the laughing and talking, it is a very pretty, though to an Englishman rather an extraordinary scene. The English ladies generally bathe at some distance from the rest.[10]

In bygone times, as we have recounted, Foz do Douro was the first port of call for foreigners landing in northern Portugal. It was a generally unsatisfactory point for landing ships due to dangers involved. The long history of the loss of ships and the cost to human life reflects the perilous nature of the arrival into Porto. One such tragedy attracted world attention:

Close to Foz is the frightful Bar of the Douro, on which so many lives have been lost. The latest and one of the most terrible accident happened on 29 March 1852. The Porto steamer, on her voyage to Lisbon was obliged to put back; she crossed the bar in safety, but struck on a sunken rock, unshipped her rudder, became unmanageable, drifted onto the rocks, and was there knocked to pieces. Sixty persons perished within a stone throw of the castle, and within hearing of the crowds who were utterly unable to render any assistance.[11]

It is not an area of industry, except for the local fishermen who day after day courageously navigate their small boats through the treacherous tides and waters at the mouth of the River Douro. Their catches are sold at the little restaurants on the narrow, cobbled streets overlooking the end of the river, often frequented by the locals. The larger fishing industry takes place further north in the port of Matosinhos, where streets full of seafood restaurants attract Portuguese and foreigners alike, most notably at the weekend. The Atlantic Ocean-facing port is now physically linked to Foz by apartment blocks that line its ocean front.

At the point where Foz starts to run into Matosinhos and at the start of the Avenida da Boavita sits the imposing Forte de Saõ Francisco Xavier, better known by locals as Castelo do Queijo (The Cheese Castle) due to its shape. Once inside the main apartment of the building we can see a document hanging on the wall that explains that the fortress was named after Francisco Xavier, the Catholic missionary that carried out much of his work in Portuguese India and Japan. 'He won so many souls for the Church and so many leagues for Portugal'.[12] The concept of the mixture of missionary aims and territorial conquest was at the very heart of the Portuguese empire. Spreading the word of God was seen as an essential part of the rationale for sailing across uncharted oceans to discover new worlds.[13] This dualism of intent was not unique to the Portuguese, and the religious elements of the empire are strongly recognised. They do not, however, fully explain the reasons for sending ships out of Porto and Lisbon to battle the waves and the storms in order to discover the new world. In a small country like Portugal, not sufficiently furnished with valuable resources, the only way to get rich was through trade and conquest. Portugal did both and the missionary element, although important, was not the driving force behind the creation of the country's global empire.

Castelo do Queijo does not only serve as a monument to Portugal's missionary past, it is a reminder of the importance of the Atlantic coastline, and the historical need to defend it against foreign invaders, sometimes including Portugal's Iberian cousins. This was particularly true during the Restoration Wars, when it had been rebuilt at great expense. The fort also served as a flashpoint in the War of the Brothers. During the war the Miguelites held the fort, which was frequently shelled by the forces loyal to Dom Pedro. By the end of the war there was not much of it left. It was partly rebuilt once again and today has become an attraction for locals and tourists to stroll around and from which to admire vistas of the ocean.

In the wider Porto coastal region there are additional reminders of the importance of the defences against invaders. One factor that favoured the Portuguese in any attack on their lands along the Porto coastline was the difficulties any invading navies encountered in trying to land men along the rocky coastline. The ocean around Castelo do Queijo is a case in point where the rocks and waves made it extremely difficult to land even in the calmest of weather.

Coming away from the fort, it is worth heading through Matosinhos towards Leça da Palmeira, an old fishing port, home today to the port of Leixões and a rather large and ugly oil refinery. The port was said to have been so badly constructed that it was continually breached by the ocean. Attempts to repair it were described in a somewhat critical tone by the travel writer Eugène E. Street:

Steam cranes whistle and groan all day long, and huge blocks of cement or of stone are swung around, lifted, lowered and shifted about. Labourers shout, swear, smoke cigarettes, and heave at chains and ropes, or press down levers, or pick away in a desultory manner with pickaxes and crows, the little engine on the little tram line that brings the materials, whistles, shrieks and puffs with enormous importance. All seems really bustle and hurry, but when the end of the day's work has come, and the gangs are called off, and cluster on the little engine and on the little trucks like a swarm of bees, a careful examination reveals that no substantial progress has been made towards keeping out the encroaching sea: preparations have only been made for the work it is intended to carry out *amanhã*.[14]

The deep-water port was eventually completed and, as previously mentioned, today serves as the prime maritime link between the Porto region and other cities. This gateway to the world continues to see Portuguese goods exported in large container ships and the importation of a range of goods from cars to foodstuffs. The sounds of the sirens as the cranes load and unload ships, and the seemingly never-ending lines of lorries waiting to collect or hand over their metal containers are testament to the importance of this very busy port.

In recent years, there has been another maritime invasion of the Porto region: by huge cruise ships that gently make their way into the futuristic Leixões Terminal. The snail-shaped building is located around 700 metres from the shoreline and was designed by the local architect Luís Pedro Silva who worked on the project for a decade.[15] The building is spectacular to look at from one of the beaches in the Matosinhos area, from where it looks like it belongs to a different era set well into the future. From inside the visitor is struck by the attention to detail with the use of one million tiles to create a unique texture and atmosphere. The building is smaller than many other terminals, a perspective that is only noticeable when a giant cruise ship is moored next to it.

From faraway the building is read...by the wavy white with fanciful nuances regarding light and atmosphere variation. Closely the arches and its texture appeal to proximity, involve movements and the body, inviting the look and the touch. At the accessible cover, the land and the ocean meet and distend the soft broadness that the calm eye can reach.[16]

263

As Porto connects with the outside world, the Leixões Terminal is a crucial addition to the city's, and the region's, infrastructure. The number of people visiting the city from cruise ships has multiplied in recent years, providing new opportunities and new challenges. Arrival in Porto by boat has come a long way since the days of disembarking at Foz in heavy seas. The terminal building makes it easy for passengers to transfer directly from ships and onto buses to head into the city.

To finish the morning, we head back into the heart of Matosinhos. The Leixões Terminal belongs to the present and the future while the old fishing port with its street of restaurants selling the freshest catches, illustrates the continued importance of this most ancient of professions. Rua Heróis de França, offers some of the best fish restaurants. The visitor can walk along, window shopping to make a choice from ten or more establishments ranging from the ultra-modern to the more traditional places to enjoy lunch. There is nothing fake about the street, no beautiful vistas to distract, rather only high-quality seafood, cooked by experts and simply presented. A reminder of everything that is good about Portuguese cuisine.

There is a timeless quality to the area, a sense of quiet contentment that for all the changes that have taken place in Matosinhos during the first decades of the twenty-first century that its core values and historical relevance remain somehow intact. For the weary visitor, out of the comfort zone of central Porto, it is a worthwhile reminder of an authentic connection that lies between the city, the river, and the ocean. Few places in the world offer such opportunities to indulge the senses and to look both back in history and forward at the same time. It is where tradition meets modernity, and where national values and traditions stand side by side with projects like the Leixões Terminal that aim to further internationalise the city.

PART EIGHT

DAY FOUR – AFTERNOON

23

The Longest Avenue

Casa da Música was a great venue to play aside – from how beautiful it is – the main thing for us is how does it sound. Most of the places we play, especially when they are involved in other forms of culture are usually set up for an orchestra, they are not set up for electric instruments. This particular place they put a lot of effort to try to incorporate contemporary music into a contemporary cultural hall... They obviously put a lot of work into trying to make the sound work for an electric instrument and drums. I would say they succeeded. It was terrific to be able to play your instrument, tune your instrument, and hear it as it's supposed to sound.[1]

Lou Reed

A N IDEAL STARTING POINT for the afternoon is to head back to Castelo do Queijo. The most scenic route is to simply follow the coastline and walk along the promenade of Matosinhos beach, whose wide golden sands and high waves are said to make it arguably the best surfers' beach in the area. In summertime it is one of the most popular in Porto, both with local sunbathers and out of towners. Once at Castelo do Queijo, we enter the start of Avenida da Boavista. The five-and-a-half-kilometre road remains one of the most important streets in Porto and has been the subject of much debate as to how to maximise its use and beauty. When originally completed in 1917 it resembled more of a genuine avenue with two rows of trees planted down the middle providing it with an elegant and slightly 'south-of-France' feel. Given the high population density in Porto, along with the desire of many to travel in motor cars and public transport from the city to the coast, the trees were eventually sacrificed in favour of creating extra space for cars and buses.

Avenida da Boavista contains a snapshot of all aspects of Porto's history, economic, and cultural life. The first area of interest is Parque da Cidade, located at the start of the Avenida. The park's statistics are impressive; occupying eighty hectares it is said to be the largest urban park in the country. The clever design of the terrain, the lakes, and the subtle coverage around its edges makes it feel like a retreat. Despite being located in a densely populated area it is difficult to hear the noises of the city. At weekends, the park is full of locals jogging or walking along its ten kilometres of paths.

Historically, the park reflects an attempt to break out of the systemic overcrowding of large parts of the city centre, which has characterised Porto since the nineteenth century. The population density has been an issue in Porto since its birth as an elegant industrial city. The geographic size of the city, and the restraints on its expansion imposed by the river and the ocean meant that the city centre has been traditionally overcrowded. This changed at the end of the twentieth century and the start of the twenty-first when there was a population shift from the centre to the suburbs. The prime reason for this was a lack of investment in buildings and infrastructure in the centre. Companies moved out of town, shopping malls started to replace traditional shopping streets, and the void was for many years not satisfactorily filled. The return to the centre has been spectacular, utilising both Portuguese and foreign investment. The restoration of the area's housing and a new transport infrastructure centred around the development of a metro system, have both contributed to a rebirth of the city centre as one of the most desirable areas in which to live.

We continue up the Avenida until the distinctive Edifício Vodafone, frequently described as an architectural icon. The building, designed by José António Barbosa and Pedro Guimarães, was chosen as one of the top twenty most creative offices in the world.[2] Its jagged edges give the impression that it has been dropped from an enormous height and smashed onto the ground. It looks at its best when lit up at sunset or in the early evening.

The office block represents the new dynamic Porto, the home of the business sector in Portugal. Its design and construction making a statement that the Avenida da Boavista is flourishing, and a centre for international companies to invest. Sometimes in architecture the spin and the publicity generated from the construction of super-buildings such as this one can outweigh their practical use. Not in this case. The eight floors are all extremely user-friendly with open-plan office space occupying the top levels. The building's opening on 29 October 2009 coincided with the start of the biggest economic crisis in Portugal since the 1930s. Investment in additional super-buildings dried up as a result leaving the Edifício Vodafone to dominate the middle section of the Avenida, sitting next to less glamorous housing and office projects.

Heading up the Avenida, the visitor takes a brief detour down Avenida do Marechal Gomes da Costa. The road is named after Manuel Gomes da Costa who commanded the Second Division of the Portuguese Expeditionary troops in France during World War I, as mentioned earlier. His division suffered heavy casualties in the notorious Battle of Lys in April 1918, but he remained one of the most internationally visible of the Portuguese military commanders during the war. Following the overthrow of the First Republic and its replacement by the dictatorship in 1926, Gomes da Costa was selected to be the second president of the era of the dictatorship. A conservative monarchist, he never fully fitted into the politics of the dictatorship and he was soon overthrown during that period of great instability. The avenue was named after him in 1930 and reflected his military record in France rather than his political achievements.

Near the top of this avenue we find the Serralves Museum which pays homage to local artistic talent and acts as a window for international names from around the world. The museum building was designed by Álvaro Siza, and its permanent collection and temporary exhibitions attract large numbers of visitors each year.

The art scene in Porto and the rest of Portugal really only took off after the 25 April Revolution in 1974, which removed censorship and provided artistic licence to a new generation of artists, sculptors, filmmakers, and photographers. Many of these artists, along with the younger post-Revolution generations, have gone on to attract world-wide attention and acclaim. The Serralves has helped establish Porto as a major player in the Portuguese, European, and world art scenes. The arts have reflected the tensions between a distinctive Portuguese identity steeped in history versus the more Eurocentric leanings of the more recent generations of artists. On additional levels, there remain questions as to whether there is a clearly defined Porto regional arts identity, distinctive to say the city's great rival Lisbon, or whether there is merely a national movement in culture, or indeed simply a European one.

In all probability, the most important decision taken in post-1974 Revolution Portugal was made in 1977 when they applied to join what was then known as the European Economic Community (EEC). At the time the Prime Minister Mário Soares explained the reasons for applying to join in a private conversation with the British Ambassador to Portugal.

Portugal has lost her African colonies and after two years of [internal political] turmoil, has by the skin of her teeth avoided a takeover by totalitarian Communists. She has made great strides in establishing a democratic structure. But now she faces formidable economic difficulties, which will demand privations and sacrifices from her people. These will only be accepted if the country is engaged in a great enterprise. This must be her integration into Western Europe, which can only be achieved through full membership of the EEC.[3]

Portugal's application for membership was not met with unanimous support from within the member states of the 'Rich Club' as the British dubbed the EEC, or indeed from inside Portugal. The biggest opposition in Europe came from the French, fearful of the potentially negative economic consequences of allowing such a poor country to join, along with similar reservations about Greece and post-fascist Spain who had also applied for membership.[4] Britain was more sympathetic towards the Portuguese application, especially after Margaret Thatcher assumed office in 1979. She felt that the best remedy for reducing the influence of Germany and France in the EEC institution was to expand the community to include countries such as Portugal.

Inside Portugal, there was strong support for the application to the EEC from the business sector, including the numerous enterprises in the Porto region, and at a generational level among young urbanities. Although in favour of joining, there were fears expressed that it would lead to Spain flooding the market with Spanish goods, especially fruit and vegetables, and taking over and buying Portuguese businesses such as banks. Some older more conservative elements were less supportive, along with the supporters of the Communists (mainly in the Alentejo region of the country). While the Communists were against joining what they viewed as a 'Capitalist Club', the older conservatives feared a loss of national identity and culture to a new more Eurocentric one. This group often recollected glorious episodes of Portugal's past, highlighting the era of the empire when Portuguese culture was a global export and its economy was bolstered by the riches from its empire. For these, the nostalgia for the 'good old days' outweighed the uncertainties of being swallowed up by the European powers. The trauma of losing the empire in such dramatic circumstances following the Revolution and the resulting immediate decolonisation of what Salazar termed as 'Portugal's overseas territories' was too much for some.

Mário Soares, however, was right; without its colonies, Portugal could not survive as a small independent state without joining the 'Rich Club' of Europe which would provide the country with an opportunity to advance economically and modernise its backward infrastructure. At the time of Portugal's application for EEC membership there was not even a motorway linking Porto with the capital city. Instead, for much of the journey, cars and lorries were forced to navigate an overcrowded and dangerous single-lane national road, making the average journey time between the two cities around the five-hour mark. Porto's links to Spain and with it the rest of Europe were just as primitive. Narrow winding roads that snaked up and over the mountain passes were slow and difficult to navigate, and only once in Spain with its flat and open plains did the journey get easier.

Portugal, along with Spain, eventually joined the EEC in January 1986. For all the debates about the plusses and minuses of membership, Portugal's infrastructure did receive a much-needed cash injection in order to modernise.[5] Porto's hugely impressive motorway system, which locals claim to be much better and more functional than Lisbon's, owes much to money from European structural funds.[6] It is now possible to drive from Porto to Lisbon in three hours, to get to the once remote Alto-Douro wine region in just over an hour, and drive to the historic cities of Braga and Guimarães in approximately one hour. The motorways are comparatively quiet and well-maintained; critics point out that this is because users have to pay some of the most expensive tolls in Europe to use them.

Two issues clouded the initial years of membership. The first was that the man on the street – and on the farm – remained bemused and sceptical of membership.[7] The country's leaders needed to show that there were immediate financial benefits to joining the 'Rich Club' in order to compensate for a feeling of a loss of national sovereignty and identity. On this score Portuguese leaders and bureaucrats were able to demonstrate right from the start that the balance of transfers were heavily in Portugal's favour. It was not all easy pickings; one European Commissioner described the first Portuguese delegation in Brussels as 'a sardine among the sharks'.[8]

The second issue centred upon Spain. There was a prevalent feeling that the old Iberian rival had been able to secure better joining terms than Portugal. This was said to be most obvious in the fishing sector where Spanish fishing quotas were better than Portuguese ones. In towns such as Matosinhos there was much bad feeling about the outcome of the negotiations on this historically important sector of the Portuguese economy.

During the initial years of membership there was a feeling among the Portuguese, largely confirmed by statistics, that they were not seeing the same level of benefits as Spain, Greece, and Ireland. This was partly explained by the British who noted that 'refreshingly, it is not the Portuguese style to rattle the begging bowl too loudly'.[9] In the long run, despite the rivalries over the division of European funds among member states, most Portuguese regard the membership of the European project as having been a great success economically. From time to time, Portugal feels slightly isolated in the community or as one official described, 'bullied by the French, swamped by the Spanish and unloved by the British, except when we want something'.[10] The country, however, was extremely proud to meet the fiscal criteria to be able to join the euro currency in the first round of its launch, culminating in the shift from escudos to euro notes and coins on 1 January 2002.

The attachment to the European project from the Porto region has been very strong. As the main location of Portuguese business, it has benefitted not only in terms of improved infrastructure, but also with the award of direct grants to companies and enterprises in the city. European funds have been at the centre of the programme of urban renewal and renovation that has helped to transform the city centre of Porto back to its original glory. On top of this, investments by individual foreigners have helped create the conditions for the restoration of houses in important streets such as Avenida da Boavista and Avenida do Marechal Gomes da Costa. The transformation of Porto into an exciting and attractive city for foreigners to not only invest, but to live in and to develop new businesses has been most impressive. The downside of the continued lack of affordable housing for locals wishing to live in the city centre (or its most desirable suburbs), has been a problem, as it is in many other successful European cities.

In addition to reflecting the tensions between national and European art and culture, the Serralves Museum highlights Porto's and Portugal's connection with the its ex-colonies. Artists from Brazil, Angola, and beyond are well-represented in the cycle of temporary exhibitions. On a deeper level, the loss of empire after the 1974 Revolution created challenges and debates over narratives surrounding Portugal's policies and actions in these countries. As we have recounted, Brazil became an independent nation long before 1974, but the continued focus in the arts and Portuguese literature on especially Portugal's African empire reflects continued dialogues and debates about achieving a better understanding of the history of the empire.

Rivalries between Porto and Lisbon also surface in the art world. Both cities are well represented by major galleries and host a good range of exhibitions. Competition in the art world is just the tip of the iceberg in the rivalry between the two. This is not a new development. Eça de Queiroz wrote in 1872 about the two cities:

> ...There is an incurable rivalry – in all things moral, social, elegant, commercial, comestible and political – between Lisbon and Porto. Lisbon envies Oporto's wealth, its trade, its fine modern streets, the comfort of its houses, the solidity of its fortunes, the seriousness of its well-being. Porto envies Lisbon because of the Court, the King, the Chambers, São Carlos and Martinho. They detest each other. Do the ladies of Lisbon laugh at the toilettes of Porto as lacking in refinement, skill, and *je ne sais quoi?* Porto red faced covers its ladies in the most sumptuous fabrics and sparkling diamonds.[11]

He goes on to write about the merits of Foz (along the Porto coast) versus Cascais (along the Lisbon coast) and the never-ending desire of each city to try to outdo the other in anything from the hosting of bullfights to poetry. In truth, not much has changed since Eça de Queiroz wrote these words. The two cities are constantly trying to better the other, often without realising what they are trying to achieve. The art world is no different, with deep rivalries over attracting international exhibitions and fierce competition over the housing of the wonderfully eclectic elements of the state-owned collections. Porto however continues to do very well in bringing in world-class exhibitions that have helped put the city firmly in the first division of the international art circuit. Several of Porto's, and the region's, own artists continue to develop global reputations maintaining the tradition of the city producing world-class art. The dialogue between local, national, and international culture remains at the very heart of Porto's efforts to host exhibitions that link the past and the present and offer insight, creativity, and direction for the future.

One of the most enjoyable parts of a visit to the Serralves remains its gardens, which provide a peaceful setting in which to contemplate the exhibits and collections just visited. There has been an important addition to the Serralves which provides a homage to a famous son of Porto, the filmmaker Manoel de Oliveira. The Álvaro Siza-designed building was inaugurated on 24 June 2019 and provides a permanent exhibition space that highlights the work and the long career of the filmmaker. There is also an area for temporary exhibits related to film and conference facilities. It is a worthy tribute to Manoel de Oliviera's work, which started in the era of the *Estado Novo* and continued in democratic Portugal until his death on 2 April 2015.

Oliveira's career included the making of dozens of feature films, shorts, and documentaries. One of his finest moments came at the start of his career with his first feature film entitled *Aniki-Bóbó*, made in the middle of World War II in 1942. The story is essentially a story of childhood love and the lives of children in Porto amidst the rigidity of the *Estado Novo*. Beautifully shot with the *Estado Novo* represented by a repressive schoolteacher and a policeman, it was a striking statement from the young director against Salazar. The film also represented the tension between social classes in Portugal and their confrontation with one each other during a period of Portuguese history in which a small highly centralised political, economic, and social elite dominated the country. In some ways, it is still surprising that the film was allowed to be screened given the strong control the censors of the *Estado Novo* exerted over cultural projects. A careful analysis of the film on a superficial level, however, indicates how the Porto filmmaker was able to get the film under the radar of the censors. Alves Costa reminds us:

...In the 1930s and 1940s the country's cinema functioned perfectly well within the regime's political objectives, mirroring the image and manners that it wants us to believe are those of the good Portuguese people – poor but joyful, sentimental and seductive, with eight centuries of history and an empire (to be respected), conformist and happy with their simplicity, their daily ration of bread, bullfights, fado and the sun shining.[12]

The brilliance of Oliveira was his ability to portray these values in the film, while at the same time introducing elements of a narrative critical towards the regime. Put simply, he made a film to pass the censors that was, in reality, making a bold statement against the *Estado Novo*.[13] The film had its premiere in the splendid Eden Cinema in Lisbon on 18 December 1942. It still remains a favourite of many Portuguese and is often shown on local television channels. Oliveira would go onto make better, more complex, films later in his career, but this portrayal of childhood in Porto, set during one of the most challenging periods in Portuguese history, remains charming, engaging, and a worthy tribute to the city of his birth.

From the picturesque gardens of the Serralves we once more join Avenida da Boavista and continue to head towards the Rotunda da Boavista that marks the end of the road. In the distance, we can see the impressive statue that towers over the rotunda. Passing through a seemingly never-ending series of traffic lights that guard the countless junctions on and off the Avenida, and passing the international hotel and designer stores, we reach Casa da Música, one of the most iconic and important buildings in Porto. Even in this city full of architectural treats, Casa da Música stands out like a shining beacon in the middle of the desert.

Not dissimilar to other major projects of this scale in Portugal there is quite a story behind the creation of this wonderful concert hall. Originally planned in 1998 as part of the celebrations to mark Porto being chosen as one of the European Cities of Culture for 2001, the design, planning, and construction phases of the project became steeped in a giant bureaucratic quagmire. The 'best of the best' in the architectural world were originally sought out by the search committee to design the building.[14] What everybody wanted to avoid was the creation of another shoe-box concert hall. There was initial controversy over whether a local architect should be chosen over an international star such as Norman Foster or Rem Koolhaas. In the end, the prize went to the Dutchman Koolhaas, whose proposal was as far away from the shoe box formula as could be imagined. Phrases used to justify the award included, 'universal adaption of internal and external spaces', 'use of easy-to-maintain materials', but most of all 'uniqueness'.[15]

At the time of the building's conception, there was a feeling in Porto that it needed to undertake a major project; one which would provide the city with a showstopping attraction. Lisbon had recently held the massively ambitious Expo 1998, a fair that had helped transform the infrastructure of the capital city as well as providing it with new venues after the Expo closed. Porto needed to be seen to be keeping up with its rival three hundred kilometres to the south. Despite the pressing need for the project to be completed, management committees came and went (five in total), problems with contractors and a change of government added to the chaos in decision-making.[16] As a result, the building did not open to the public until the spring of 2005 when the American singer Lou Reed gave one of the opening performances.

In truth, Casa da Música was worth the wait. *The Guardian* was among the long list of foreign newspapers that offered glowing praise:

> The Casa da Música is a remarkably compact, angular, white concrete mushroom that explodes every preconception of what a concert hall should be, and how it should look. It faces a big civil space, surrounded on three sides by a mix of buildings, ranging from the banal to the ramshackle and the stately... Koolhaas may

like to claim that he does not want to invent more that he has to. But the Casa da Música is nevertheless a ruthlessly inventive building. It is the only concert hall in the world with two walls made entirely of glass.[17]

The corrugated glass facades are located at each end of the major auditorium, which seats 1,300 concertgoers, and opens the hall to the wonderful soft Atlantic light of Porto as a beautiful backdrop for the music.[18] The choice of Rotunda as the location was an interesting one for such an ambitious project as much of the area is still in need of rejuvenation. Years after it opened, there is still a strange mixture of old or derelict buildings that surround Porto's architectural and musical calling-card to the world. Casa da Música remains a slightly eerie, but beautifully engaging, oasis in an area that still very much retains its working-class roots.

The building's reputation has been further enhanced by its use as a location for fashion shoots. The most famous was for Vogue, shot by the Peruvian photographer Mario Testino using the model Gigi Hadid and the actor Domhnall Gleeson. The famous shoot was not restricted to the Casa da Música. Other buildings and locations that we have visited in this book also hosted the Vogue shoot: the Yeatman Hotel produced the famous 'Angel Face' photograph of Hadid wearing the Iconic British brand Burberry, the Serralves hosted 'A Moment in the Sun', a shot of the two models kissing, 'Take me to the Church' was shot in the cloisters of Sé do Porto, 'Heartstrings' in Praça da Ribeiro and 'Black Magic' in front of the Igreja do Carmo.[19] Perhaps, the most beautiful photograph is 'Bringing Back the Bling' taken in the splendour of the blue, green, and white-tiled Renaissance Room at Casa da Música.[20]

Casa da Música has proven to be good for Porto, placing it firmly on the international map just as the Frank Gehry-designed Guggenheim building did for Bilbao. It was a bold and brave statement for a city to make at a time when its process of rejuvenation was just starting. Such has been its influence that it is difficult to imagine a time when it was not dominating the skyline at Rotunda. The introduction of a strong music programme for the building, ranging from classical to jazz, has meant that its relatively modest-sized concert hall is usually filled.

Across the road from Casa da Música, in the middle of Boavista Rotunda we find a tall monument that competes with it to dominate the area. The forty-five-metre high column, entitled the Heroes of the Peninsular War, commemorates the victory over the French forces that invaded Portugal. At the top of the column is a lion, symbolising the Portuguese victory, bringing down the French imperial eagle, marking its defeat in Portugal. Despite the heavy traffic, it is possible to sit in the gardens of Rotunda in relative quietness and contemplate the events that led to the last time that Porto was invaded by a foreign army. The battles that took place during the Peninsular War were among some of the bloodiest witnessed in the city. Sitting by the monument it is difficult not to imagine the terror and fear of the fighting that led to the fall of the city. From the false start caused by the huge thunderstorm that struck in the middle of the night, the ringing of the church bells, and the sounds of the French Infantry sharpening their bayonets, to the intense push into the city past the defensive lines onwards to the riverside. The monument, and the recollections of the Peninsular War, serves as the perfect point to conclude our historical tour of the city.

24

Conclusions: Taking Stock

A great city, whose image dwells in the memory of man,
is the type of some great idea. Rome represents conquest;
Faith hovers over the towers of Jerusalem; and Athens
embodies the pre-eminent quality of the antique world,
Art. In modern ages, Commerce has created London;
while Manners, in the most comprehensive sense of the
word, have long found a supreme capital in the airy and
bright-minded city of the Seine.[1]

Benjamin Disraeli

HOW BEST TO REMEMBER Porto? Clearly, trade created
Porto and made it the pre-eminent city of Portugal in this
area. As its commercial potential developed, so the city
became a magnet for foreigners and their ambitions to cultivate ties
between the city and the outside world. Local and foreign merchants
developed global networks during the era of the Portuguese empire
and in recent centuries the Porto wine trade has come to identify
the city in the minds of most people. Walk into any decent bar in the
world and the chances are somewhere on one of their shelves they
will have at least one bottle of Port wine. The strong connection in
identity between the wine and the city means that Porto is known
the world over, even by people who have never visited it. Of course,
this does not tell the whole story.

Porto, and its surrounding region, has throughout the ages
proven to be an extremely important strategic point for foreign

nations and their armies. From its humble beginnings with its location next to the River Douro and close to the Atlantic Ocean, Porto has offered advantages of climate, food, water, and minerals that rewarded and maintained its first settlers and helped expand their communities into larger more sustainable societies. In the Iberian continent, much of which has been characterised by poor quality of soil and land, the Porto region has been a haven for the growing of food, fishing and the development of larger farming projects.

Over the centuries the growth of the settlement and subsequently the city has been stunted by wars ancient and modern. The most striking characteristic of the city and its people through the ages has been resilience; an ability to survive setbacks such as wars or disease and to re-emerge somehow stronger and more determined to rebuild the city. This was most certainly the case in the years following the French invasions and after the bloody and divisive War of the Brothers. The Siege of Porto illustrated the inhabitants of the city's ability to resist even when surrounded by hostile forces. It also revealed important cleavages in society between absolutists and liberals that tell us much about the development of Portuguese society.

Porto's success has largely stemmed from its engagement with the outside world. The Golden Age of the Portuguese Empire, with the arrival of the gold from Brazil, helped transform the city. It was, however, the city's ties with British merchants and the development of the Port wine trade that offered the greatest potential for advancement. The imposition of taxes by Pombal on these traders helped to fund the dramatic improvements in infrastructure in the city during the eighteenth century. It was not always good news, however; the much-hated Methuen Treaty clearly damaged the Portuguese economy, although not as much as claimed by some local historians. Relations between the ancient allies of Portugal and Britain have often been complicated with Britain pursuing a policy of national self-interest, damaging Portuguese interests. The effective British rule over Portugal following the Peninsular War was a case in point.

What is perhaps most striking about Porto in recent centuries has been its political and economic divergence from Lisbon. In ancient times, Porto gave its name to Portugal, but the emergence of Lisbon as the capital city, the seat of the Crown, the Courts, and the government meant the city needed to find a role for itself. The development of industry and commerce has been so impressive that Porto and its region is firmly installed as the economic powerhouse of Portugal. Over the centuries, the city's politics have been shaped by different events, elites, and processes to those in Lisbon, or indeed in the rest of Portugal. In many respects, Porto has been at the forefront of the political changes that have shaped Portugal from ancient to modern times. On occasion, the city has suffered from this position; it is no coincidence that the War of the Brothers was fought in the Porto region.

Today, the rivalry with Lisbon is largely played out on the football field with the city proud of its home team FC Porto. The competition reaches fever pitch twice a year when the team plays Benfica, the most successful side from Lisbon. Victory over the Reds is a source of great local pride: defeat is a disaster. Either way the games are talked about and analysed in bars across the city for days afterwards. FC Porto have also enjoyed success in European competitions, introducing the city to new audiences in the process. With the exception of Port wine, the football club has become the most recognisable brand related to the city. Difficult moments in the city's recent history have been made all the easier to take if the local team is doing well in Portuguese and European competitions.

Kofi Annan, Margaret Thatcher, and countless other leaders and smart thinkers have heralded and toasted the success of the city of Porto. Its recent rehabilitation and reinvention as a major centre for tourism has helped secure its position as a successful city. There is more to Porto however than pretty monuments, beautiful parks, riverbank walks, and beach holidays. The city is now very much a European one, making the most of its opportunities to conduct trade and commerce with its global partners. The future looks very bright for Porto as it takes its place in the first division of international cities, diversifying and dealing with the environmental and infrastructure challenges that this new-found place at the top table brings.

For centuries, Porto has been the gateway to the world for Portugal. Its role in the discovery of the new world, the establishment of the first global trading empire, and the resulting development of international trade in a wide range of commodities, minerals, and ores highlights this position. The internationalisation of the city is physically present for all to see. The use of Italian, British, and most recently Dutch, architects to design key buildings and contribute to the urban planning of the city alongside their Portuguese counterparts has created an eclectic city centre full of architectural surprises. Not many places in Europe can offer such shifts in style that are present in a number of Porto's main streets. See for example, the changes on Rua do Infante Dom Henrique from the British Factory House and the Palácio da Bolsa to the Igreja de São Francisco. Porto contains brilliant examples of many different and contrasting styles of buildings, which somehow when joined together work to create a visually attractive palate of colour and shapes.

At the heart of the city lies the golden River Douro which has played such a prominent role in the history of the city. Difficult to enter from the ocean, the river has been the scene of many tragedies and triumphs. The collapse of the Bridge of Boats as local inhabitants tried to flee the advancing French army, with the resulting huge loss of life, represented one of the saddest disasters. It also provided a stark reminder of the power of the currents in the river as people were soon swept away and pulled under the surface. The brilliantly improvised military operation launched by the British to cross the river unseen by the French forces occupying the city was, in contrast, a triumph.

The American poet, Walt Whitman wrote, 'A great city is that which has the greatest man or woman'.[2] Porto has had plenty of great sons and daughters, arguably the most important being Infante Dom Henrique, whose vision, persistence, and desire to explore the unknown helped Portugal acquire one of the most important and lucrative trading empires in the history of the world. Today, all appears quiet along the riverbank as boats containing sightseers cruise up and down the river. After centuries of conflicts, uprisings, rebellions, revolutions, and upheavals, the city of Porto is at peace, not only with itself but with its role in Portugal, Europe, and in the wider world. The gateway to the world offers the city new horizons and challenges, which the resilient and down-to-earth people of Porto will no doubt rise to meet.

25

Afterword: Further Afield

A cold damp mist lay over the whole district, but as we left the lowlands and ran between the hills and woods, the sun came out and in the station by Coimbra it shone with southern warmth: a warmth that was clearly in the people too. Here was the bustle, noise and disorder of a thronged Neapolitan town...Coimbra rises up on the hillside, one street higher than the other. Many of the houses jut out, three or four stories above those below. The streets are narrow, twisting and forever mounting...There are lots of shops and bookstalls. Everywhere are students.[1]

Hans Christian Andersen

W ITH THE CONSTRUCTION OF the new network of motorways, tunnels, bridges, and flyovers that originated from Portugal's membership of the EEC (later known as the EC and EU) it is now possible to travel from Porto to a wealth of interesting places and return the same day. Cities, ancient villages, secluded beaches, and national parks offering beautiful scenic escapes are now much more accessible from Porto. Most of these locations can be reached in just over an hour from the city centre by motor car, or slightly longer if using public transport. The areas that lie to the south of Porto, northwards to the border with Spain, and east to the Douro are rich in Portuguese history. Much of this is linked to the same conquests, wars, and trade that we have covered in the book relating to the immediate Porto region. The visitor, as a result, would find it rewarding to devote a whole week to their travels: four days in Porto and three making day trips to explore the wider region.

The university city of Coimbra lies just over one hour's drive along the main Porto to Lisbon motorway. Upon arriving in the city, the visitor notes the Kafkian dominance of the university buildings, so carefully perched on top of the city's high ground. There are in truth, two Coimbras: the first is the university where many of the characters in this book were educated, often forming long-lasting cultural, political, or religious links with fellow students. The other Coimbra is the historic city that once served as the capital of Portugal. It is difficult to get away from history in Coimbra, from the joys of the magnificent Biblioteca Joanina (Joanina Library) to the timeless Santa Cruz café, where students still mingle with locals and tourists. It is said, that there are more doctors and lawyers in the city than anywhere else in Portugal. Despite worthy attempts to modernise the university, it is these two ancient disciplines that attract the greatest interest and require the highest academic scores to enter the near-sacred faculties. Many graduates simply find it too difficult to leave the city after they have completed their studies, choosing instead to make their careers there. The expansion and rebuilding of parts of the university during the *Estado Novo* era meant that it was left with the soulless, rather ugly, and imposing buildings that sit uncomfortably with the few older ones that are left.

For the visitor intrigued by the Peninsular Wars, a detour from Coimbra is worthwhile to visit the scene of one of the major battles in Portugal, at Bussaco in 1810. Standing on the elevated ground it is possible to imagine the assaults of the French as they tried to dislodge the British and Portuguese forces from their positions. The fighting marked the first time that the reconstituted Portuguese army had fought alongside its British allies. Today, it is a much calmer scene with a beautiful hotel, attractive gardens, and from the summit, far-reaching views towards the Atlantic coastline.

Two of the most historic Portuguese cities, Braga and Guimarães, lie to the north-east of Porto and are reachable by car along direct motorways in approximately an hour. There is also a fast train service that links the two cities with Porto and continues onto Lisbon. Visits to both cities present further opportunities to understand the history of Portugal. Braga is one of the spiritual homes of the Catholic Church in the country and was also important in medieval Christianity. The city is the capital of the beautiful Minho district, much of which remains rural and unspoilt by the industrialisation that damaged parts of the Portuguese countryside in the centre of the country.

During the era of the Roman rule of Lusitania, the city was known as Bracara Augusta. The city is full of historic sites including Roman ruins and a cathedral dating from the twelfth century. Braga was also an important location in the Peninsular War and its fall to French forces proved to be the prelude to the invasion and occupation of Porto. In more recent times, it was the place where General Gomes da Costa (we recently visited the Avenida in Porto named after the General) announced the proclamation of the military uprising against the First Republic on 28 May 1926. It was also from this city that the march on Lisbon by the rebel military unit began, which led to the overthrow of the parliamentary First Republic.[2] In recent years, the Braga-based University of the Minho has undergone a resurgence, expanding into new areas of scientific research that has led to major joint research projects from universities across the globe.

The city of Guimarães is of no less historical importance than that of Braga. Attractive and mysterious on misty mornings, the city is best known as the cradle of the nation with its origins predating both the nation and the monarchy. It was in Guimarães that the first *Cortes* were held that, in 1093 gave the rule of the country of Portugal to Count Henry, the father of Afonso Henriques – the first king of Portugal who was born in the city in around 1109. The main attraction in the city is the granite castle, with all its links to the early years of the history of Portugal. There are also many other monuments to see in the city, including historic churches and palaces both inside the city and in the surrounding countryside. The historic city centre remains one of the most charming areas to wander around, to browse in the shops and take lunch in one of the many restaurants around the central square.

To the east of Porto, we find the Douro and the winemaking area of the Alto-Douro. The most interesting town in the lower Douro to visit is the historically important and pleasingly picturesque, Amarante, which we mentioned at the start of the book. The town proved to be very important during the French invasions of Portugal during the Peninsular Wars. With the River Tâmega running through the town, the French forces, commanded by Marshal Soult fought a number of battles to try to secure control over Amarante as well as the strategically important area around it.

The fighting in the area was extremely brutal with the French burning a number of neighbouring villages. One of the largest confrontations in the town took place in April 1809. After the French forces had defeated the Portuguese army outside the town, the local army retreated back into the town across its bridge. The town and the bridge were held with the help of Colonel Patrick, a British officer, who commanded a battalion that was able to establish a presence in buildings around the bridge and offer resistance to the advancing French. Local commanders then were able to establish artillery positions that commanded the bridge. The next day battles were just as intense.

> Loison [a French commander] stormed the buildings at the bridge-head, but found that he could get no further forward. The town was his, but he could not debouch from it, as the bridge was palisaded, built up with a barricade of masonry and raked by Portuguese artillery. Marshal Soult now sent up to aid Loison still further reinforcements...Thus no less than 9,000 French troops, nearly half the army in Portugal, were concentrated in Amarante.[3]

Overall it took the French army twelve days to force their way through the defences. From 20 April to 2 May the Portuguese defenders had been able to occupy the attentions of some 9,000 out of the 21,000 men under Soult's command in Portugal. For the French commander, it was the first time that his men had lost the momentum since entering Portugal. The timing of events in Amarante proved crucial as on 22 April Sir Arthur Wellesley (Duke of Wellington) had landed in Portugal, along with a large contingent of English reinforcements. By the time Loison had finally taken the bridge at Amarante, the British forces with their Portuguese irregulars were already marching to Coimbra and Porto to engage Soult.[4] By distracting and holding off such a large French force at Amarante, the Portuguese had performed a great service to Wellesley and his men.

Today the town of Amarante is a most pleasant place to visit, particularly so in summertime when the addition of pontoon bridges makes it easy to cross the river at different points adding to the experience of being close to the river. The town centre also offers the Museu Municipal Amadeo de Souza-Cardoso, which is well worth a visit. Most of all, however, it is a pleasant place to stroll and walk by the river, perhaps thinking of the heroics of the Portuguese forces with their British support in holding the town against French forces who occupied much of the important strategic ground around the town.

In the past, Amarante served as one of the gateways to the wine producing areas of the Douro. Drivers would then have to navigate narrow, twisty roads that went up and over mountain ranges. Although the views were often spectacular it was a time-consuming drive and not really possible to reach areas such as the Alto-Douro and return the same day to Porto. The opening of the tunnel at Marão, not too far along the motorway from the junction for Amarante has changed all of this, now making it possible to reach the start of the Alto-Douro in an hour and a half from the city centre in Porto.

Other day trips from Porto are Pinhão, which we have already discussed, the historic town Peso da Régua which dates back to the Romans, and the pretty mountain-top village of Provesende which offers elevated views over the river and mountain ranges. The road from Peso da Régua to Pinhão has been described as one of the most scenic in Europe, hogging the bank of the River Douro, with Port wine lodges appearing on either side. Well-placed picnic spots are located by the side of the road, but there are excellent restaurants in the area, including the Michelin-starred chef Rui Paula's riverside restaurant, DOC.

For many, however, a day trip to one of the most beautiful and unspoilt parts of Europe is not sufficient. Longer stays are recommended for visitors to enjoy the many Port wine lodges of the major companies, to see the remote parts of the Alto-Douro and to embrace the slower pace of life that the extreme summer heat dictates. The abundance of top-quality Douro wines, Port wine, and world-class gastronomy, with many of the ingredients locally grown and produced, make for a unique experience that deserves an extended stay. Watching the sunset in the Alto-Douro after a fiery hot sunny day as the light softens and starts to fade towards Porto in the west is most certainly worth an overnight stay. The Alto-Douro offers a respite from an overcrowded world offering a feeling of remoteness, calmness, and space. There are few such places remaining in mainland Europe that can offer similar sensations, as well as providing such good quality wine and food.

Taking a northerly direction from Porto, there are a number of interesting historical places for the visitor to see. The extension of the motorway to the Spanish border has made it possible to reach many of these locations in a driving time of an hour or less. Vila do Conde, located some twenty-five kilometres north-west of Porto, offers a long golden beach and a pleasant promenade to walk along. The Convent of Santa Clara, sits on a hill high above the town; its façade was erected in the eighteenth century while the church dates from much earlier – the fourteenth century.[5]

The town and its beach runs directly into old fishing port of Póvoa de Varzim, known for its seafood restaurants and attractive wide beach, which in summertime is one of the busiest in the region.[6] Although the building of high-rise blocks along the beachfront and the rise of ugly industrial units in the towns hinterland has won it few friends in recent years.

Around one hour from Porto, along the same motorway, we find the city of Viana do Castelo, which sits at the mouth of the River

Lima. The city has been important since ancient times. Widely settled in the era of Roman rule it was an important port during the voyages of discovery and the Portuguese empire. Many of the city's key buildings originate from this period when the riches of the empire entered Portugal. We have already recounted Viana do Castelo's importance to the development of the Portuguese wine trade, and how it was the first location where British merchants settled, prior to moving to Porto. The wine trade dried up, but the docks remained important. During the *Estado Novo*, the city became one of the important ports for the cod fishing industry. It remains an attractive place to visit, with nice buildings; the Misericordia in the main square has been much written about.[7]

The coastline above Viana do Castelo is worth visiting, especially the parish of Afife, which has one of the prettiest beaches in Portugal and is worth visiting at any time of year. The wide beach also contains several small coves that can be reached by the natural wooden walkway that follows the contours of the sands. Like Viana do Castelo and much of the rest of the coast towards the Spanish border, Afife has a history that dates back to ancient times; some historians suggest that the Celts and Phoenicians settled in the area, and there are some interesting archaeological monuments.[8]

There are two places of great interest that can be reached either from the direction of Viana do Castelo or from the motorway north of Braga. The first of these is Ponte de Lima, considered to be one of the most attractive small towns in Portugal. The bridge over the River Lima was built by the Romans to help them link Braga with the north and there are Roman influences in the town, including the remains of six Roman arches.[9] Today, it is a pleasant place to visit, although during the holiday seasons it tends to fill up with coachloads of visitors who spend a couple of hours walking around the town. Despite these incursions, it remains relatively unspoilt and has considerable charm.

Finally, the visitor can discover the great unspoilt wilderness and stunning scenery of the historically important, Peneda-Gerês National Park. While reaching the park by car is relatively straightforward from Porto, it is only really possible to explore all the many delights of the parks on foot. It is possible to drive to some of the historic sites, but narrow roads and at times slow-moving traffic can hinder progress. On a day trip, the visitor should limit their programme and select what they wish to see in advance. Most opt for visiting a sample of the unique rock formations and a few of the beautiful waterfalls. The air in Portugal's only National Park is extremely invigorating and draining, even for the fittest of visitors. The area of the park also experiences extreme rainfall with on average more than 130 wet days per year. Nonetheless, the monuments, the scenery, and the breath-taking views reward the effort of the journey.

In truth, the range of places to visit to the north, east, and south of Porto is most impressive and varied. During the course of this book, we have charted the development of transport infrastructure in the Porto region. Within the city itself, the first attempts to construct a crossing over the River Douro with the crude, and in the end tragic, Bridge of Boats, the first road bridge, railway bridge, and then double level crossings. The development of the road system has been no less impressive: first within the city's boundaries and then towards Lisbon in the south, and to the east, the interior and eventually Spain. To the northeast and the northwest the progress was no less impressive. Today, a phrase you read more frequently about many parts of the region is that they are located just under or just over an hour from Porto airport. The opening up of the region has brought new challenges and opportunities, but most of all, it offers the visitor an opportunity to see so much more history and beautiful scenery than at any point in the past. And that has to be considered a positive development.

THE END.

Notes

Introduction

1 'Dear Europe: Letters from JK Rowling, Neil Gaiman, Mary Beard and More', *The Guardian*, 26 October 2019.

2 United Nations Archives (UNA), The Secretary-General Toast to Dinner Given by the Mayor of Porto, 7 August 1998.

3 Ibid.

4 Margaret Thatcher Archives (MTA), Speech to Oporto Industrial Association, Palacio da Bolsa, Porto, 19 April 1984.

5 For more information of this and the resulting Taylor's Fladgate led 'Porto Protocol' see the website: https://climatechange-porto.com/porto-protocol/

6 Sarah Bradford, *Portugal*, London, Thames and Hudson, 1973, p.9.

7 H. V. Livermore, *Portugal: A Short History*, Edinburgh, Edinburgh University Press, 1973, p.120.

Chapter 1

1 Francisco Sá Carneiro, Citações de Francisco Sá Carneiro, Instituto Francisco Sá Carneiro, 22 July 1974.

2 William Kingston, *Lusitanian Sketches of the Pen and Pencil, Vol. 1*, London, John Parker, 1845, p.20.

3 William Kingston, *Lusitanian Sketches of the Pen and Pencil, Vol. 1*, p.21.

4 Ian Robertson, *A Traveller's History of Portugal*, London, The Armchair Traveller, 2011, p.4.

5 Leonor Freire Costa, Pedro Lains and Susana Munch Miranda, *An Economic History of Portugal, 1143-2010*, Cambridge, Cambridge University Press, 2018, p.311.

6 Henri Cartier-Bresson, *Europeans*, London and New York, Thames and Hudson, 2011, p.56.

CHAPTER 2

1 José Hermano Saraiva, *Portugal: A Companion History*, Manchester, Carcanet, 1997, p.1.
2 James M. Anderson, *The History of Portugal*, Westport, Connecticut and London, Greenwood Press, 2000, p.20.
3 A. H. De Oliveira Marques, *History of Portugal, Volume 1*. New York, Columbia University Press, 1976, p.20.
4 José Hermano Saraiva, *Portugal*, p.3.
5 David Birmingham, *A Concise History of Portugal*, Cambridge, Cambridge University Press, 2007, p.14.
6 James M. Anderson, *The History of Portugal*, p.21.
7 José Hermano Saraiva, *Portugal: A Companion History*, p.9.
8 James M. Anderson, *The History of Portugal*, p.23.
9 José Hermano Saraiva, *Portugal: A Companion History*, p.10.
10 James M. Anderson, *The History of Portugal*, p.23.
11 José Hermano Saraiva, *Portugal: A Companion History*, p.11.
12 A. H. De Oliveira Marques, *History of Portugal*, P.25.
13 Ibid.
14 José Hermano Saraiva, *Portugal: A Companion History*, p.11.
15 A. H. De Oliveira Marques, *History of Portugal*, P.27.

CHAPTER 3

1 Charles Sellers, Oporto: Old and New, Being a Historical Record of the Port Wine Trade and a Tribute to British Commercial Enterprise in the North of Portugal, London, Herbert E. Harper, 1899, p.286.
2 Charles Oman, *A History of the Peninsular War: Volume II, January-September 1909, From the Battle of Corunna to the End of the Talavera Campaign*, London, Greenhill Books, 1995, p.241.
3 Charles Sellers, Oporto: Old and New, p.285.
4 Charles Oman, *A History of the Peninsular War: Volume II*, p.240.
5 There remains some debate over numbers here, especially with reference to the 9,000 inhabitants of Porto armed and willing to fight. This is considered to be an exaggerated number.
6 W. F. P. Napier, *History of the War in the Peninsula and in the South of France from the Year 1807 to the Year 1814, Volume II*, London, Constable, 1992, p.203.
7 Charles Oman, *A History of the Peninsular War: Volume II*, p.242.

8   Charles Sellers, Oporto: Old and New, p.286.
9   Charles Oman, *A History of the Peninsular War: Volume II*, p.246.
10 W. F. P. Napier, *History of the War in the Peninsula*, p.206.
11 Charles Esdaile, *The Peninsular War*, London, Penguin, 2002, p.164.
12 Charles Oman, *A History of the Peninsular War: Volume II*, p.248.
13 W. F. P. Napier, *History of the War in the Peninsula*, p.207.
14 Charles Oman, *A History of the Peninsular War: Volume II*, p.248.
15 Leonor Freire Costa, Pedro Lains and Susana Munch Miranda, *An Economic History of Portugal, 1143-2010*, p.232.
16 W. F. P. Napier, *History of the War in the Peninsula*, p.231.
17 Charles Esdaile, *The Peninsular War*, London, Penguin, 2002, p.164.

CHAPTER 4

1   W. F. K. Thomson (editor), London, Michael Joseph, *An Ensign in the Peninsular War: The Letters of John Aitchison*, 1981, p.44.
2   Public Records Office (PRO)/FO/608/119/From Ronald Graham to Foreign Office, 24 January 1919.
3   Julian Rathbone, *Wellington's War: His Peninsular Dispatches*, London, Michael Joseph, 1994, p.48.
4   W. F. K. Thomson (editor), *An Ensign in the Peninsular War*, p.44.
5   Julian Rathbone, *Wellington's War: His Peninsular Dispatches*, p.46.
6   Charles Oman, *A History of the Peninsular War: Volume II*, p.332.
7   Michael Glover, *Wellington as a Military Commander*, London , Penguin, 1966, p.118.
8   Charles Oman, *A History of the Peninsular War: Volume II*, p.334.
9   Julian Rathbone, *Wellington's War: His Peninsular Dispatches*, p.44.
10 Charles Oman, *A History of the Peninsular War: Volume II*, p.337.
11 Charles Oman, *A History of the Peninsular War: Volume II*, p.339.
12 Charles Esdaile, *The Peninsular War*, p.194.
13 Julian Rathbone, *Wellington's War: His Peninsular Dispatches*, p.49.

CHAPTER 5

1   Rose Macaulay, *They Went to Portugal*, London, Penguin, 1985, p.283.
2   Charles Sellers, Oporto: Old and New, p.305.
3   Eric Solsen (editor), *Portugal: A Country Study*, Washington DC, Library of Congress, 1993, p.43.
4   Sarah Bradford, *Portugal*, p.65.

5   José Hermano Saraiva, *Portugal: A Companion History*, p.92.
6   James M. Anderson, *The History of Portugal*, p.129.
7   José Hermano Saraiva, *Portugal: A Companion History*, p.92.
8   Eric Solsen (editor), *Portugal: A Country Study*, p.43.
9   Eric Solsen (editor), *Portugal: A Country Study*, p.44.
10 James M. Anderson, *The History of Portugal*, p.131.
11 H. V. Livermore, *A New History of Portugal*, Cambridge, Cambridge University Press, 1966, p.265.
12 James M. Anderson, *The History of Portugal*, p.131.
13 A British Officer of the Hussars (Anonymous), *The Civil War in Portugal and the Siege of Oporto*, London, Edward Moxon, 1836, pp.13-14.
14 Eric Solsen (editor), *Portugal: A Country Study*, p.44
15 James M. Anderson, *The History of Portugal*, p.131.
16 Eric Solsen (editor), *Portugal: A Country Study*, p.44.
17 H. V. Livermore, *A New History of Portugal*, p.266.
18 James M. Anderson, *The History of Portugal*, p.131
19 H. V. Livermore, *A New History of Portugal*, p.266.

CHAPTER 6

1   A British Officer of the Hussars (Anonymous), *The Civil War in Portugal and the Siege of Oporto*, p.25.
2   H. V. Livermore, *A New History of Portugal*, p.269.
3   Eric Solsen (editor), *Portugal: A Country Study*, p.45.
4   H. V. Livermore, *A New History of Portugal*, p.269.
5   H. V. Livermore, *A New History of Portugal*, p.270.
6   Rose Macaulay, *They Went to Portugal*, p.283.
7   Eric Solsen (editor), *Portugal: A Country Study*, p.45
8   H. V. Livermore, *A New History of Portugal*, p.271.
9   William Bollaert, *The Wars of Succession of Portugal and Spain from 1826 to 1840, Volume I*, London, Edward Stanford, 1861, p.61.
10 Charles Sellers, Oporto: Old and New, p.302.
11 José Hermano Saraiva, *Portugal: A Companion History*, p.97.
12 Neill Lochery Archives (NLA)/DEN/1832-1833, *The Diary of Elizabeth Noble*, entry date, 7 July 1832.
13 There are different estimates to the exact number of Pedro's force, ranging from 7000 to 7,500 men.

14 NLA/DEN/1832-1833, *The Diary of Elizabeth Noble*, entry date, 9 July 1832.

15 Charles Sellers, Oporto: Old and New, p.302.

CHAPTER 7

1 Letter from Thomas Sorell, British Consul at Porto, *The Times*, 6 July 1833.

2 NLA/DEN/1832-1833, *The Diary of Elizabeth Noble*, entry date, 10 July 1832.

3 NLA/DEN/1832-1833, *The Diary of Elizabeth Noble*, entry dates, 12, 14, 15 July 1832.

4 Charles Sellers, Oporto: Old and New, p.265.

5 Charles Sellers, Oporto: Old and New, p.266.

6 A British Officer of the Hussars (Anonymous), *The Civil War in Portugal and the Siege of Oporto*, p.97.

7 A British Officer of the Hussars (Anonymous), *The Civil War in Portugal and the Siege of Oporto*, p.98.

8 A British Officer of the Hussars (Anonymous), *The Civil War in Portugal and the Siege of Oporto*, p.99.

9 Charles Napier, *An Account of the War in Portugal between Dom Pedro and Dom Miguel, Vol. I*, London T. & W. Boone, 1836, p.49.

10 Charles Napier, *An Account of the War in Portugal between Dom Pedro and Dom Miguel, Vol. I*, pp.48-49.

11 Neill Lochery Archives (NLA)/DEN/1822-1833, *The Diary of Elizabeth Noble*, entry date, 25 July 1832.

12 William Bollaert, *The Wars of Succession of Portugal and Spain from 1826 to 1840, Volume I*, p.105.

13 Ibid.

14 Charles Napier, *An Account of the War in Portugal between Dom Pedro and Dom Miguel, Vol. I*, p52.

15 NLA/DEN/1822-1833, *The Diary of Elizabeth Noble*, entry dates, 8 and 9 August 1832.

16 A British Officer of the Hussars (Anonymous), *The Civil War in Portugal and the Siege of Oporto*, p.110.

17 Charles Napier, *An Account of the War in Portugal between Dom Pedro and Dom Miguel, Vol. I*, p64.

18 Ibid.

19 William Bollaert, *The Wars of Succession of Portugal and Spain from 1826 to 1840, Volume I*, p.111.

20 William Bollaert, *The Wars of Succession of Portugal and Spain from 1826 to 1840, Volume I*, p.114.

21 A British Officer of the Hussars (Anonymous), *The Civil War in Portugal and the Siege of Oporto*, p.132.

22 William Bollaert, *The Wars of Succession of Portugal and Spain from 1826 to 1840, Volume I*, p.132.

23 Ibid.

24 NLA/DEN/1822-1833, *The Diary of Elizabeth Noble*, entry date, 17 December 1832.

25 Ibid.

26 A British Officer of the Hussars (Anonymous), *The Civil War in Portugal and the Siege of Oporto*, p.141.

27 Bollaert, William, *The Wars of Succession of Portugal and Spain from 1826 to 1840, Vol. I*, p. 132.

28 NLA/DEN/1832-1833, *The Diary of Elizabeth Noble*, entry date, 17 December 1832.

CHAPTER 8

1 NLA/DEN/1832-1833, *The Diary of Elizabeth Noble*, entry date, 4 March 1833.

2 NLA/DEN/1832-1833, *The Diary of Elizabeth Noble*, entry date, 17 January 1833.

3 NLA/DEN/1832-1833, *The Diary of Elizabeth Noble*, entry dates, 8 and 9 March 1833.

4 The Fladgate Partnership Archives (TFPA), Unsigned Letter Addressed to 'My Dear Friends' on the Subject of Mr. Wright's Left Arm Amputated, 9 March 1833.

5 NLA/DEN/1832-1833, *The Diary of Elizabeth Noble*, entry date, 19 February 1833.

6 A British Officer of the Hussars (Anonymous), *The Civil War in Portugal and the Siege of Oporto*, p.204.

7 H. V. Livermore, *A New History of Portugal*, p.276.

8 A British Officer of the Hussars (Anonymous), *The Civil War in Portugal and the Siege of Oporto*, p.208.

9   Charles Napier, *An Account of the War in Portugal between Dom Pedro and Dom Miguel, Vol. I*, pp.158-159.

10 Charles Napier, *An Account of the War in Portugal between Dom Pedro and Dom Miguel, Vol. I*, p.163.

11 A British Officer of the Hussars (Anonymous), *The Civil War in Portugal and the Siege of Oporto*, p.206.

12 Charles Napier, *An Account of the War in Portugal between Dom Pedro and Dom Miguel, Vol. I*, p181.

13 NLA/DEN/1832-1833, *The Diary of Elizabeth Noble*, entry date, 12 June 1833.

14 NLA/DEN/1832-1833, *The Diary of Elizabeth Noble*, entry date, 23 June 1833.

15 NLA/DEN/1832-1833, *The Diary of Elizabeth Noble*, entry date, 29 June 1833.

16 H. V. Livermore, *A New History of Portugal*, p.276.

17 A British Officer of the Hussars (Anonymous), *The Civil War in Portugal and the Siege of Oporto*, pp.218-19.

18 NLA/DEN/1832-1833, *The Diary of Elizabeth Noble*, entry date, 9 July 1833.

19 NLA/DEN/1832-1833, *The Diary of Elizabeth Noble*, entry date, 10 July 1833.

20 NLA/DEN/1832-1833, *The Diary of Elizabeth Noble*, entry date, 14 July 1833.

21 A British Officer of the Hussars (Anonymous), *The Civil War in Portugal and the Siege of Oporto*, p.221.

22 H. V. Livermore, *A New History of Portugal*, p.276.

23 William Bollaert, *The Wars of Succession of Portugal and Spain from 1826 to 1840, Volume I*, p.306.

24 Ibid, p. 310.

25 Corporal Knight, *The British Battalion at Oporto with Adventures, Anecdotes and Exploits in Holland, Waterloo and in the Expedition to Portugal*, Glasgow, Thomas Murray, 1834, p.112.

26 Charles Napier, *An Account of the War in Portugal between Dom Pedro and Dom Miguel, Vol. I*, p228.

27 William Bollaert, *The Wars of Succession of Portugal and Spain from 1826 to 1840, Volume I*, p.321.

28 Charles Napier, *An Account of the War in Portugal between Dom Pedro and Dom Miguel, Vol. I*, p.247-248.
29 William Bollaert, *The Wars of Succession of Portugal and Spain from 1826 to 1840, Volume I*, p.312.
30 William Bollaert, *The Wars of Succession of Portugal and Spain from 1826 to 1840, Volume I*, p.324.

CHAPTER 9

1 Baron Forrester quoted in Charles Sellers, Oporto: Old and New, p.265.
2 NLA/DEN/1832-1833, *The Diary of Elizabeth Noble*, entry date, 4 August 1833.
3 Baron Forrester quoted in Charles Sellers, Oporto: Old and New, p.266.
4 William Bollaert, *The Wars of Succession of Portugal and Spain from 1826 to 1840, Volume I*, p.342.
5 A British Officer of the Hussars (Anonymous), *The Civil War in Portugal and the Siege of Oporto*, p.241.
6 William Bollaert, *The Wars of Succession of Portugal and Spain from 1826 to 1840, Volume I*, p.344.
7 A British Officer of the Hussars (Anonymous), *The Civil War in Portugal and the Siege of Oporto*, p.242.
8 William Bollaert, *The Wars of Succession of Portugal and Spain from 1826 to 1840, Volume I*, pp.342-343.
9 William Bollaert, *The Wars of Succession of Portugal and Spain from 1826 to 1840, Volume I*, pp.344-345.
10 A British Officer of the Hussars (Anonymous), *The Civil War in Portugal and the Siege of Oporto*, p.242.
11 A British Officer of the Hussars (Anonymous), *The Civil War in Portugal and the Siege of Oporto*, p.243.
12 Baron Forrester quoted in Charles Sellers, Oporto: Old and New, p.267.
13 NLA/DEN/1832-1833, *The Diary of Elizabeth Noble*, entry date, 16 August 1833.
14 A British Officer of the Hussars (Anonymous), *The Civil War in Portugal and the Siege of Oporto*, p.243.
15 NLA/DEN/1832-1833, *The Diary of Elizabeth Noble*, entry date, 18 August 1833.

16 William Bollaert, *The Wars of Succession of Portugal and Spain from 1826 to 1840, Volume I*, p.346.

17 NLA/DEN/1832-1833, *The Diary of Elizabeth Noble*, entry date, 18 August 1833.

18 William Bollaert, *The Wars of Succession of Portugal and Spain from 1826 to 1840, Volume I*, p.346.

19 A British Officer of the Hussars (Anonymous), *The Civil War in Portugal and the Siege of Oporto*, p.246.

20 A British Officer of the Hussars (Anonymous), *The Civil War in Portugal and the Siege of Oporto*, p.249.

21 H. V. Livermore, *A New History of Portugal*, p.276.

22 H. V. Livermore, *A New History of Portugal*, p.277.

23 Eric Solsen (editor), *Portugal: A Country Study*, p.46.

24 Leonor Freire Costa, Pedro Lains and Susana Munch Miranda, *An Economic History of Portugal, 1143-2010*, pp.272-273.

25 A British Officer of the Hussars (Anonymous), *The Civil War in Portugal and the Siege of Oporto*, p.282.

26 NLA/DEN/1832-1833, *The Diary of Elizabeth Noble*, entry date, 29 August 1833.

CHAPTER 10

1 William Kingston, *Lusitanian Sketches of the Pen and Pencil, Vol. 1*, P.30.

2 H. V. Livermore, *A New History of Portugal*, p.281.

3 Eric Solsen (editor), *Portugal: A Country Study*, p.46.

4 H. V. Livermore, *A New History of Portugal*, p.281.

5 Eric Solsen (editor), *Portugal: A Country Study*, p.46.

6 H. V. Livermore, *A New History of Portugal*, p.281.

7 H. V. Livermore, *A New History of Portugal*, p.282.

8 José Hermano Saraiva, *Portugal: A Companion History*, p.100.

9 H. V. Livermore, *A New History of Portugal*, p.284.

10 José Hermano Saraiva, *Portugal: A Companion History*, p.101.

11 James M. Anderson, *The History of Portugal*, p.135.

12 H. V. Livermore, *A New History of Portugal*, p.285.

13 José Hermano Saraiva, *Portugal: A Companion History*, p.101.

14 James M. Anderson, *The History of Portugal*, p.136.

15 H. V. Livermore, *A New History of Portugal*, p.285.

16 Ibid.

17 James M. Anderson, *The History of Portugal*, p.136.

18 H. V. Livermore, *A New History of Portugal*, p.287.
19 Eric Solsen (editor), *Portugal: A Country Study*, p.48.
20 H. V. Livermore, *A New History of Portugal*, p.287.
21 Eric Solsen (editor), *Portugal: A Country Study*, p.48.
22 José Hermano Saraiva, *Portugal: A Companion History*, p.104.

CHAPTER 11

1 Fontes Pereira de Melo, Launch of Government and Reform Programme, 1852.
2 A. H. De Oliveira Marques, *History of Portugal, Volume 2*, New York, Columbia University Press, 1976, pp.7-8.
3 Leonor Freire Costa, Pedro Lains and Susana Munch Miranda, *An Economic History of Portugal, 1143-2010*, p.253.
4 H. V. Livermore, *A New History of Portugal*, p.289.
5 H. V. Livermore, *A New History of Portugal*, p.290.
6 David Birmingham, *A Concise History of Portugal*, p.135.
7 A. H. De Oliveira Marques, *History of Portugal, Volume 2*, p.8.
8 Eric Solsen (editor), *Portugal: A Country Study*, p.47.
9 A. H. De Oliveira Marques, *History of Portugal, Volume 2*, p.8.
10 David Birmingham, *A Concise History of Portugal*, p.136.
11 A. H. De Oliveira Marques, *History of Portugal, Volume 2*, p.8.
12 A. H. De Oliveira Marques, *History of Portugal, Volume 2*, p.9.
13 David Birmingham, *A Concise History of Portugal*, p.136.
14 A. H. De Oliveira Marques, *History of Portugal, Volume 2*, p.10.
15 A. H. De Oliveira Marques, *History of Portugal, Volume 2*, p.20.
16 David Birmingham, *A Concise History of Portugal*, p.139.
17 H. V. Livermore, *Portugal: A Short History*, p.168.
18 PRO/FO/608/119/From Ronald Graham to Foreign Office, 24 January 1919.
19 PRO/FO/608/119/From The Earl Curzon of Kedleston to Foreign Office, 21 February 1919.
20 H. V. Livermore, *Portugal: A Short History*, p.168.
21 Eric Solsen (editor), *Portugal: A Country Study*, p.49.
22 H. V. Livermore, *Portugal: A Short History*, p.169.
23 Ibid.
24 Eric Solsen (editor), *Portugal: A Country Study*, p.49.
25 H. V. Livermore, *Portugal: A Short History*, p.170.

26   Ibid.
27   David Birmingham, *A Concise History of Portugal*, p.148.
28   Eric Solsen (editor), *Portugal: A Country Study*, p.50.

CHAPTER 12

1   'Military Revolt in Oporto', *The Times*, 2 February 1891.
2   José Hermano Saraiva, *Portugal: A Companion History*, p.105.
3   'Rebels Quickly Subdued', *New York Times*, 1 February 1891.
4   'Military Revolt in Oporto', *The Times*, 2 February 1891.
5   'Rebels Quickly Subdued', *New York Times*, 1 February 1891.
6   'Military Revolt in Oporto', *The Times*, 3 February 1891.
7   'Military Revolt in Oporto', *The Times*, 2 February 1891.
8   'Military Revolt in Oporto', *The Times*, 3 February 1891.
9   Jorge Martins Ribeiro, 'The City of Oporto at the End of the Nineteenth Century as Viewed by American Diplomats in Portugal', *Mediterranean Studies*, Volume 4, 1994, p.151.
10   'Military Revolt in Oporto', *The Times*, 5 February 1891.
11   'Military Revolt in Oporto', *The Times*, 4 February 1891.
12   'King Charles Congratulated', *New York Times*, 3 February 1981.
13   Douglas L. Wheeler, *Republican Portugal: A Political History, 1910-1926*, Madison, The University of Wisconsin Press, 1978, p.34.
14   H. V. Livermore, *Portugal: A Short History*, p.177.
15   José Hermano Saraiva, *Portugal: A Companion History*, p.105.
16   H. V. Livermore, *Portugal: A Short History*, p.177.
17   José Hermano Saraiva, *Portugal: A Companion History*, p.105.
18   H. V. Livermore, *Portugal: A Short History*, p.177.
19   David Birmingham, *A Concise History of Portugal*, p.151.
20   Eric Solsen (editor), *Portugal: A Country Study*, p.50.
21   José Hermano Saraiva, *Portugal: A Companion History*, p.106.
22   Douglas L. Wheeler, *Republican Portugal: A Political History, 1910-1926*, p.43.
23   Eric Solsen (editor), *Portugal: A Country Study*, p.50.
24   Douglas L. Wheeler, *Republican Portugal: A Political History, 1910-1926*, p.44.
25   H. V. Livermore, *Portugal: A Short History*, p.179.
26   Douglas L. Wheeler, *Republican Portugal: A Political History, 1910-1926*, p.44.

27 H. V. Livermore, *Portugal: A Short History*, p.179.
28 Douglas L. Wheeler, *Republican Portugal: A Political History, 1910-1926*, p.44.
29 'The Revolution in Portugal', *The Times*, 6 October 1910.
30 H. V. Livermore, *Portugal: A Short History*, p.179.
31 José Hermano Saraiva, *Portugal: A Companion History*, p.105.
32 Douglas L. Wheeler, *Republican Portugal: A Political History, 1910-1926*, p.48.
33 'Rumoured Revolution in Portugal', *The Times*, 5 October 1910.
34 Ibid.
35 H. V. Livermore, *Portugal: A Short History*, p.181.
36 Foreign Relations of the United States (FRUS), Minister Gage to Secretary of State, 4 October 1910.
37 Douglas L. Wheeler, *Republican Portugal: A Political History, 1910-1926*, p.48.
38 NLA/FO/Portugal/Ambassador to Foreign Office, 5 October 1910.
39 FRUS, Gaye to Secretary of State, 5 and 6 October 1910.
40 FRUS, Gaye to Secretary of State, 10 October 1910.
41 Ibid.
42 'The Revolution in Portugal', *The Times*, 6 October 1910.
43 H. V. Livermore, *Portugal: A Short History*, p.181.

CHAPTER 13

1 Sophia de Mello Breyner Andresen, 'A Country within a Country', in Eugénio de Andrade (editor), *Daqui Houve Nome Portugal*, Porto, Asa Editores, 2004, pp.291-292.
2 John Delaforce, *The Factory House in Oporto: Its Historic Role in the Port Wine Trade*, London, Christie's Wine Publications, 1990, pp.23-24.
3 John Delaforce, *The Factory House in Oporto: Its Historic Role in the Port Wine Trade*, p.24.
4 Elaine Sanceau, *The British Factory Oporto*, Barcelos, Companhia Editora do Minho, 1970, p.50.
5 John Delaforce, *The Factory House in Oporto: Its Historic Role in the Port Wine Trade*, p.25.
6 José Manuel Lopes Cordeira, 'O Palacio dos Carrancas', *Publico*, 29 July 2001.
7 NLA/DEN/1822-1833, *The Diary of Elizabeth Noble*, entry date, 11 August 1832.

8 José Manuel Lopes Cordeira, 'O Palacio dos Carrancas', *Publico*, 29 July 2001.

9 Erik Hitters, 'Porto and Rotterdam as European Capitals of Culture: Toward the Festivalisation of Urban Cultural Policy', *Cultural Tourism: Global and Local Perspectives*, Philadelphia, Haworth Press, 2007, pp.294-295.

10 PRO/FO/370/1454/History of the Oporto Chaplaincy, 14th January 1948, p.1.

11 PRO/FO/370/1454/History of the Oporto Chaplaincy, 14th January 1948, p.2.

12 PRO/FO/370/1454/History of the Oporto Chaplaincy, 14th January 1948, p.3.

13 Sarah Bradford, *The Story of Port*, London, Christie's Wine Publications, 1978, p.63.

14 Sarah Bradford, *The Story of Port*, p.64.

15 Sarah Bradford, *The Story of Port*, p.65.

16 http://www.museusoaresdosreis.gov.pt/pt-PT/coleccao/autoresrepresentados/ContentDetail.aspx?id=530

CHAPTER 14

1 PRO/FO/608/119/From Carnegie to Earl Curzon, 30 January 1919.

2 Eric Solsen (editor), *Portugal: A Country Study*, p.53.

3 José Hermano Saraiva, *Portugal: A Companion History*, p.109.

4 H. V. Livermore, *Portugal: A Short History*, p.186.

5 José Hermano Saraiva, *Portugal: A Companion History*, p.109.

6 H. V. Livermore, *Portugal: A Short History*, p.186.

7 Douglas L. Wheeler, *Republican Portugal: A Political History, 1910-1926*, p.152.

8 PRO/FO/608/119/From Carnegie to Earl Curzon, 30 January 1919.

9 Ibid.

10 Douglas L. Wheeler, *Republican Portugal: A Political History, 1910-1926*, p.153.

11 Ibid.

12 PRO/FO/608/119/From Carnegie to Earl Curzon, 30 January 1919.

13 PRO/FO/608/119/From Earl Curzon to Carnegie, 23 January 1919.

14 PRO/FO/608/119/From Earl Curzon to Carnegie, 23 January 1919, p.1.
15 PRO/FO/608/119/From Earl Curzon to Carnegie, 23 January 1919. p.3.
16 Leonor Freire Costa, Pedro Lains and Susana Munch Miranda, *An Economic History of Portugal, 1143-2010*, p.295.
17 José Hermano Saraiva, *Portugal: A Companion History*, p.109.
18 PRO/FO/608/119/Hardinge to King and War Cabinet, 6 February 1919.
19 H. V. Livermore, *Portugal: A Short History*, p.198.
20 H. V. Livermore, *Portugal: A Short History*, p.186.
21 José Hermano Saraiva, *Portugal: A Companion History*, p.109.
22 H. V. Livermore, *Portugal: A Short History*, p.187.
23 For more details on this proposal and detailed documentary evidence outlining its development and eventual rejection see, Douglas L. Wheeler, *Republican Portugal: A Political History, 1910-1926*, p.199.
24 Eric Solsen (editor), *Portugal: A Country Study*, p.53.
25 H. V. Livermore, *Portugal: A Short History*, p.187.
26 José Hermano Saraiva, *Portugal: A Companion History*, p.110.
27 Douglas L. Wheeler, *Republican Portugal: A Political History, 1910-1926*, p.242
28 H. V. Livermore, *Portugal: A Short History*, p.187.

CHAPTER 15

1 Hugh Kay, Salazar and Modern Portugal, New York, Hawthorn Books, 1970, pp.42-43.
2 'Revolt of Oporto Troops', *The Times*, 4 February 1927.
3 Ibid.
4 'The Oporto Revolt: Reported Surrender of the Rebels', *The Times*, 5 February 1927.
5 'The Oporto Revolt: City Bombarded', *The Times*, 7 February 1927.
6 'Oporto Again Bombarded', *The Times, 8 February 1927*.
7 'The Revolt in Portugal', *The Times*, 10 February 1927.
8 Hugh Kay, Salazar and Modern Portugal, p.41.
9 José Hermano Saraiva, *Portugal: A Companion History*, p.110.
10 Hugh Kay, Salazar and Modern Portugal, p.44.
11 H. V. Livermore, *Portugal: A Short History*, p.188.

12 Hugh Kay, Salazar and Modern Portugal, p.48.
13 Hugh Kay, Salazar and Modern Portugal, p.49.
14 José Hermano Saraiva, *Portugal: A Companion History*, p.111.
15 Filipe Ribeiro de Meneses, *Salazar: A Political Biography*, New York, Enigma Books, 2009, p.588.
16 Hugh Kay, Salazar and Modern Portugal, p.25.
17 PRO/FO/371/66288/O'Malley to Bevin, 7 November 1946.
18 Ibid.
19 PRO/FO/371/66288/Kemball to Embassy in Lisbon, 5 November 1946.
20 PRO/FO/371/66288/Situation in Portugal, 20 November 1946.
21 PRO/FO/371/66288/ O'Malley to Millar, 7 November 1946, p. 3.
22 Eric Solsen (editor), *Portugal: A Country Study*, p.57.
23 Leonor Freire Costa, Pedro Lains and Susana Munch Miranda, *An Economic History of Portugal, 1143-2010*, p.311.
24 Ibid.
25 A. H. De Oliveira Marques, *History of Portugal, Volume 2*, p.237.
26 Neill Lochery, *Lisboa: A Cidade Vista de Fora, 1933-1974*, Lisbon, Editorial Presença, 2013, pp.177-178.
27 José Hermano Saraiva, *Portugal: A Companion History*, p.115.
28 A. H. De Oliveira Marques, *History of Portugal, Volume 2*, p.237.
29 José Hermano Saraiva, *Portugal: A Companion History*, p.115.
30 A. H. De Oliveira Marques, *History of Portugal, Volume 2*, p.238.
31 José Hermano Saraiva, *Portugal: A Companion History*, p.115.
32 PRO/FCO/9/2275/Annual Review for Portugal for 1974, 8 January 1975, p.1.

CHAPTER 16

1 F. C. C. Egerton, *Salazar Rebuilder of Portugal*, London, Hodder and Stoughton, 1943, p.13.
2 Filipe Ribeiro de Meneses, *Salazar: A Political Biography*, p.243.
3 F. C. C. Egerton, *Salazar Rebuilder of Portugal*, London, Hodder and Stoughton, 1943, p.17.
4 C. R. Boxer, *The Portuguese Seaborne Empire, 1415-1825*, Manchester, Carcanet, 1991.
5 A. R. Disney, *A History of Portugal and the Portuguese Empire: From Beginnings to 1807 (2 Volumes)*, Cambridge, Cambridge University Press, 2009

and A. J. R. Russell-Wood, *The Portuguese Empire, 1415-1808: A World on the Move*, Baltimore and London, The John Hopkins University Press, 1998.

6   José Hermano Saraiva, *Portugal: A Companion History*, p.35.

7   C. R. Boxer, *The Portuguese Seaborne Empire, 1415-1825*, p.17.

8   A. H. De Oliveira Marques, *History of Portugal, Volume 1*, p.142

9   José Hermano Saraiva, *Portugal: A Companion History*, p.36.

10 C. R. Boxer, *The Portuguese Seaborne Empire, 1415-1825*, p.17.

11 Stanley G. Payne, *A History of Spain and Portugal, Volume 1*, Madison, The University of Wisconsin Press, 1973, p.194.

12 Stanley G. Payne, *A History of Spain and Portugal, Volume* 1, p.193.

13 A. H. De Oliveira Marques, *History of Portugal, Volume 1*, p.144.

14 José Hermano Saraiva, *Portugal: A Companion History*, p.36.

15 C. R. Boxer, *The Portuguese Seaborne Empire, 1415-1825*, p.27.

16 H. V. Livermore, *Portugal: A Short History*, p.73.

17 José Hermano Saraiva, *Portugal: A Companion History*, p.38.

18 C. R. Boxer, *The Portuguese Seaborne Empire, 1415-1825*, p.27.

19 H. V. Livermore, *Portugal: A Short History*, p.73.

20 H. V. Livermore, *Portugal: A Short History*, p.72.

21 José Hermano Saraiva, *Portugal: A Companion History*, p.38.

22 José Hermano Saraiva, *Portugal: A Companion History*, p.33.

23 H. V. Livermore, *Portugal: A Short History*, p.72.

24 José Hermano Saraiva, *Portugal: A Companion History*, p.33.

25 José Hermano Saraiva, *Portugal: A Companion History*, p.34.

26 H. V. Livermore, *Portugal: A Short History*, p.72.

27 A. H. De Oliveira Marques, *History of Portugal, Volume 1*, p.158.

28 A. H. De Oliveira Marques, *History of Portugal, Volume 1*, p.149.

29 José Hermano Saraiva, *Portugal: A Companion History*, p.50.

30 L. M. E. Shaw, *Trade, Inquisition and the English Nation in Portugal, 1650-1690*, Manchester, Carcanet Press, 1989, p.96.

31 Chronology from José Hermano Saraiva, *Portugal: A Companion History*, p.160.

Chapter 17

1   John Croft, *A Treatise on the Wines of Portugal*, York, Crask and Lund, 1787, p.19.

2   John Delaforce, The British in the North of Portugal in the 18th Century, with Special Reference to the Port Factory and Its Roles

in the Social and Commercial Life of Oporto, and an Assessment of the Influence of John Whitehead on the Architecture of the City, Porto, University of Porto, undated, p.201.

3   Sarah Bradford, *The Story of Port*, London, p.24.

4   A. H. De Oliveira Marques, *History of Portugal, Volume 1*, pp.109-110.

5   John Delaforce, The British in the North of Portugal in the 18th Century, p.202.

6   Charles Sellers, Oporto: Old and New, p.19.

7   Ibid.

8   John Croft, *A Treatise on the Wines of Portugal*, p.5

9   Sarah Bradford, *The Story of Port*, London, p.26.

10   John Croft, *A Treatise on the Wines of Portugal*, p.5

11   Charles Sellers, Oporto: Old and New, p.20.

12   PRO/FO/63/427/Report Relating to the Factory House of Oporto, Consul John Crispin, 6 October 1830.

13   John Delaforce, *The Factory House at Oporto: Its Historic Role in the Port Wine Industry*, p.17.

14   Sarah Bradford, *The Story of Port*, London, p.27.

15   Ibid.

16   David Birmingham, *A Concise History of Portugal*, p.64.

17   A. D. Francis, *The Methuens and Portugal, 1691-1708*, Cambridge, Cambridge University Press, 1966, pp.185-185.

18   H. V. Livermore, *Portugal: A Short History*, p.121.

19   Stanley G. Payne, *A History of Spain and Portugal, Volume* 2, p.402.

20   A. D. Francis, *The Methuens and Portugal, 1691-1708*, p.198.

21   H. V. Livermore, *Portugal: A Short History*, p.120.

22   A. D. Francis, *The Methuens and Portugal, 1691-1708*, p.204.

23   Leonor Freire Costa, Pedro Lains and Susana Munch Miranda, *An Economic History of Portugal, 1143-2010*, p.198.

24   A. D. Francis, *The Methuens and Portugal, 1691-1708*, p.202.

25   Ibid.

26   Ibid.

27   C. R. Boxer, *The Portuguese Seaborne Empire, 1415-1825*, pp.167-168.

28   Stanley G. Payne, *A History of Spain and Portugal, Volume* 2, p.402.

29   H. V. Livermore, *Portugal: A Short History*, p.120.

30   Leonor Freire Costa, Pedro Lains and Susana Munch Miranda, *An Economic History of Portugal, 1143-2010*, p.198.

31   Stanley G. Payne, *A History of Spain and Portugal, Volume* 2, p.402.

32   C. R. Boxer, *The Portuguese Seaborne Empire, 1415-1825*, p.168.
33   A. D. Francis, *The Methuens and Portugal, 1691-1708*, p.23.

CHAPTER 18

1   Joseph James Forrester, *Speech Delivered at the Wine Proprietors and Public Authorities of the Wine District of the Alto-Douro*, 8 October 1844, London, Royston and Brown, 1844, pp.13-14.
2   A. D. Francis, *The Methuens and Portugal, 1691-1708*, p.217.
3   John Croft, *A Treatise on the Wines of Portugal*, pp.6-7.
4   Sarah Bradford, *The Story of Port*, London, p.33.
5   John Delaforce, The British in the North of Portugal in the 18th Century, p.203.
6   Ibid.
7   PRO/FO/370/1454/The British Chaplaincy at Oporto, 14 January 1948, p.3.
8   PRO/FO/63/427/Report Relating to the Factory House of Oporto, Consul John Crispin, 6 October 1830, p.3.
9   Ibid.
10   PRO/FO/63/427/Report Relating to the Factory House of Oporto, Consul John Crispin, 6 October 1830, p.4.
11   PRO/FO/63/427/Report Relating to the Factory House of Oporto, Consul John Crispin, 6 October 1830, p.5.
12   Ibid.
13   John Delaforce, The British in the North of Portugal in the 18th Century, p.203.
14   Sarah Bradford, *The Story of Port*, London, p.34.
15   Sarah Bradford, *The Story of Port*, London, p.37.
16   John Delaforce, The British in the North of Portugal in the 18th Century, p.203.
17   John Delaforce, The British in the North of Portugal in the 18th Century, p.204.
18   Sarah Bradford, *The Story of Port*, London, p.37.
19   Nicholas Shrady, *The Last Day: Wrath, Ruin and Reason in The Great Lisbon Earthquake of 1755*, New York, Penguin, 2008, p.190.
20   John Delaforce, The British in the North of Portugal in the 18th Century, p.204.
21   John Croft, *A Treatise on the Wines of Portugal*, p.11.
22   Sarah Bradford, *The Story of Port*, London, p.39.

23 John Delaforce, The British in the North of Portugal in the 18th Century, p.204.

24 PRO/FO/63/427/Report Relating to the Factory House of Oporto, Consul John Crispin, 6 October 1830, p.5.

25 John Delaforce, *The Factory House in Oporto: Its Historic Role in the Port Wine Trade*, p.19.

26 PRO/FO/63/427/Report Relating to the Factory House of Oporto, Consul John Crispin, 6 October 1830, p.5.

27 Ibid.

28 Ibid.

29 John Delaforce, *The Factory House in Oporto: Its Historic Role in the Port Wine Trade*, p.52.

30 John Delaforce, *The Factory House in Oporto: Its Historic Role in the Port Wine Trade*, p.24.

CHAPTER 19

1 C. R. Boxer, *The Portuguese Seaborne Empire, 1415-1825*, pp.160-164.

2 Leonor Freire Costa, Pedro Lains and Susana Munch Miranda, *An Economic History of Portugal, 1143-2010*, p.203.

3 Leonor Freire Costa, Pedro Lains and Susana Munch Miranda, *An Economic History of Portugal, 1143-2010*, p.207.

4 C. R. Boxer, *The Portuguese Seaborne Empire, 1415-1825*, p.164.

5 Ibid.

6 H. V. Livermore, *Portugal: A Short History*, p.121.

7 Stanley G. Payne, *A History of Spain and Portugal, Volume 2*, p.409.

8 Ibid.

9 A. H. De Oliveira Marques, *History of Portugal, Volume 1*, p.420.

10 Ibid.

11 Stanley G. Payne, *A History of Spain and Portugal, Volume 2*, p.410.

12 Ibid.

13 H. V. Livermore, *Portugal: A Short History*, p.123.

14 Nuno Ferreira and Manuel Joaquim Morreira da Rocha, 'Etapes de Consolidacão da Paisagem Urbana do Porto Contemporaneo', p.191, https://repositorio-aberto.up.pt/handle/10216/78025.

15 John Delaforce, *The Factory House in Oporto: Its Historic Role in the Port Wine Trade*, p.52.

16 Joaquim Jaime Ferreira-Alves, 'João de Almada e Melo (1703-1786): O Homem e a Cidade', p.187, http://hdl.handle.net/10216/20416.

CHAPTER 20

1 'The World's Greatest Bookshops', Lonely Planet, 2012. https://www.lonelyplanet.com/articles/the-worlds-greatest-bookshops.
2 "Rectory Building of University of Porto", www.sigarra.up.pt.
3 "Brief History of the University of Porto", www.sigarra.up.pt.
4 Eric Solsen (editor), *Portugal: A Country Study*, p.103.
5 Eric Solsen (editor), *Portugal: A Country Study*, p.104.
6 "Brief History of the University of Porto", www.sigarra.up.pt.
7 A. H. De Oliveira Marques, *History of Portugal, Volume 2*, p30.
8 Eric Solsen (editor), *Portugal: A Country Study*, p.104.
9 A. H. De Oliveira Marques, *History of Portugal, Volume 2*, p30.
10 David Birmingham, *A Concise History of Portugal*, p.141.
11 A. H. De Oliveira Marques, *History of Portugal, Volume 2*, p141.
12 A. H. De Oliveira Marques, *History of Portugal, Volume 2*, p142.
13 "Brief History of the University of Porto", www.sigarra.up.pt.
14 Ibid.
15 "University of Porto Famous Alumni", www.sigarra.up.pt.
16 A. H. De Oliveira Marques, *History of Portugal, Volume 2*, p37.
17 A. H. De Oliveira Marques, *History of Portugal, Volume 2*, p38.
18 Neill Lochery, *Lisboa: A Cidade Vista de Fora, 1933-1974*.
19 "Rogério dos Santos Azevedo", www.sigarra.up.pt.
20 "Vogue Café Has already Opened in Baixa", *Time Out Porto*, 19 April 2018.
21 "José Neves Nets $1.2 Billion in Farfetch IPO", *The Business of Fashion*, 21 September 2018.
22 "Grande Hotel do Porto Welcomes Eça de Queirós", *Correio da Manhã*, 19 October 2017.
23 A. H. De Oliveira Marques, *History of Portugal, Volume 2*, p.39.
24 Ibid.
25 Douglas L. Wheeler, *Republican Portugal: A Political History, 1910-1926*, p.138.
26 "Pérola do Bolhão, Cem Anos de Porta Aberta", *Publico*, 28 May 2017.

CHAPTER 21

1 Eugénio de Andrade (editor), *Daqui Houve Nome Portugal*, 2004, pp.119-120.
2 "Reports from Oporto", *The Times*, 26 October 1932.

3 'A Luz Voltou à Mais Antiga Oficina de Vitrais', *Jornal de* Notícias, 19 October 2008.

4 "Vitrais, uma Vida a Pintar Luz", *Sol*, 6 November 2010.

5 *Jornal de* Notícias, 19 October 2008.

6 http://pin.amp.pt/recurso/170.

7 http://patrimoniocultural.gov.pt.

8 *Oporto and the Jews*: Israel Community of Oporto, undated.

9 H. V. Livermore, *Portugal: A Short History*, p.125.

10 "Olival Jewish Quarter", http://portoby.livrarialello.pt/en/judiaria-do-olival

11 H. V. Livermore, *Portugal: A Short History*, p.126.

12 José Hermano Saraiva, *Portugal: A Companion History*, p.45.

13 H. V. Livermore, *Portugal: A Short History*, p.86.

14 Saraiva, José Hermano, *Portugal: A Companion History*, p. 45.

15 H. V. Livermore, *Portugal: A Short History*, p.86

16 James M. Anderson, *The History of Portugal*, p.69.

17 H. V. Livermore, *Portugal: A Short History*, p.88.

18 Ibid.

19 F. Almeida, *Historia da Igreja em Portugal, Vol. IV*, Porto, 1923, p.442.

20 *Oporto and the Jews*: Israel Community of Oporto, undated, p.20.

21 António José Saraiva, *The Marrano Factory: The Portuguese Inquisition and Its New Christians, 1536-1765*, Leiden, Brill, 2001, p.9.

22 H. V. Livermore, *Portugal: A Short History*, p140.

23 On the workings of the courts and the organisations of the punishments see, António José Saraiva, The Marrano Factory: The Portuguese Inquisition and Its New Christians, 1536-1765, Leiden, Boston, Koln, Brill, 2001, pp.100-122.

24 Elvira de Azevedo Mea and Inacio Steinhardt, "The Contributions of Captain Barros Basto, 'Apostle of the Marranos'" *Shofar*, Vol. 18, No.1, Special Issue, Crypto-Judaism, Fall 1999, p.67.

25 For more on the refugees in Portugal see, Neill Lochery, *Lisbon: War in the Shadows of the City of Light, 1939-1945*, New York and London, Public Affairs, 2011.

26 Neill Lochery, *Lisbon: War in the Shadows of the City of Light*, p.106.

27 The rescue work of the local Porto Jewish community in World War Two is documented in the United States Holocaust Memorial Museum. General details of the collection can be accessed at: https://collections.ushmm.org/search/catalog/irn72603

28 Neill Lochery, *Lisbon: War in the Shadows of the City of Light*, p.113.
29 Sérgio B. Gomes, 'O Capitão Barros Basto Escondia um Segredo', *Publico*, 16 November 2014.

CHAPTER 22

1   Interview with Álvaro Siza: Beauty is the Peak of Functionality, *Arch Daily*, http://archdaily.com/803250
2   Igreja de São Francisco, *Lonely Planet*. http://lonelyplanet.com/portugal/porto/attractions
3   https://www.ccalfandegaporto.com
4   Rita Almeida de Carvalho, 'Ideology and Architecture in the Portuguese *Estado Novo*: Cultural Innovation within a Para-Fascist State, 1932-1945', *Journal of Comparative Fascist Studies*, Vol.7. No.2, Brill, October 2018, p.149.
5   Rita Almeida de Carvalho, 'Ideology and Architecture in the Portuguese *Estado Novo*', p.147.
6   Interview with Álvaro Siza: Beauty is the Peak of Functionality.
7   Ibid.
8   Eduardo Souto de Moura: I Look Beyond Solution; I Look for an Expression https://www.archdaily.com/885229
9   Ibid.
10 *A Handbook for Travellers in Portugal: A Complete Guide for Lisbon, Cintra, Mafra, the British Battlefields, Alcobaça, Batalha, Oporto, &c.* London, John Murray, 1864, pp.161-162.
11 *A Handbook for Travellers in Portugal*, p.162.
12 Stuart B. Schwartz, 'The Economy of the Portuguese Empire' in Francisco Bethencourt and Diogo Ramada Curto (Editors, *Portuguese Oceanic Expansion, 1400-1800*, Cambridge, Cambridge University Press, 2007, p.19.
13 Ibid.
14 Eugène E. Street, *A Philosopher in Portugal*, London, T. Fisher Unwin, 1903, pp.67-68.
15 'Terminal de Leixões é uma Linha Curva com um Milhão Azulejos', *Publico*, 23 July 2015.
16 https://www.archdaily.com/779868/porto-cruise-terminal-luis-pedro-silva-arquitecto

Chapter 23

1   Interview with Lou Reed, http://strangeharvest.com
2   'Sede do Vodafone no Porto é um dos Mais Surpreendentes Escritórios Criativos do Mundo', *Publico*, 28 January 2011.
3   FCO/NLA/Portugal: Annual Review for 1977, 3 January 1978, pp.1-2.
4   Ibid.
5   FCO/NLA/Portugal: Annual Review for 1986, 31 December 1986, p.3.
6   Ibid.
7   Ibid.
8   Ibid.
9   FCO/NLA/Portugal: Annual Review for 1987, p.2.
10 FCO/NLA/Portugal: Annual Review for 2003, p.2.
11 Eça de Queiroz, 'To the Soul of Dom Pedro IV in the Elysian Fields', in Eugénio de Andrade (editor), *Daqui Houve Nome Portugal*, Porto, Asa Editores, 2004, p.159.
12 Alberto Mira and Román Gubern (Editors), *The Cinema of Spain and Portugal*, London, Wallflower Press, 2005, p.41.
13 Alberto Mira and Román Gubern (Editors), *The Cinema of Spain and Portugal*, p.49.
14 https://www.casadaMúsica.com/pt/a-casa-da-Música/a-obra/#10024?lang=pt
15 Ibid.
16 'We Got Rid of the Shoe Box', *The Guardian*, 10 April 2005.
17 Ibid.
18 https://www.archdaily.com/619294/casa-da-Música-oma
19 https://www.vogue.com/slideshow/gigi-hadid-domhnall-gleeson-lace
20 Ibid.

Chapter 24

1   Benjamin Disraeli, *Coningsby: Or the New Generation, Volume 2*, London, Henry Colburn, 1884, pp.1-2.
2   Walt Whitman, Song of the Broad-Axe, *Leaves of Grass and Other Writings*, New York, W. W. Norton, 2002.

CHAPTER 25

1 Hans Christian Andersen, *A Visit to Portugal: 1866*, London, Peter Owen, 1972, pp.58-59.
2 Douglas L. Wheeler, *Historical Dictionary of Portugal*, N. J. and London, The Scarecrow Press including Metuchen, 1993, p.45.
3 Charles Oman, *A History of the Peninsular War: Volume II*, p.268.
4 Ibid.
5 Ann Bridge and Susan Lowndes, *The Selective Traveller in Portugal*, London, Chatto and Windus, 1967, p.195.
6 David Wright and Patrick Swift, *Minho and North Portugal: A Portrait and a Guide*, London, Barrie and Rockliff, 1968, p.211.
7 Ann Bridge and Susan Lowndes, *The Selective Traveller in Portugal*, p.241.
8 http://jf-afife.com/historia
9 Brian and Eileen Anderson, *Northern Portugal*, London, A & C Black, 1996, p.126.

Acknowledgements

I am very grateful to the all the archivists who kindly helped me navigate archives in Porto, Lisbon, London, Washington DC, New York, Madrid, Berlin, and Edinburgh. This book would not have been written without the support of Adrian Bridge whose drive, energy, and passion for the city of Porto and Portugal shines through in everything he does. I would to thank my wife, Emma for her help in editing the book and with the photographic research. She has a very good eye for the photographs, art and, maps that adds much to the book. My children Benjamin and Hélèna are both keen historians and have been good sounding boards for the material used in the book. I would also like to extend a big thank you to the Portuguese people who have talked to me about the book in Porto and Portugal. Their opinions and insights have been very useful in adding important details to the narrative. It goes without saying that any mistakes in the book are the sole responsibility of myself as the author.

Professor Neill Lochery
Porto, February 2020.

A Brief Note About Sources

The book makes use of a mixture of primary source documentation from the extensive research conducted in the archives listed in the bibliography. Parts of this documentation have not yet been released to the public and I am grateful to the people have given permission to me to use in this book. The Freedom of Information Act also proved useful in obtaining the release of documentation in the United Kingdom not yet due for release under the thirty-year rule.

Several of the accounts of the key phases in the history of Porto have been drawn from the accounts of the participants in memoirs and drawn from official documentation. There is always a risk of political or personal bias in using this type of material, as well as memory issues, but wherever possible multiple sources have been used. Leading historians of the Peninsular War warned me that many of the eye-witness accounts of the war were highly unreliable, often based on gossip and hearsay. In choosing the sources for this part of the book, I have been careful to use widely accepted accounts, cross referencing them with narratives written by historians of a later era.

Right from the outset of the research I was struck by the richness of the sources in many of the subject areas covered in the book and the volume of documentation, memoirs, and secondary source material available in Portuguese and English. The ancient alliance has certainly produced a great volume of documentation over the years. I was particularly pleased to read the diaries and memoirs written about the 'War of the Brothers', which on a personal note I have always considered to have been one of the most avoidable wars in Portuguese history.

A Brief Note About Sources

When undertaking the task of trying to distil a huge amount of material, covering a period of time from ancient to modern times, there are always endless decisions to be made about what to include, or equally importantly what to leave out. Many of the topics in this book could constitute full studies in their own right, and this is something I would like to return to in future years.

CREDITS

Biblioteca Nacional de Portugal
Section 1, photos: 1–3, 5–10, 12–17, 25. Section 2, photo: 24

The Fladgate Partnership Archive
Section 1, photo: 11

Biblioteca de Arte, Fundação Calouste Gulbenkian
Back cover. Section 1, photos: 18–22, 24

Library of Congress, Washington DC
Section 1, photo: 4

Neill Lochery Photographic Archive
Front cover. Section 1, photos: 23, 26–35. Section 2, photos: 1–23, 25–31

Maps: Vitor Costa, ProjetoVimoc D&Co. Portugal

Bibliography

Archives

Archive Histórico Nacional, Madrid.
Arquivo Histórico da Presidência da Republica, Lisbon.
Arquivo Municipal Sophia de Mello Breyner, Vila Nova de Gaia.
Arquivo Municipal de Lisboa, Lisbon.
Arquivo Nacional Brazil, Rio de Janeiro.
Arquivo Nacional Torre do Tombo, Lisbon.
Biblioteca Nacional de Portugal, Lisbon.
British Library, London.
Centro Português de Fotografia, Porto.
CIA Library, Washington DC.
Das Bundesarchiv, Koblenz.
Foreign Broadcast Information Service (FBIS), on-line.
Gulbenkian Archives, Lisbon.
Historical Archives of the European Union, San Domenico di Fiesole, Italy.
JDC Archives, New York.
Jimmy Carter Presidential Library and Museum, Atlanta, Georgia.
Library of Congress, Washington DC.
Lochery Archives, London and Porto.
Margaret Thatcher Foundation, London.
Museum of the City of New York, New York.
National Archives (Public Records Office), Kew London.
National Archives and Records Administration (NARA), College Park, Maryland.
National Archives of Scotland, Edinburgh.
New York Times Archives, New York.
Office of the Historian, State Department, Washington DC.
RTP Archives, Lisbon.

Bibliography

Selby Papers, University of Oxford.
Fladgate Partnership Archives, Porto.
The Times of London Archives, London.
United Nations Archives and Records Management, New York.
United States, Holocaust Memorial Museum Archives, Washington DC.
Wiener Library, London.
William J. Clinton Presidential Library and Museum.
Yad Vashem, Jerusalem.

BOOKS

A British Officer of the Hussars (Anonymous). *The Civil War in Portugal and the Siege of Oporto*, London: Edward Moxon, 1836
Aires Oliveira, Pedro. *Armindo Monteiro: Uma biografia política, 1896-1955.* Venda Nova: Bertrand Editora, 2000
Almeida de Carvalho, Rita. Correspondência 1928-1968. Porto: Círculo de Leitores e Temas e Debates, 2010
Alves, Afonso Manuel and Luís Leiria de Lima. *Algarve: Southern Lands.* Lisbon: Dom Quixote, 1989
Andersen, Hans Christian. *A Visit to Portugal, 1866.* London: Peter Owen, 1972
Anderson, Brian and Eileen. *Northern Portugal.* London: A & C Black, 1996
Anderson, James M. *The History of Portugal.* Westport: Greenwood Press, 2000
Araujo, Rui. *O Diário Secreto que Salazar Não Leu.* Cruz Quebrada: Oficina do Livro, 2008
Atkinson, William C. *A History of Spain and Portugal.* London: Penguin, 1960
Avelãs Nunes, João Paulo. *O Estado Novo e o Volframio, 1933-1947* Coimbra: Coimbra University Press, 2010
Azenha, Abadarao, a. *História de Portugal, Vol. 11: Dicionário de Personalidades.* Matosinhos: QuidNovi, 2004
Barreto, António and Joana Pontes. *Portugal, Um Retrato Social, Vol. 1: Gente Diferente, Quem Somos, Quantos Somos e Como Vivemos.* Lisbon: RTP, 2007
Barreto, António and Joana Pontes. *Portugal, Um Retrato Social, Vol. 2: Ganhar o Pão, O Que Fazemos.* Lisbon: RTP, 2007
Barreto, António and Joana Pontes. *Portugal, Um Retrato Social, Vol. 3: Mudar de Vida, O Fim da Sociedade Rural.* Lisbon: RTP, 2007

Barreto, António and Joana Pontes. *Portugal, Um Retrato Social, Vol. 4: Nós e os Outros, Uma Sociedade Plural.* Lisbon: RTP, 2007

Barreto, António and Joana Pontes. *Portugal, Um Retrato Social, Vol. 5: Cidadãos, Direitos Políticos e Sociais.* Lisbon: RTP, 2007

Barreto, António and Joana Pontes. *Portugal, Um Retrato Social, Vol. 6: Igualdade e Conflito, As Relações Sociais.* Lisbon: RTP, 2007

Barreto, António and Joana Pontes. *Portugal, Um Retrato Social, Vol. 7: Um País Como os Outros.* Lisbon: RTP, 2007

Beamish, Huldine. *Cavaliers of Portugal.* London: Geoffrey Bles, 1966

Bermeo, Nancy Gina. *The Revolution within the Revolution: Workers' Control in Rural Portugal.* New Jersey: Princeton University Press, 1986

Bethencourt, Francisco & Ramada Curto, Diogo. *Portuguese Oceanic Expansion, 1400-1800.* New York, Cambridge University Press, 2007

Birmingham, David. *A Concise History of Portugal.* Cambridge & NY: Cambridge University Press, 1993

Bloch, Michael. *Operation Willi: The Nazi Plot to Kidnap the Duke of Windsor, July 1940.* London: Weidenfeld & Nicolson, 1984

Bollaert, William. *The Wars of Succession of Portugal and Spain from 1826 to 1840, Volume I,* London: Edward Stanford, 1861.

Bower, Tom. *Nazi Gold: The Full Story of the Fifty-Year Swiss-Nazi Conspiracy to Steal Billions from Europe's Jews and Holocaust Survivors.* New York: HarperCollins, 1997

Boxer, C.R. *The Dutch Seaborne Empire, 1600-1800.* London: Penguin, 1989

Boxer, C.R. *The Golden Age of Brazil, 1695-1750. Growing Pains of a Colonial Society.* Berkeley & LA: University of California Press, 1969

Boxer, C.R. *The Portuguese Seaborne Empire, 1415-1825.* Manchester: Carcanet, 1991

Bradford, Sarah. *Portugal and Madeira.* London & Sydney: Ward Lock, 1969

Bradford, Sarah. *Portugal.* London: Thames and Hudson, 1973

Bradford, Sarah. *The Story of Port.* London: Christie's Wine Publications, 1978

Bridge, Ann, Susan Lowndes. *The Selective Traveller in Portugal.* London: Chatto & Windus, 1967

Bruce, Neil. *Portugal: The Last Empire.* London: David & Charles, 1975

Buttery, David. *Wellington Against Junot: The First Invasion of Portugal, 1807-1808.* Barnsley: Pen & Sword Military, 2011

Cabral de Mello, Carlos Ernesto. *Ferreira: Branding Image*. Vila do Conde: QuidNovi, 2013

Caetano, Marcello. *Minhas Memórias de Salazar*. Lisbon: Verbo, 1977

Campbell, Christy. *Phylloxera: How Wine was Saved for the World*. London: HarperCollins, 2004

Cartier-Bresson, Henri. *Europeans*, London and New York: Thames and Hudson, 2011

Carvalho, Manuel. *A Guide to the Douro and to Port Wine*. Porto: Edicoes Afrontamento, 1995

Castanheira, Jose Pedro, Antonio Caeiro, Natal Vaz: *A Queda de Salazar: O Princípio do Fim da Ditadura*. Lisbon: Edições tinta-da-china, 2018

Castro Brandão, Fernando, de. António de Oliveira Salazar: Uma Cronologia. Lisbon: Prefácio, 2011

Castro Henriques, Mendo, Goncalo de Sampaio e Mello. *Pensamento e Doutrina Política: Textos Antológicos, António de Oliveira Salazar*. Lisbon: Verbo, 2010

Castro Leal, Ernesto. *António Ferro: Espaço Politico e Imaginário Social, 1918-1932*. Lisbon: Edições Cosmos, 1994

Cavaco Silva, Aníbal. *Quinta-Feira e Outros Dias*. Porto, 2: Porto Editora, 2018

Cavaco Silva, Aníbal. *Quinta-Feira e Outros Dias*. Porto: Porto Editora, 2017

Cidade, Hernâni. *História de Portugal, Vol. 7: Implantação do Regime Liberal – da Revolução de 1820 à Queda da Monarquia*. Matosinhos: QuidNovi, 2004

Correia Filho, João. *Lisbon in Person: A Tour and Literary Guide of the Portuguese Capital*. Alfragide: Livros d'Hoje, 2011

Costa, Fernando. *Portugal e a Guerra Anglo-Boer: Política Externa e Opinião Pública, 1899-1902*. Lisbon: Edições Cosmos, 1998

Croft-Cooke, Rupert. *Port*. London: Putnam, 1957

Croft, John. *A Treatise on the Wines of Portugal*, York: Crask and Lund, 1787.

Crowley, Roger. *Conquerors: How Portugal Seized the Indian Ocean and Forged the First Global Empire*. London: Faber & Faber, 2015

Cruzeiro, Maria Manuela. *Costa Gomes: O Último Marechal*. Alfragide: Dom Quixote, 1998

Dacosta, Fernando. *Máscaras de Salazar*. Cruz Quebrada: Casa das Letras, 1997

Dacosta, Fernando. *Salazar: Fotobiografia*. Alfragide: Casa das Letras, 2000 das Neves, Jose Manuel. *Portuguese Contemporary Wine Architecture*. Lisbon: Uzina Books, 2016

de Oliveira Marques, A.H. *Daily Life in Portugal in the Late Middle Ages*. Wisconsin & London: The University of Wisconsin Press, 1971

Delaforce, John. *Anglicans Abroad: The History of the Chaplaincy and Church of St James at Oporto*. London: SPCK, 1982

Delaforce, John. *The Factory House at Oporto: Its Historic Role in the Port Wine Trade*. Bromley: Christopher Helm Publishers, 1990

Disney, A.R. *A History of Portugal and the Portuguese Empire: From Beginnings to 1807, Vol 1*. New York: Cambridge University Press, 2009

Disney, A.R. *A History of Portugal and the Portuguese Empire: From Beginnings to 1807, Vol 2*. New York: Cambridge University Press, 2009

Duffy, James. *Portugal in Africa*. Middlesex: Penguin, 1962

Edwards, Michael. *The Finest Wines of Champagne: A Guide to the Best Cuvées, Houses and Growers*. London: Aurum Press, 2009

Egerton, F.C.C. *Salazar: Rebuilder of Portugal*. London: Hodder & Stoughton, 1943

Eliade, Mircea: *The Portugal Journal*. Albany: State University of New York, 2010

Eppstein, John. *Portugal: The Country and its People*. London: Queen Anne Press, 1967

Esdaile, Charles. *The Peninsular War*. London & NY: Penguin, 2003

Fernandes, Filipe S. *Os Empresários de Marcello Caetano*. Alfragide: Casa das Letras, 2018

Fielding, Henry. *Jonathan Wild and The Voyage to Lisbon*. London & NY: Everyman's Library, 1932

Fisher, Stephen. *Lisbon as a Port Town, the British Seaman and other Maritime Themes*. Exeter: University of Exeter, 1988

Fletcher, Wyndam. *Port: An Introduction to its History and Delights*. London: Sotheby Parke Bernet Publications, 1978

Flunser Pimentel, Irene. *Cardeal Cerejeira: O Príncipe da Igreja*. Lisbon: A Esfera dos Livros, 2010

Flunser Pimentel, Irene. *Judeus em Portugal durante a II Guerra Mundial: Em Fuga de Hitler e do Holocausto*. Lisbon: A Esfera dos Livros, 2006

Forrester, Joseph James. *Portugal and its Capabilities*. London: John Weale, 1860

Francis, A.D. *The Methuens and Portugal 1691-1708*. London & NY: Cambridge University Press, 1966

Bibliography

Francis, A.D. *The Wine Trade*. London: A & C Black, 1972

Freire Costa, Leonor, Pedro Lains and Susana Munch Miranda. *An Economic History of Portugal, 1143-2010*. Cambridge: Cambridge University Press, 2016

Freitas do Amaral, Diogo. *Da Lusitânia a Portugal: Dois mil anos de história*. Lisbon: Bertrand Editora, 2018

Galvão, Henrique. *Santa Maria: My Crusades for Portugal*. Cleveland & NY: The World Publishing Company, 1961

Glover, Michael. *The Peninsular War, 1807-1814: A Concise Military History*. London: Penguin, 2001

Glover, Michael. *Wellington as Military Commander*. London: Penguin, 2001

Gurriarán, José Antonio. *Um Rei no Estoril: Dom Carlos e a família real espanhola no exílio português*. Lisbon: Dom Quixote, 2001

Halley, Ned. *Sandeman: Two Hundred Years of Port and Sherry*. London: The House of Sandeman, 1990

Harsgor, Michael. *The Washington Papers: Portugal in Revolution*. Beverly Hills & London: SAGE Publications, 1976

Harvey, Robert. *Portugal: Birth of a Democracy*. London: The Macmillan Press, 1978

Hibbert, Christopher. *A Soldier of the Seventy-first: A Journal of a Soldier in the Peninsular War*. Gloucestershire: Windrush Press, 1996

Hogg, Anthony. *Traveller's Portugal*. West Sussex: Solo Mio Books, 1983

Howkins, Ben. *Real Men Drink Port...and Ladies Do Too!* Shrewsbury: Quiller, 2011

Hyland, Paul. *Backwards Out of the Big World: A Voyage into Portugal*. London: HarperCollins, 1996

Jeffreys, Henry. *Empire of Booze: British History through the Bottom of a Glass*. London: Unbound, 2016

Jenkins, Simon (editor). *Insight on Portugal: The Year of the Captains*. London: André Deutsch Ltd, 1975

Johnson, Hugh. *Hugh Johnson's Wine Companion: The Encyclopedia of Wines, Vineyards & Winemakers*. London: Michael Beazley, 2010

Joseph, Robert. *French Wines: The Essential Guide to the Wines and Wine-growing Regions of France*. London: Dorling Kindersley Books, 1999

Kaplan, Marion. *The Portuguese: The Land and its People*. Manchester: Carcanet Press, 1991

Kay, Hugh. *Salazar and Modern Portugal*. New York: Hawthorn Books, 1970

Kendrick, T.D. *The Lisbon Earthquake.* Philadelphia & NY, JB Lippincott Company, 1955

Kennan, George F. *Memoirs, 1925-1950.* New York: Atlantic, Little Brown, 1967

Kingston, William. *Lusitanian Sketches of the Pen and Pencil, Vol. 1,* London: John Parker, 1845

Knight, Corporal. *The British Battalion at Oporto with Adventures, Anecdotes and Exploits in Holland, Waterloo and in the Expedition to Portugal,* Glasgow: Thomas Murray, 1834

Leitz, Christian. *Nazi Germany and Neutral Europe during the Second World War.* Manchester: Manchester University Press, 2000

Liddell, Alex and Janet Price. *Port Wine Quintas of the Douro.* London: Sotheby's Publications, 1992

Livermore, H.A. *Portugal: A Short History.* Edinburgh: Edinburgh University Press, 1973

Livermore, H.V. *A New History of Portugal.* Cambridge: Cambridge University Press, 1966

Livermore, Harold. *Portugal: A Traveller's History.* Woodbridge: The Boydell Press, 2004

Lochery, Neill. *Lisboa: A Cidade Vista de Fora, 1933-1974.* Barcarena: Editorial Presenca, 2013

Lochery, Neill. *Lisbon: War in the Shadows of the City of Light, 1939-1945.* New York: PublicAffairs, 2011

Lochery, Neill. *Out of the Shadows: Portugal from Revolution to the Present Day.* London: Bloomsbury, 2017

Louçã, António, Isabelle Paccaud. *O Segredo da Rua d'o Século: Ligações perigosas de un dirigente judeu com a Alemanha nazi, 1935-1939.* Portugal: Fim de Século, 2007

Lovat Corbridge, Sylvia. *We Go to Portugal.* London: George G Harrap & Co, 1969

Macaulay, Rose. *They Went to Portugal Too.* Manchester: Carcanet Press, 1990

Macaulay, Rose. *They Went to Portugal.* London: Penguin Books, 1985

Macaulay, Rose. *They Went to Portugal.* Middlesex: Penguin, 1985

Macedo, Newton, de. *História de Portugal, Vol. 3: A Epopeia dos Descobrimentos – A Dinistia de Avis e a Expansão Ultramarina.* Matosinhos: QuidNovi, 2004

Macedo, Newton, de. *História de Portugal, Vol. 4: Glória e Declíno do Império – de D. Manuel I ao Domínio dos Filipes.* Matosinhos: QuidNovi, 2004

Bibliography

Machado de Sousa, Maria Leonor. *A Guerra Peninsular em Portugal – Relatos Britânicos*. Casal de Cambra: Caleidoscópio, 2007

Marjay, F.P. *Porto: e Seu Distrito, suas Belezas e seus Encantos*. Lisbon: Livraria Bertrand, 1955

Martins, João Paulo. *A Wine Lover's Guide to Port: the inside story of a unique fortified wine*. Lisbon: Dom Quixote, 2001

Matos, Helena. *Salazar: A Construção de Mito 1928-1933*. Porto: Círculo de Leitores e Temas e Debates, 2010

Matos, Helena. *Salazar: A Propaganda 1934-1938*. Porto: Círculo de Leitores e Temas e Debates, 2010

Mattoso, Jose, Suzanne Daveau, Duarte Belo. *Portugal: O Sabor da Terra*. Porto: Círculo de Leitores e Temas e Debates, 2010

Maxwell, Kenneth (editor). *Portugal in the 1980s: Dilemmas of Democratic Consolidation*. New York: Greenwood Press, 1986

Maxwell, Kenneth (editor). *The Press and the Rebirth of Iberian Democracy*. New York: Greenwood Press, 1983

Maxwell, Kenneth R. *Conflicts and Conspiracies: Brazil and Portugal 1750-1808*. London & NY: Cambridge University Press, 1973

Maxwell, Kenneth. *The Making of Portuguese Democracy*. New York: Cambridge University Press, 1995

Mayhill, Henry. *Portugal*. London: Faber & Faber, 1972

Mayson, Richard. *Port and the Douro*. London: Michael Beazley, 2004

Mayson, Richard. *Port and the Douro*. Oxford: Infinite, 2013

McWhirter, Kathryn and Charles Metcalfe. *Encyclopedia of Spanish and Portuguese Wines*. New York: Fireside Book, 1991

Mendes, Nuno. *Lisboeta: Recipes from Portugal's City of Light*. London & NY: Bloomsbury, 2017

Metcalfe, Charles and Kathryn McWhirter. *The Wine and Food Lover's Guide to Portugal*. Haywards Heath: Inn House Publishing, 2007

Milgram, Avraham. *Portugal, Salazar e os Judeus*. Lisbon: Gravida, 2010

Mira, Alberto (editor). *The Cinema of Spain and Portugal*. London: Wallflower Press, 2005

Mocatta, Frederic David. *The Jews of Spain and Portugal and the Inquisition*. General Books, 2009

Moleksy, Mark. *This Gulf of Fire: The Destruction of Lisbon, or Apocalypse in the Age of Science and Reason*. New York: Knopf, 2015

Moura, Fatima. *Portugal: O Melhor Peixe do Mundo*. Lisbon: Assírio & Alvim, 2011

Napier, W. F. P. *History of the War in the Peninsula and in the South of France from the Year 1807 to the Year 1814, Volume II*, London: Constable, 1992

Nogueira Pinto, Jaime. *António de Oliveira Salazar: O Outro Retrato.* Lisbon: A Esfera dos Livros, 2007

Nogueira Pinto, Jaime. *O Fim do Estado Novo e as Origens do 25 de Abril.* Algés: DIFEL, 1999

Nunes Ramalho, Miguel. *Sidónio Pais: Diplomata e Conspirador, 1912-1917.* Lisbon: Edições Cosmos, 2001

Nuno Rodrigues, Luís. *Salazar-Kennedy: A Crise de uma Aliança.* Lisbon: Editorial Notícias, 2002

Oldenburg, Henrik. *Port.* Copenhagen: SMAG & BEHAG, 1999

Oliveira Marques, A.H, de. *History of Portugal.* New York: Columbia University Press, 1976

Oliveira Marques, A.H, de. *History of Portugal.* New York: Columbia University Press, 1972

Oman, Charles. *A History of the Peninsular War, Vol. 1: 1807-1809, From the Treaty of Fontainebleau to the Battle of Corunna.* London: Greenhill Books, 1995

Oman, Charles. *A History of the Peninsular War, Vol. 2: January-September 1809, From the Battle of Corunna to the End of the Talavera Campaign.* London: Greenhill Books, 1995

Oman, Charles. *A History of the Peninsular War, Vol. 3: September 1809 – December 1810, Ocaña, Cadiz, Bussaco, Torres Vedras.* London: Greenhill Books, 1996

Oman, Charles. *A History of the Peninsular War, Vol. 4: December 1810 – December 1811, Massena's Retreat, Fuentes de Oñoro, Albuera, Tarragona.* London: Greenhill Books, 1996

Oman, Charles. *A History of the Peninsular War, Vol. 5: October 1811 – August 1812, Valencia, Ciudad Rodrigo, Badajoz, Salamanca, Madrid.* London: Greenhill Books, 1996

Oman, Charles. *A History of the Peninsular War, Vol. 6: September 1, 1812 – August 5, 1813, Siege of Burgos, the Retreat from Burgos, the Campaign of Vittoria, the Battle of the Pyrenees.* London: Greenhill Books, 1996

Oman, Charles. *A History of the Peninsular War, Vol. 7: August 1813 – April 14, 1814, St. Sebastain, Invasion of France, The Nivelle, The Nive, Orthez, Toulouse.* London: Greenhill Books, 1996

Opello Jr, Walter C. *Portugal: From Monarchy to Pluralist Democracy.* Boulder, San Francisco: Westview Press, 1991

Paice, Edward. *Wrath of God: The Great Lisbon Earthquake of 1755*. London: Quercus, 2008

Palla, Victor and Costa Martins. Lisboa: Cidade Triste e Alegre. Pierre von Kleist Editions, 2015

Parkinson, Roger. *The Peninulsar War*. Ware: Wordsworth Editions, 2000

Payne, Stanley G. *A History of Spain and Portugal, Vol 1*. Madison: The University of Wisconsin Press, 1973

Payne, Stanley G. *A History of Spain and Portugal, Vol 2*. Madison: The University of Wisconsin Press, 1973

Pessoa, Fernando. *Lisbon: What the Tourist Should See*. Exeter: Shearsman Books, 2008

Petropoulos, Jonathan. *Royals and the Reich: The Princes von Hessen in Nazi Germany*. New York: Oxford University Press, 2009

Pillement, Georges. *Unknown Portugal*. London: Johnson Publications, 1967

Pinheiro, Magda. *Biografria de Lisboa*. Lisbon: A Esfera dos Livros, 2011

Pintao, Manuel and Carlos Cabral. *Dicionário Ilustrado do Vinho do Porto*. Porto: Editora Porto, 2014

Pinto Janeiro, Helena. *Salazar e Pétain: Relações Luso-Francesas durante a II Guerra Mundial, 1940-1944*. Lisbon: Edições Cosmos, 1998

Postgate, Raymond. *Portuguese Wine*. London: J.M Dent & Sons, 1969

Proper, Datus C. *The Last Old Place: A Search Through Portugal*. London & NY: Simon & Schuster, 1992

Queiroz, Eça, de. *Alves & Co. and other stories*. Sawtry: Dedlus, 2012

Queiroz, Eça, de. *The City and the Mountains*. Sawtry: Dedlus, 2008

Queiroz, Eça, de. *The Relic*. Sawtry: Dedalus, 1994

Rasquilho, Rui. Portugal. Geneva, Editions Minerva S.A, 1983

Rathbone, Julian. *Wellington's War: His Peninsular Dispatches*. London: Michael Joseph, 1994

Read, Jan. *The Wines of Portugal*. London: Faber & Faber, 1982

Reis Torgal, Luís. *O Cinema sob o olhar de Salazar*. Porto: Círculo de Leitores e Temas e Debates, 2001

Reis, Rogério. *Route of Port Wine: The Wealth of Wine and Panoramic Views*. Barcelona: Editorial Escudo de Oro, 1986

Rezola, Maria Inácia. *25 de Abril: Mitos de um Revolução*. Lisbon: A Esfera dos Livros, 2007

Ribeiro de Meneses, Filipe. *Salazar: A Political Biography*. New York: Enigma Books, 2009

Ribeiro de Meneses, Filipe. *União Sagrada e Sidonismo: Portugal em Guerra, 1916-18*. Lisbon: Edições Cosmos, 2000

Ribeiro, Ângelo and Hernâni Cidade. *História de Portugal, Vol. 6: A Monarquia Absolutist – da Afirmação do Poder às Invasões Francesas*. Matosinhos: QuidNovi, 2004

Ribeiro, Ângelo. *História de Portugal, Vol. 1: A Formação do Território – da Lusitânia ao Alargamento do País*. Matosinhos: QuidNovi, 2004

Ribeiro, Ângelo. *História de Portugal, Vol. 2: A Afirmação do País – da Conquista do Algarve à Regência de Leonor Teles*. Matosinhos: QuidNovi, 2004

Ribeiro, Ângelo. *História de Portugal, Vol. 5: A Restauração da Independência – O Incío da Dinastia de Bragança*. Matosinhos: QuidNovi, 2004

Robertson, George. *Port*. London & Boston: Faber & Faber, 1978

Robertson, Ian. *A Traveller's History of Portugal*. London: The bookHaus, 2002

Robertson, Ian. *Portugal*. London: A & C Black, 1988

Robinson, Janis. *The Oxford Companion to Wine*. Oxford: Oxford University Press, 2015

Robinson, R.A.H. *Contemporary Portugal: A History*. London: George Allen & Unwin, 1979

Ros Agudo, Manuel. *A Grande Tentação: Os Planos de Franco para Invadir Portugal*. Alfragide: Casa das Letras, 2009

Rosas, Fernando. *História de Portugal Vol. 7: O Estado Novo*. Portugal: Editorial Estampa, 1998

Russell-Wood, A.J.R. *The Portuguese Empire, 1415-1808*. Baltimore & London: The Johns Hopkins University Press, 1992

Salavisa, Eduardo. *Caderno do Porto*. Porto: Edicoes Afrontamento, 2018

Salter, Cedric. *Portugal*. London: BT Batsford, 1970

Sanceau, Elaine. *The British Factory House*. Barcelos: Companhia Editora do Minho, 1970

Saraiva, Arnaldo. *A Feeling For Porto*. Portugal: Campo das Letras, 2001

Saraiva, José António. *Política à Portuguesa: Ideias, pessoas e factos*. Cruz Quebrada: Oficina do Livro, 2007

Saraiva, José Hermano. *História de Portugal, Vol. 10: A Terceira República – do 25 de Abril aos Nosso Dias*. Matosinhos: QuidNovi, 2004

Saraiva, José Hermano. *História de Portugal, Vol. 8: A Primeira República – do 5 de Outubro à Crise Partidária*. Matosinhos: QuidNovi, 2004

Saraiva, José Hermano. *História de Portugal, Vol. 9: A Segunda República – de António Salazar ao Marcelismo*. Matosinhos: QuidNovi, 2004

Saraiva, José Hermano. *Portugal: A Companion History*. Manchester: Carcanet, 1997

Saramago, José. *Journey to Portugal: In Pursuit of Portugal's History and Culture*. New York: Harcourt, 1990

Saramago, José. *Journey to Portugal: In Pursuit of Portugal's History and Culture*. London & NY: Harcourt Books, 1990

Saramago, José. *The Notebook*. London & NY: Verso, 2010

Savelli, Luciana. *Oporto: Northern Portugal*. Florence: Bonechi, 2001

Sellers, Charles. *Oporto Old and New*. London: Herbert E Harper, 1899

Shaw, L.M.E. *Trade, Inquisition and the English Nation in Portugal, 1650-1690*. Manchester: Carcanet, 1989

Shrady, Nicholas. *The Last Day: Wrath, Ruin & Reason in The Great Lisbon Earthquake of 1755*. New York: Viking Penguin, 2009

Siegner, Otto. *This Is Portugal: An Art Book*. Munich: Ludwig Simon

Silva, Germano. *Porto: História e Memórias*. Porto: Editora Porto, 2010

Silva, Germano. *Porto: Nos Lugares da História*. Porto: Editora Porto, 2011

Simon, André L. *Port*. London: Wine & Food Society, 1948

Solsen, Eric (editor). *Portugal: A Country Study*, Washington DC: Library of Congress, 1993.

Spence, Godfrey. *The Port Companion: A Connoisseur's Guide*. London: Apple Press, 1997

Stanislawski, Dan. *Landscapes of Bacchus: The Vine in Portugal*. Austin & London: University of Texas Press, 1970

Stevenson, Tom. *The New Sotheby's Wine Encyclopedia: A Comprehensive Reference Guide to the Wines of the World*. London: Dorling Kindersley, 1997

Stone, Glyn. *The Oldest Ally: Britain and the Portuguese Connection, 1936-1941*. Suffolk & NY: The Boydell Press, 1994

Stoop, Anne, de. *Living in Portugal*. Paris: Flammarion, 1995

Suckling, James: *Vintage Port: The Wine Spectator's Ultimate Guide for Consumers, Collectors and Investors*. San Francisco: The Wine Spectator, 1990

Sykes, John. Portugal & Africa: The People and the War. London: Hutchinson, 1971

Taber, George. *Judgement of Paris: California vs France and the Historic 1976 Paris Tasting That Revolutionized Wine*. New York: Scribner, 2005

Taber, George. *To Cook or Not to Cook*. New York: Scribner, 2007

Tavares Dias, Marina. *Lisboa nos Anos 40: Longe da Guerra*. Lisbon: Quimera Editores, 1997

Taylor, Patrick E. *Making it into Port: for gold medal amateur wines*. Sausalito & Geyserville: Patrick Ellsworth Taylor Publishing, 2015

Telo, António José. *A Neutralidade Portuguesa e o Ouro Nazi*. Lisbon: Quetzal Editores, 2000

Telo, António. *Portugal na Segunda Guerra, 1941-1945, Vol. 1*. Lisbon: Documenta Historica, 1991

Telo, António. *Portugal na Segunda Guerra, 1941-1945, Vol. 2*. Lisbon: Documenta Historica, 1991

Thompson, W.F.K. *An Ensign in the Peninsular War: The Letters of John Aitchison*. London: Michael Joseph, 1991

Thomson, W.F.K. (editor). *An Ensign in the Peninsular War: The Letters of John Aitchison*, London: Michael Joseph 1981.

Trabulo, António. *O Diario de Salazar*. Lisbon: Parceria A. M. Pereira, 2008

Trend, J.B. *Portugal*. London: Ernest Benn Ltd, 1957

Various. *Whence Cometh the Name Portugal: About Oporto, an anthology of Poetry and Prose*. Porto: ASA Editores, 2004

Vicente, Ana. *Portugal: Visto Pelo Espanha, Correspondência Diplomática 1939-1960*. Lisbon: Assírio & Alvim, 1992

Vieira, Edite. *The Taste of Portugal: A Voyage of Gastronomic Discovery combined with Recipes, History and Folklore*. London: Grub Street, 2000

Ward Davies, Susan (editor). *Port to Port*. London: LB Publishing, 1996

Warner Allen, H. *The Wines of Portugal*. London: George Rainbird, 1962

Wheeler, Douglas. *Historical Dictionary of Portugal*. London: The Scarecrow Press, 1993

Wheeler, Douglas. *Republican Portugal: A Political History 1910-1926*. Wisconsin & London: The University of Wisconsin Press, 1978

Wiarda, Howard J., Margaret MacLeish Mott. *Catholic Roots and Democratic Flowers: Political Systems in Spain and Portugal*. Connecticut & London: Praeger, 2001

Wilcken, Patrick. *Empire Adrift: The Portuguese Court in Rio de Janeiro, 1808-1821*. London: Bloomsbury, 2004

Wright, Carol. *Portuguese Food*. London: JM Dent & Sons, 1975

Wright, David and Patrick Swift. *Algarve: A Portrait and a Guide*. London: Barrie & Rockliff, 1965

Wright, David and Patrick Swift. *Lisbon: A Portrait and a Guide*. London: Barrie & Jenkins, 1975

Bibliography

Wright, David and Patrick Swift. *Minho and North Portugal: A Portrait and a Guide*. London: Barrie & Rockliff, 1968

Young, George. *Portugal Old and Young: An Historical Study*. London: Oxford University Press, 1917

Younger, William & Elizabeth. *Blue Moon in Portugal*. London: Eyre & Spottiswoode, 1956

CATALOGUES

Amorim: A Family History, 1870-1953. Portugal: Amorim

Amorim: A Family History, 1953-1997. Portugal: Amorim

Barao de Forrester: Razao e Sentimento, Uma Historia do Douro 1831-1861. Croft Porto. The Fladgate Partnership, 2008

Douro River – Golden Heritage. José Cruz, Andre Pregitzer, Manuel Granja 2005

Fonseca Porto. The Fladgate Partnerhsip, 2012

Joshua Benoliel, Photojounalist, 1873-1932. LisboaPhoto & CM-Lisboa, 2005

Memorias do Vinho. Maria João de Almeida and Paulo Laureano. Civilizacao Editora.

Our World Is Cork. Portugal: Amorim

Porto Vintage. Gaspar Martins Pereira & Joao Nicolou de Almeida. Campo das Letras, 2005

Portugal Around the World Program. American Geographical Society. Doubleday, 1968

Portugal. Tiger Books International

Portuguese Pavilion: 1998 Lisbon World Exposition. Official Catalogue

Spared Lives: the actions of three diplomats in world war II. Portugal: Ministry of Foreign Affairs, September 2000.

Taylor's: The Story of a Classic Port House. The Fladgate Partnership, 2011

The Future is our Present: Amorim. Portugal: Amorim

The Port Wine Heritage: Cellars of Gold. Matosinhos: QuidNovi, 2006

VIDEO

Jornal Português: Revista Mensal de Actualidades, 1938-1951. Cinematica Portuguesa-Museu do Cinema, 2015

Index

Index

335

Index

Index